Key Cases in Psychotherapy

KEY CASES IN PSYCHOTHERAPY

Edited by
Windy Dryden
Department of Psychology
Goldsmiths' College,
University of London

CROOM HELM
London & Sydney

© 1987 Windy Dryden,
Croom Helm Ltd, Provident House, Burrell Row,
Beckenham, Kent BR3 1AT

Croom Helm Australia, 44–50 Waterloo Road,
North Ryde, 2113, New South Wales

British Library Cataloguing in Publication Data

Key cases in psychotherapy.
   1. Psychotherapy — Case Studies
   I. Dryden, Windy
   616.89'14'0926   RC465

ISBN 0-7099-4501-9

Filmset by Mayhew Typesetting, Bristol, England
Printed and bound in Great Britain
by Billing & Sons Limited, Worcester.

To the memory of Don Bannister

Contents

List of Contributors	ix
1 Key Cases in Psychotherapy: An Introduction *Windy Dryden*	1
2 A Psychotherapist at the Crossroads: A Personal and Professional Turning Point *James K. Morrison*	5
3 The Process of Being Known and the Initiation of Change *Mark Aveline*	21
4 Beyond the Core Conditions *Brian Thorne*	48
5 An Even More Offensive Theory *Daniel B. Wile*	78
6 Siding with the Client *John Rowan*	103
7 Better the Devil You Know *Trevor Butt and Don Bannister*	127
8 On the Origin and Development of Rational-Emotive Therapy *Albert Ellis*	148
9 Listening to Oneself: Cognitive Appraisal Therapy *Richard L. Wessler*	176
10 When More is Better *Arnold A. Lazarus*	213
11 From Prescription to Integration *James O. Prochaska*	227
12 Key Cases in Psychotherapy: Concluding Issues *Windy Dryden*	253
Index	263

List of Contributors

Mark Aveline, F.R.C. Psych., is Consultant Psychotherapist to the Nottingham Health Authority, England, and Clinical Teacher in the Medical School. His research and clinical publications are on teaching dynamic psychotherapy, reforming the membership examination of the Royal College of Psychiatrists, group therapy, action techniques and diabetes. He is co-editor (with Windy Dryden) of the forthcoming book — *Group Therapy in Britain* (London: Harper and Row).

Don Bannister was a prominent figure in the development and promotion of personal construct psychology. He wrote and edited numerous publications in the field and in 1985 was the President of the International Congress of Personal Construct Psychology at Cambridge.

His radical approach to psychology permeated his work as a Psychotherapist, Teacher and Researcher as well as the five novels he wrote. The courage with which he lived his life and faced his death was an inspiration to the many who loved him. He died on July 11th 1986.

Trevor Butt is a Clinical Psychologist who teaches in the Department of Behavioural Sciences at Huddersfield Polytechnic; his previous publications have been concerned with the theory and practice of behavioural therapy. He practices as a Personal Construct Psychotherapist and is interested in all aspects of personal change.

Windy Dryden is Senior Lecturer in the Department of Psychology, Goldsmiths' College, University of London. He is co-editor of the *Journal of Cognitive Psychotherapy: An International Quarterly* and has authored and edited numerous publications in the field of psychotherapy including *Therapists' Dilemmas* (London: Harper & Row, 1985) and *Cognitive-Behavioural Approaches to Psychotherapy* (with William L. Golden) (London: Harper & Row, 1985).

Albert Ellis is Executive Director of the Institute for Rational-Emotive Therapy in New York City. He has written or edited more than fifty books and over 600 articles and chapters in the fields of psychotherapy, sex, and marital and family relations, including *A New Guide to Rational Living* (Hollywood: Wilshire Books, 1975 with Robert Harper) and *Overcoming Resistance: Rational-Emotive Therapy with Difficult Clients* (New York: Springer, 1985).

Arnold A. Lazarus is Distinguished Professor in the Graduate School of Applied and Professional Psychology, Rutgers — The State University of New Jersey. He has authored or edited 11 books and has published over 150 articles and chapters. His most recent publication is 'The multimodal approach (with adult outpatients)' in N.S. Jacobson (ed.) *Psychotherapists in Clinical Practice: Cognitive and Behavioral Perspectives* (New York: Guilford, 1987).

James K. Morrison is in the full-time private practice of psychotherapy in the Latham, New York area. A clinical associate professor in the Department of Psychiatry at Albany Medical College, he is the author of over one hundred professional journal articles, as well as of the book *A Consumer Approach to Community Psychology* (Nelson-Hall, 1978).

James O. Prochaska is Professor of Psychology and Director of the Self-Change Laboratory at the University of Rhode Island. He has authored numerous clinical, empirical and theoretical publications including: *Systems of Psychotherapy: A Transtheoretical Analysis* (Chicago: Dorsey, 1984) and the *Transtheoretical Approach: Crossing Traditional Boundaries of Therapy* (with Carlo C. DiClemente) (Chicago: Dow Jones/Irwin, 1985).

John Rowan is a psychotherapist in private practice, and also teaches at the Institute of Psychotherapy and Social Studies in Hampstead. He is a founder member of the Association of Humanistic Psychology Practitioners, and a member of the Accreditation Panel of the British Association for Counselling. He has written books including *The Reality Game: A Guide to Humanistic Counselling and Therapy* (RKP 1983) and *Ordinary Ecstasy: Humanistic Psychology in Action* (2nd edition, RKP in press).

Brian Thorne is Director of Student Counselling at the University of East Anglia, Norwich and a founding Partner of the Norwich Centre for Personal and Professional Development. He is Associate Editor of the *Person-Centred Review: an International Quarterly* and has published widely in the fields of therapy and education. His publications include *Intimacy* (Norwich: Norvicare, 1982) and *Student Counselling in Practice* (with Audrey Newsome and Keith L. Wyld) (London: U.L.P., 1973).

Richard L. Wessler is Professor of Psychology and Chairman of the department at Pace University, Pleasantville, New York, and practises cognitive psychotherapy in New York City. He is co-author of *The Principles and Practice of Rational-Emotive Therapy* (San Francisco: Jossey-Bass, 1980) and many other publications.

Daniel B. Wile is in private practice in Oakland, California. He has written several articles on psychoanalysis, psychotherapy, and couples therapy, has given numerous courses, workshops, and demonstrations on couples therapy, and is the author of *Couples Therapy: A Nontraditional Approach* (New York: Wiley, 1981).

1

Key Cases in Psychotherapy: An Introduction

Windy Dryden

In this book a number of noted practitioners write about cases that have led them to revise their thinking about psychotherapy and/or to change some aspect of their clinical practice. The idea for the book emerged as I was completing a previous book entitled *Therapists' dilemmas* (Dryden, 1985). In that book, well-known therapists discussed dilemmas of therapeutic work and often pointed to specific cases that provoked conflict and precipitated change in their thinking about therapy and how they practised it. I wondered, at that time, whether there existed any books that had as their central theme therapists discussing 'key' cases, which are here defined as 'those cases which led therapists to experience a significant degree of conflict but out of which emerged important new developments in their theorising about psychotherapy and/or their practice of it'.

Although numerous casebooks have been published, some even describing so-called 'great cases' (e.g. Wedding and Corsini, 1979), none of these dealt with such 'key' cases (as defined above) in a systematic manner, with contributors being asked to address similar issues outlined in a common chapter structure.

At the time I was having these thoughts, I received a preprint of a research study which, among other things, considered the use that American psychotherapists make of different sources of information on therapy (Morrow-Bradley and Elliott, 1986). It was found that 48 per cent of the total sample of almost 300 therapists rated 'ongoing experience with clients' as their most important source of information about psychotherapy. This finding reinforced my belief that a book on 'key' cases would be timely, particularly when compared with the other sources given 'top billing' by smaller proportions of the total research sample:

- 'theoretical/practical books/articles': rated as most important by 10 per cent
- 'through experience of being a client': rated as most important by 8 per cent
- 'supervision/consultation with others': rated as most important by 7 per cent

Given these findings, I decided to put together a book that attempts to show how noted therapists have learned from their ongoing experience with clients. I believe that this book is timely precisely because we know very little about this aspect of therapists' learning. Obviously, more research needs to be done on this subject, but if we can generalise from another finding obtained by Morrow-Bradley and Elliott (1986), only 4 per cent of psychotherapists will rate such research as their most important source of learning about psychotherapy, whereas 10 per cent will view a book like this as such.

In the present book, contributors could choose to present either a single 'key' case or, if they deemed it more relevant, a series of cases. This latter option was chosen by several writers, particularly those who wished to discuss more than one important shift in their theorising and/or practice (e.g. Albert Ellis and Arnold Lazarus).

I asked all contributors to adhere to a common chapter structure in writing their chapters. I did this (a) to have them all deal with issues that several colleagues wished to see addressed in a book of this nature, and (b) to help readers to make meaningful comparisons among the chapters. Contributors were asked to write on four themes:

(a) *Prior theory and practice.* First, contributors were asked to describe their ideas on therapy and the mode of practice that characterises their work before the 'key' case(s), particularly emphasising elements of theory and practice that were later revised.
(b) *Description of the 'key' case(s).* Then, contributors were asked to give a full description of the case(s) as it (they) unfolded over time. They were particularly asked to highlight the conflicts that they experienced during the case(s) and what steps (if any) they took to resolve these conflicts.
(c) *Emergent new developments.* Next, contributors were asked to describe fully the new developments in theory and/or practice that emerged from the case(s) and to outline the subsequent

impact that these developments had on their professional life.
(d) *Implications for other therapists.* Finally, contributors were asked to discuss how the learning which they derived from the case(s) described could benefit other practitioners.

I shall discuss each chapter in greater detail in Chapter 12, but a few orienting remarks are in order at this point. The reader will note that contributors differ concerning the type of learning that is discussed in their chapters. Several contributors highlight the personal learning that they derived from their 'key' case(s) (Aveline, Thorne) or, in one instance, before the case (Morrison), and show how such learning influenced their conceptual thinking about therapy and their mode of practising therapy. Other contributors focus directly on the conceptual learning that they derived from the case(s). Thus, Butt and Bannister describe the gradual but radical shift in conceptual thinking that Butt experienced, as does Wessler who traces his change over a period of a decade; Ellis describes shifts in his ideas about the nature and determinants of psychological disturbance; Prochaska discusses revisions in his views about therapeutic change; Wile shows how his theory was paradoxically strengthened by his case; and Rowan's case demonstrates how he resolved a conflict raised by the possibility of making a particular intervention by making a distinction between 'therapy' and 'therapeutic'. Whereas all the contributors who made conceptual revisions show how these led to developments in their practice, only Wessler and, to some extent, Wile discuss the impact of these revisions on their personal experience. The remaining chapter, that of Lazarus, has a more technical focus. Lazarus's concern with 'what works' led him to broaden the scope of his therapeutic approach and thence to make certain modifications in his thinking about therapy.

Only two contributors (Prochaska and, to a lesser extent, Morrison) discuss the role that their own research played in the learning process. It is noteworthy in this regard that Morrow-Bradley and Elliott (1986) found that only 3 per cent of their sample rated 'doing psychotherapy research' as the most useful source of learning about psychotherapy.

In summary, whereas all contributors discuss conceptual and practical changes as instructed, only half of them discuss personal issues or point to personal implications of the case(s). The reader should note, however, that the contributors were not specifically asked to address themselves to personal material.

The reader will note that there are no female contributors in the book. Before I am wrongly accused of being a sexist editor, it should be understood that invitations to contribute to the book were issued to more than a dozen women. Only one accepted, but was unable to complete her chapter.

Sadly, Don Bannister died shortly after completing his chapter with Trevor Butt and I dedicate this book to his memory.

REFERENCES

Dryden, W. (1985). *Therapists' dilemmas.* London: Harper & Row

Morrow-Bradley, C. and Elliott, R. (1986). Utilization of psychotherapy research by practising psychotherapists. *American Psychologist, 41*, (2), 188–97

Wedding, D. and Corsini, R.J. (1979). *Great cases in psychotherapy.* Itasca, IL: Peacock

2

A Psychotherapist at the Crossroads: A Personal and Professional Turning Point

James K. Morrison

Exactly how a psychotherapist has evolved the theory and clinical techniques used in practice remains a mystery in most cases. It is unfortunate that so few psychotherapists take the time and effort to delineate this gradual unfolding process, because there is much to be gained by tracing one's theoretical and practical approach from early training to present practice.

One way to approach this process is to think in terms of the event or clinical case that most affected one's theory and practice. Is there one client with whom the clinical transactions led to a change of direction in the clinician; a change carried over into practice thereafter? Such questions, posed by the editor of this volume, have led to this chapter, which is a description of how I evolved as a psychotherapist due to the influence of a key case. After first outlining my clinical approach at the conclusion of my professional training, I will then proceed to discuss the two crucial experiences, one personal and one professional, which became the crucible for change in my development as a psychotherapist.

PRIOR THEORY AND PRACTICE

My theoretical position at the conclusion of my training (graduate course, clinical internship), and for the first few months of my first clinical position with a community mental health centre, is best described as that of cognitive-learning theory. In an article written during my internship and published two years later (Morrison, 1974), I outlined and referenced this approach (e.g. Harris, Johnston, Kelley and Wolf, 1964; Hawkins, Peterson, Schweid and Bijou, 1966; and especially Kanfer and Phillips, 1970 and Kanfer and Saslow, 1965).

At that time the importance of cognitive factors in behaviourism was not as clearly recognised as it is today. An emphasis was placed on what was happening in the present, rather than what had happened in the past. The clinical techniques that I was taught included behavioural analysis, assertive training, thought stopping, anxiety management training, treatment contracts, systematic desensitisation, modelling, and aversive conditioning. Mackay (1984) provides an excellent summary of most of these techniques. Psychoanalytic theory and techniques were openly ridiculed by the professors; Gestalt therapy and rational-emotive therapy were largely ignored. A few professors underlined the utility of client-centred therapy (Rogers, 1951), but most of the faculty tended to encourage graduate students to move in the direction of behaviourism. However, some limited eclecticism was not totally discouraged.

During my clinical internship, I soon discovered the unsuitability of the behavioural approach to my personality. I had always been an impatient person and found that the repetitive work of behavioural analysis and technique application (e.g. systematic desensitisation) was a tedious and too often boring process. Although I would readily admit the process was effective enough, especially with clients with phobias and other anxiety disorders, it seemed to take a longer amount of time than I thought was reasonable. Too often I found clients unwilling to do their homework assignments (e.g. practising relaxation techniques). Although I felt that behavioural approaches were superior to psychoanalysis in their efficient use of time, I was still searching for methods that were for me more interesting than behavioural ones, and ones that were more efficient as well.

My dissatisfacation with the results of behavioural techniques with the commonly reported problems of depression was another reason for my search for new methods. I found that even though behavioural methods were appropriate to reduce certain symptoms of depression, all too often the overall depression remained.

To sum up, I wanted to get more deeply into a client's psyche without practising psychoanalysis which, at the time, was not a short-term methodology. Only a short-term insight-oriented, emotionally involving (for the client) process would seem to satisfy my personal needs at the time.

Perhaps it is a more personal reason which actually was the driving force behind my gradual rejection of the behavioural approach. Thus, because behavioural theory was not personally helpful in explaining the cognitive side of my neurotic conflict (to be explained later), such a theory was not to my liking. To explain my past, with all the emotional underpinnings, in terms of reinforcement contingencies seemed too arid and unreal to satisfy my curiosity.

It should also be mentioned that although clinical supervisors seemed happy enough with my work, I was not. They seemed patient with my progress. Again, I was not. So, gradually, I became a therapist in search of a different theoretical and operational approach. I was quickly approaching a crossroads in my professional career, a point where my neurotic conflict would trigger some personal insights which would enable me to try a new approach with a certain client. Both of these events would be key in my evolution as a psychotherapist.

DESCRIPTION OF THE KEY EVENTS

The personal experience

Despite my dissatisfaction with both the theoretical and practical aspects of my work, I had at the time made no decision to change these until faced with what I have called a 'peak experience' (Maslow, 1976) — an event which turned out to be unusually enlightening and therapeutic for me and which later led to drastic changes in my clinical work with clients. I was not able to change my work until then because I had not yet found a better alternative.

A few months after my internship, and while I was working full time as a community psychologist and completing my doctoral dissertation, I read Arthur Janov's (1970) *The primal scream.* This book, one with which I violently disagreed concerning the author's theory and techniques, offered a number of case studies which must have raised my anxiety level. These case histories, with their emphasis on early traumatic experiences, began to stir up in me unconscious memories of certain childhood events. However, before I went to sleep that night, I was only minimally aware of the anxiety the book was evoking.

At 2.30 a.m. I suddenly awoke with a vivid image and a powerful feeling. After I became a little more conscious I began to experience an eruption of tremendous anger associated with the image. The image was that of my mother, standing in the cellar of our house, with a knife in her right hand and a crazed, desperate and depressed look in her eyes. Right then and there an incredible anger burst forth and I found myself shouting out loud over and over to my father: 'You son of a bitch!' It was only then, at the age of 32, that I realised that for 27 years I had been blaming my father for driving my mother close to a nervous breakdown. Now I began to understand for the first time why I had rebelled against my father most of my life and why I had made most of the major life decisions I had. It seemed as if in five minutes I understood, for the first time, my family's dynamics, why I was attracted to women I needed to save or heal, and why I thus chose the two professions (the ministry and psychology) I had. I also experienced a rush of childhood memories, most of which I had forgotten or repressed, which confirmed my conclusions.

My anger quickly subsided and suddenly I began to see my father's perspective for the first time. I never experienced real anger at my father again after this. I also seemed to lose most of my need to save depressed females, a need which I feel made me a less effective therapist with women clients. Before this experience, all too often in trying to 'save' these women clients I was apparently so emotionally involved in the process that such clients were misled into believing that I was in love with them. Then, as I realised that they began to fantasise a different relationship with me, I began to be stiff and cold with them to discourage this. My behaviour then provoked anger and, at times, termination from therapy.

My personal life changed significantly after I had that experience, to the extent that I was better able to predict my experiences with clients and people in general. Thus, I do not get surprised about how people react to me. Also, and of more relevance to this chapter, this experience opened the door to a different approach to psychotherapy which seemed to fit my personality style better.

As a result of this imagery experience, I was very impressed with how an image (of my mother in a suicidal state) could provoke strong, repressed feelings which could then lead to powerful insights and noticeable personality change. I naturally wondered how the provocation of vivid images might work with some of the clients I had been seeing. At the time I began to work with Joan (not her real name), I was a therapist armed with techniques but without a theory which really seemed to explain why the techniques seemed to work the way they did. I needed a cognitive frame of reference to explain logically how the way I construed or conceptualised a person (e.g. my father) could reorder my entire cognitive frame of reference to accomodate that construction. Thus, in a child's construction of events, if my father had treated my mother badly, then he must be my 'enemy' as well. As described subsequently, it was only after my work with Joan that I 'discovered' how neatly the construct theory of George Kelly (1955) meshed with my techniques.

The case of Joan

Several months before my 'peak experience', described earlier, I had begun to see Joan for individual psychotherapy. She was a 30-year-old married housewife who had been variously diagnosed, during her long history of episodes of psychiatric hospitalisation, as 'manic-depressive' and 'schizophrenic', among others. She seemed to have more potential for insight than many of the community mental health centre's outpatients, although she was far from the ideal therapy client, most especially because she was poorly educated. But her rather frequent, vivid dreams made me think she might be good at imagery work.

True to form, about the time I decided to use my imagery methods with Joan, I discovered that inadvertently I had been trying to rework on her my 'rescue fantasy', which originated with my need to save my mother from my father. Sharaf (1960) has suggested that the development of 'intraceptive capacities' (an amazing ability to respond intuitively and sensitively to others) in men, such as male therapists (Farber, 1985), is often related to a certain family pattern in which mother and son have an emotionally intimate and intense relationship, the father being excluded.

After my life-changing personal experience, I found that I no longer had to 'save' this client. Rather, I discovered that I could do effective work with her while being emotionally disengaged from her to an appropriate degree. I discussed with the client the new techniques I wished to use and she agreed to try them. I spent the first few sessions taking her back to various early developmental periods in her life. Although nothing dramatic happened, I was collecting valuable information about her childhood which helped me to guide her through imagery in her fourth session. This session yielded a clinical breakthrough.

In this particular hour of therapy, I asked the client to close her eyes and take long deep breaths to relax. After a few minutes the client began to see clear vivid images. At this point she must have entered into a hypnotic trance on her own — at the time I had not yet learned hypnosis — because she began to talk like a five-year-old. She related detail by detail how she was in her backyard at home and her older sister was pushing her around in a wheelbarrow. Her narration sounded like those described by Penfield and Roberts (1959) in their pre-operation brain stimulations. Suddenly the client became frightened as her sister was about to dump her out of the wheelbarrow and over the embarkment on one side of their property. The client reported falling, getting cut on her arms and crying loudly. Her father, who worked nights and was awakened from sleep, was very angry and dragged her into the house. The client felt very frightened but could not remember what happened next. Sensing that we might be focusing on something important, I had her hyperventilate for 30 seconds to stimulate a state of fear, hoping this would trigger the repressed memory. I did this because hyperventilation seemed to have unlocked certain early experiences during my 'peak experience' described earlier.

Suddenly the client shook visibly with fear and dread. The image was clear. She finally knew — no one had ever told her before — why she had horribly ugly scars on each hip. Her father, in a rage at being awakened, had actually lifted her up to his electric table saw and cut her on each hip 'to teach her a lesson'! The client seemed to have blacked out with pain and could not remember what happened immediately after this gruesome incident.

Joan did remember that, when she awakened, her hips were wrapped in bandages and she was lying on her bed. She could feel and see blood on her legs and was still afraid. She heard her mother and father arguing in the next room. Her mother was understandably terribly upset at what her father had done.

When Joan finally got out of bed a short time after hearing the argument, she walked by the open bathroom and saw her mother standing on some newspapers. Blood was running down her legs on to the paper. Joan did not know it at the time but her mother was having a miscarriage. Apparently her mother was so upset over what had happened that she aborted. The image of her bleeding mother terrified Joan. She thought her mother was dying.

Now so enraged at the consequences of what her father had done, Joan went into her parent's bedroom, grabbed a photo of her father and ripped it to pieces. She then went out the back door and hid under the porch until she was found there sometime later. After this incident, her aunt and uncle took her to live with them for a while.

Following this imagery experience the client began to understand the problems of her life. She had married a violent man like her father, as if to recreate the earlier traumatic scene so that this time she could 'get Daddy to love her' through her husband. But things worked out the same (she felt unloved) and she believed events had again proved her to be 'unlovable'. Following this session the client ended her periodic hospitalisations, threw her husband out, found a job and for the first time supported herself. She also ceased to report her usual long list of psychosomatic complaints (e.g. headaches, nervous stomach). The change in her was really quite startling and I began theoretically and clinically to conclude, albeit tentatively, that I must have discovered something important.

When I began to use imagery methods with other clients, I found that the results were surprisingly consistent. To check whether these results were due to a new-found enthusiasm in my work or to the techniques themselves, I began to conduct research on therapy process and outcome. After a series of early studies (Morrison and Teta, 1978; Morrison and Cometa, 1979; Morrison, Becker and Isaacs, 1981; Morrison, Becker and Heeder, 1983a), I began to conclude that my results were consistent and quite impressive. Briefly, evidence indicated that my approach was successful as a short-term form of therapy in that significant symptom change was evident after only five sessions, and that as a therapeutic method it was significantly more effective in reducing problem behaviour and anxiety than didactic self-help seminars.

At this point, as I began to write professionally about the therapy I was doing, I felt the need to come up with a name for the therapy I was developing. I began to call it Emotive-Reconstructive Therapy (ERT); 'emotive' to emphasise the importance of using techniques to induce strong feelings which had been repressed; 'reconstructive' to emphasise the importance of a client conceptualising self and others in a new and constructive way as a result of the emotional process.

EMERGENT NEW DEVELOPMENTS

Emotive-reconstructive therapy

As I recall it, at first I was a psychotherapist with 'new' techniques (although later I realised that some of these techniques were to some extent similar to some employed in psychoanalysis and imagery therapy) in search of a theory to explain why the techniques seemed to work. About this time, a graduate student in psychology, whom

I was supervising during his clinical training, pointed out to me how the personal construct theory of George Kelly (1955) was, in part, quite explanatory of my techniques. The more I immersed myself into Kelly's writings, the more persuaded I was of its relevance. I liked the emphasis on the cognitive factors involved in psychotherapy, something which at the time seemed greatly lacking in behavioural theory and Gestalt theory, two theoretical systems I had looked at carefully and rejected as unsuitable for me. Such systems, although of course emphasising some cognitive features in behaviour change, did not, in my opinion, go far enough in elaborating how past events become conceptualised in such a way as to change our perspective of the present and the future. Cognitive-learning theory, at that time still in its still in its infancy, did not emphasise the importance of traumatic events for present thinking in the way construct theory could.

ERT is generally based on a cognitive model of personality (Kelly, 1955; Sarbin, Taft and Bailey, 1960; Bannister and Fransella, 1971; Piaget, 1972) and includes the notion of intrapersonal variations in the level of reticular activating system (RAS) arousal (Hebb, 1955; Mamlo, 1959; Fiske and Maddi, 1961; Schachter and Singer, 1962; Dember, 1965). A person is viewed as an active individual constantly engaged in the process of monitoring and interpreting experiences so as to maintain an orderly view of the world and, concomitantly, an optimal level of arousal (Fiske and Maddi, 1961).

From the perspective of ERT, clients are viewed as persons 'victimised' by their apparent inability to construe themselves, and others, in a congruent, personally satisfying manner, especially during the early developmental years (e.g. ages 3–12). Their later constructs and roles are often influenced by the simplistic constructs they formed in their early years. Thus, inadequate self-constructs and dysfunctional roles frequently have their source in early childhood experiences (Morrison, 1977) which are poorly encoded in a person's memory system, and thus are retrievable only with difficulty.

For the purposes of this chapter,[1] it will suffice to summarise the following theoretical propositions as central to ERT. Early childhood experiences, especially those that are stressful (e.g. parent suicide, long hospitalization, divorce of parents, etc.), often induce children to use simplistic contructs to understand persons and events. These constructs usually have to be altered or even radically changed before a person can change the destructive patterns of his or her adult life. To create the conditions for change, it is usually very useful to elicit the sensorial content (visual images, sounds, smells, etc.) which accompanies the memory of events.

Once these memories, which continue to cause stress through rigid and simplistic construct systems, are recreated, analysed and reconstructed by the more complex mind of the adult (client), the construct system changes in such a way as to reduce stress and facilitate new behaviour patterns more consonant with this more complex and predictive construct system. For example, if an adult, despite current evidence to the contrary, continues to see a father as 'cold and rejecting' and the mother as 'warm and loving', it may be necessary to do a 'life review', which the ERT process basically is, in order to induce the client to look at the evidence in the memory system about both parents. Often memories are triggered which contradict long-held, simplistic and stereotyped conclusions about parents, and the client's construct system changes to accomodate these new data. Thus, the client in the example might conclude, depending on circumstances, that his mother was not as warm and loving, nor his father as cold and rejecting, as he had previously thought. Because of these construct changes, he begins to treat both his father and mother in a more realistic and healthier manner. More detailed explanation of the theory behind ERT, along with citations of relevant research, can be found elsewhere (Morrison, 1977, 1979a, 1980b; Morrison and Cometa, 1977, 1980, 1982).

The techniques of ERT

The clinical techniques of ERT are varied. Imagery techniques (some similar to those described in Singer, 1974) — at times combined with hypnosis, deep breathing exercises and/or role playing — are of prime importance in including vivid images of the type which I consider leads to an expression of a repressed emotion and, subsequently, a reconstruction of self, others and certain events. Some people need to learn how to evoke vivid images;[2] others (e.g. artists) seem to do it naturally.

In a typical session, a client will close his/her eyes, be asked to focus on some familiar *place* (e.g. the kitchen of home, a classroom of a school), or *object* (e.g. a doll, a toy gun, etc.), or *person* (parent, sibling, relative, teacher) and describe in detail not only what he or she sees, but also, when relevant, sounds, odours, tastes or bodily sensations which are connected to them. Usually such images provoke a strong feeling which erupts into consciousness and leads to a constructive insight. (When they do not, the therapist may have to train the client to focus more and more clearly on such images.) Often role playing (e.g. 'Talk to your mother who is making you feel guilty') or deep breathing exercises (e.g. 'Take long deep breaths to get the strength to say what you have to say to your sister'; 'Breathe rapidly or hyperventilate for 30 seconds to stimulate physiologically what you must have felt like when you were so upset') are employed. After approximately 25-30 minutes of imaging and, hopefully, some emoting, clients are asked to open their eyes and the emotive-constructive therapist helps them to develop new constructs to understand their emotional experiences. For example, a client who as a child often thought of one parent as the 'good guy' and the other as the 'bad guy' is guided to re-evaluate both in view of the new data retrieved from the emotional catharsis in such a way as to see parents with more complex constructs. Often the client ceases to see one parent as the 'good' parent and the other as the 'bad' parent. Usually a perusal of the past reveals a more complex pattern of behaviour which needs to be reinterpreted.

ERT can be combined with other traditional forms of therapy (supportive insight-oriented therapy, behaviour therapy, Gestalt therapy, etc.) where the therapist decides that some aspect of behaviour change is complemented by certain techniques. Thus, for example, where construct change does not easily lead to a timid person becoming more assertive, assertiveness training would be a useful process. Furthermore, a therapist of a persuasion other than ERT may want to use certain ERT techniques with certain clients (e.g. artists, clients needing to grieve)[3], where other techniques do not seem to work in a particular case, to induce a breakthrough session.

It is important to stress that ERT can only be fully understood within the context of the consumer-oriented approach to therapy in which it is rooted. Such an approach underlines the need to protect a therapy client from entering unclear and perhaps even fraudulent 'unwritten contracts' with psychotherapists. Probably since the therapeutic approach evolved from my own personal experience with images as well as from my work with clients, I feel that the therapist must ensure that the client's rights are protected during the kind of emotional experience which ERT often provokes.

It has been my clinical observation that if clients really want to change their views of themselves, they must dig down to the inner depth of their psyches and go through an intense and painful process.[4] Construct change is not easy for any client. To get the client's full consent it is usually necessary to outline the methods used, the theory behind the techniques, and the possible side effects (positive and negative). One can, of course, reveal too much, but a consumer approach emphasises that you can also reveal too little. I know that I personally would not become a client undergoing ERT unless I knew an awful lot about this process. It is too painful to trust a 'stranger' (i.e. the therapist, at least in the early stages) with such emotion and such moments of vulnerability. A further explanation of this consumer-oriented approach to therapy can be found elsewhere (Morrison, 1979b, 1980a, 1984a, b).

Besides early research studies cited previously, more recent research efforts (Morrison and Heeder, 1984, 1984–85; Morrison and Holdridge-Crane, 1984) continue to reinforce the conclusion that ERT is an effective *short*-term mode of therapy over a long period of follow-up and is superior to some other therapeutic treatments (e.g. self-help instruction). Some statistical data (see Morrison, 1979a) might also be of relevance here. Only 23 per cent of those who complete at least 15 sessions of ERT need to have more than 15 sessions. Ninety-six per cent of those clients who complete at least 15 sessions of ERT report at least some overall positive change, as measured by regularly administered symptom checklists or measures of construct change, upon completion of ERT. Among those clients who complete at least 15 sessions, 73 per cent report a symptom reduction of at least 50 per cent of those original symptoms (e.g. headaches, suicidal thoughts, excessive alcohol intake, etc.).

IMPLICATIONS FOR OTHER PSYCHOTHERAPISTS

Because of the way the theory and practice of ERT evolved, I feel very strongly about the importance of a therapist finding a theoretical and practical approach which suits his or her personality. Certainly in my case, behavioural approaches did not fit my personality or needs. Such an approach, if maintained, would perhaps — were it not for my dream — only have helped to shore up my defences against any underlying memories. I find that now I am driven to understand the causes behind a client's symptom, just as I was, at least unconsciously, always driven to understand myself. I never felt that behaviour therapy got to the heart of who I was. I do not believe that any novice in the field of therapy should just learn one type of therapy and apply one set of techniques, especially if these are handed down by some professor in graduate school. I believe that such therapists should constantly weigh different approaches and try different techniques until they find the most comfortable *and* effective approach for themselves. If a therapist finds the clinical approach he or she uses is uncomfortable — for example, a *Gestalt* approach for a therapist who is uncomfortable with a client expressing feelings — undoubtedly the client is going to be uncomfortable with that approach as well. And such discomfort is going to affect the client-therapist relationship which is often the key to the effectiveness of the therapy.

A second implication of my experience in developing the type of therapy best suited for me is that, unlike the experience of all too many therapists, I have never even approached 'psychological burnout'. I believe that the entire process of first questioning one's approach and then finding one more suitable as well as more effective tends to make the actual application of theory and techniques that much more creative, fulfilling, interesting and enjoyable for the therapist. Once one begins the process of questioning one's work, as a result of personal experiences and 'key cases', one tends to continue this valuable process. I firmly believe that such a process keeps therapy sessions from becoming routine because, even if some of the clients are not very interesting, the creative process of refining one's theory and techniques is.

A third implication is that there is a necessary (in my opinion) de-emphasis on diagnostic procedures. I have long been impressed by the unscientific nature of our diagnostic procedures (see Mischel, 1968), and discovering my own pathology has impressed me with how difficult it is to sum up a person's real problem with a few words. After all, even great novelists such as Dostoevski were dissatisfied with their descriptions of a central character, even after writing about such a character with millions of words. However, sometimes it takes a 'key' case to induce a psychotherapist to really appreciate how sterile our diagnostic word-game can become.

Another effect of my change in therapeutic style is the increased need to research the effectiveness of techniques. Had I been content to remain with the behavioural approach I initially adopted, I could have rationalised not doing outcome and process research as due to the fact that a virtual plethora of studies exists demonstrating the effectiveness of such techniques with a wide variety of problems. However, since the personal and professional experiences outlined in this chapter compelled me to change my therapeutic style, I was now faced with a new challenge: how to demonstrate that my new style was effective over time. This challenge led me to a new interest in research (almost abandoned after completing my doctoral dissertation!) and this in turn led me to ask the kinds of question that continually make my practice stimulating and interesting.

Lastly, this 'key' case convinced me of the necessity of developing what I have termed a consumer-oriented approach, where the therapist actively ensures the protection of the client's rights within psychotherapy. I could see how I had within myself the crucial set of data I needed to understand myself and change myself. And Joan, my client, had the data she needed. We just needed the right method to allow these memories to surface. So often psychotherapists do not listen to clients like Joan. They write them off as unsuitable for therapy. A consumer-oriented philosophy helps to avoid such errors. I have asked former clients to come together in a group to discuss my theory and techniques so that I could learn from them about their impressions of what seemed to help them the most. I treasure such client-therapist seminars (see Morrison, 1980a) as more intellectually stimulating and productive than any graduate-school course, thesis, book or article with which I have become acquainted.

In my present practice — and this has been so since I began my private practice — I accept all clients who call. A consumer-oriented approach seems to dictate that I not turn down people because of their personality, their problems, or even because of their lack of money. Only when I feel I am incompetent to handle a particular problem, and the client understands and accepts this, do I refer a client elsewhere.

It is my hope that I will not forget these implications of the experiences that I have outlined. Because of my vivid images from that dream about my mother, I doubt that I ever will.

NOTES

1. For a more elaborate discussion of the key concepts of 'memory' and 'early childhood experiences', as well as that of 'stress', see Morrison (1979a).
2. When clients have great difficulty forming vivid images, to enhance a client's ability to image a therapist can offer the person some imagery training (e.g. focusing on an object with eyes open and then trying to retain the image long after eyes are closed) or the use of hypnosis. Only a few clients fail to respond to these extra efforts.

3. Further details on techniques used with various clients (e.g. depressed and anxious artists, homosexual clients, persons who need to grieve the loss of a loved one, etc.) can be found elsewhere (Morrison, 1978, 1980c, 1981a, b, 1986a,b).

4. Most clients find it painful to retrieve memories that have been purposely relegated to a minimum level of awareness since the retrieval of such 'repressed' memories seems to carry with it the painful emotion that caused the clients to repress in the first place.

REFERENCES

Bannister, D. and Fransella, F. (1971). *Inquiring man: the theory of personal constructs*. Baltimore: Penguin Books

Dember, W.N. (1965). The new look in motivation. *American Scientist, 53*, 409-27

Farber, B.A. (1985). The genesis, development, and implications of psychological-mindedness in psychotherapists. *Psychotherapy: Theory, Research and Practice, 22*, 170-7

Fiske, D. and Maddi, S. (1961). *Functions of varied experience*. Homewood, IL: Dorsey Press

Harris, F.R., Johnston, M.K., Kelley, S.C. and Wolf, M.M. (1964). Effects of positive social reinforcement on regressed crawling of a nursery school child. *Journal of Educational Psychology, 55*, 35-41

Hawkins, R.P., Peterson, R.F., Schweid, E. and Bijou, S.W. (1966). Behavior therapy in the home: amelioration of problem parent-child relations in a therapeutic role. *Journal of Experimental Child Psychology, 4*, 99-107

Hebb, D.O. (1955). Drives and the C.N.S. *Psychological Review, 62*, 243-54

Janov, A. (1970). *The primal scream*. New York: Dell

Kanfer, F.H. and Phillips, J.S. (1970). *Learning foundations of behavior therapy*. New York: Wiley

Kanfer, F.H. and Saslow, G. (1965). Behavioral analysis: an alternative to diagnostic classification. *Archives of General Psychiatry, 12*, 529-38

Kelly, G. (1955). *The psychology of personal constructs* (2 vols). New York: Norton

MacKay, D. (1984). Behavioural psychotherapy. In W. Dryden (Ed.), *Individual therapy in Britain*. London: Harper & Row

Malmo, R.B. (1959). Activation: a neuropsychological dimension. *Psychological Review, 66*, 367-8

Maslow, A.H. (Ed.) (1976). Education and peak experiences. In A.H. Maslow, *The further reaches of human nature*. New York: Penguin

Mischel, W. (1968). *Personality and assessment*. New York: Wiley

Morrison, J.K. (1974). Labeling: the case of an 'autistic' child. *Journal of Family Counseling, 2*, 71-80

Morrison, J.K. (1977). The family heritage: dysfunctional constructs and roles. *International Journal of Family Counseling, 5*, 54-8

Morrison, J.K. (1978). Successful grieving: changing personal constructs through mental imagery. *Journal of Mental Imagery, 2*, 63-8

Morrison, J.K. (1979a). Emotive-reconstructive therapy: changing constructs by means of mental imagery. In A.A. Sheikh and J.T. Shaffer (Eds), *The potential of fantasy and imagination*. New York: Brandon House

Morrison, J.K. (1979b). A consumer-oriented approach to psychotherapy. *Psychotherapy: Theory, Research and Practice, 16*, 381–4

Morrison, J.K. (1980a). Client-psychotherapist seminars for refining theory and practice. *Professional Psychology, 11*, 696–9

Morrison, J.K. (1980b). Emotive-reconstructive therapy: a short-term psychotherapeutic use of mental imagery. In. J.E. Shorr, J. Connelly, G. Sobel and T. Robin (Eds), *Imagery: its many dimensions and applications* (vol. 1). New York: Plenum

Morrison, J.K. (1980c). Homosexual fantasies and the reconstructive use of imagery. *Journal of Mental Imagery, 4*, 165–8

Morrison, J.K. (1981a). The use of imagery techniques in family therapy. *American Journal of Family Therapy, 9*, 52–6

Morrison, J.K. (1981b). Using death imagery to induce proper grieving: an emotive-reconstructive approach. In E. Klinger (Ed.), *Imagery: concepts, results, and applications* (vol. II). New York: Plenum

Morrison, J.K. (1984a). Eight steps toward protecting the psychotherapy client from 'consumer fraud'. In J. Hariman (Ed.), *Does psychotherapy really help people?* Springfield, IL: Charles C. Thomas

Morrison, J.K. (1984b). A consumer approach to clinical practice. In P.A. Keller and L.G. Ritt (Eds), *Innovations in clinical practice: a source book* (vol. III). Sarasota, FL: Professional Resource Exchange, Inc.

Morrison, J.K. (1986a). The emotive-reconstructive use of imagery to induce psychotherapeutic grieving. In A.A. Sheikh (Ed.), *Death before life: growth potential of death imagery*. Farmingdale, NY: Baywood

Morrison, J.K. (1986b). The artist in imagery therapy: a picture is worth a thousand words. *Journal of Communication Therapy*

Morrison, J.K. and Cometa, M.S. (1977). Emotive-reconstructive psychotherapy: a short-term cognitive approach. *American Journal of Psychotherapy, 31*, 294–301

Morrison, J.K. and Cometa, M.S. (1979). Emotive-reconstructive therapy and client problem resolution: periodic accountability to the consumer. In J.K. Morrison (Ed.), *A consumer approach to community psychology*. Chicago: Nelson-Hall

Morrison, J.K. and Cometa, M.S. (1980). A cognitive, reconstructive approach to the psychotherapeutic use of imagery. *Journal of Mental Imagery, 4*, 35–42

Morrison, J.K. and Cometa, M.S. (1982). Variations in developing systems. In J.C. Mancuso and J. Adams-Webber (Eds), *The construing person*. New York: Praeger

Morrison, J.K. and Heeder, R. (1984). Follow-up study of the effectiveness of emotive-reconstructive therapy. *Psychological Reports, 54*, 149–50

Morrison, J.K. and Heeder, R. (1984–85). Feeling-expression ratings by psychotherapist as predictive of imagery therapy outcome: a pilot study. *Imagination, Cognition and Personality, 4*, 219–23

Morrison, J.K. and Holdridge-Crane, S. (1984). Emotive-reconstructive therapy and the reduction of artists' problem behaviors and negative self-constructs: a pilot study. *Psychological Reports, 54,* 505-6

Morrison, J.K. and Teta, D.C. (1978). Simplified use of the Semantic Differential to measure psychotherapy outcome. *Journal of Clinical Psychology, 34,* 751-3

Morrison, J.K., Becker, R.E. and Isaacs, K. (1981). Comparative effectiveness of individual imagery psychotherapy vs. didactic self-help seminars. *Psychological Reports, 49,* 923-8

Morrison, J.K., Becker, R.E. and Heeder, R. (1983a). Individual imagery psychotherapy vs didactic self-help seminars: comparative effect on problem behaviors. *Psychological Reports, 52,* 709-10

Morrison, J.K., Becker, R.E. and Heeder, R. (1983b). Reduction of anxiety: comparative effectiveness of imagery psychotherapy vs self-help seminars. *Psychological Reports, 53,* 417-18

Penfield, W. and Roberts, L. (1959). *Speech and brain mechanisms.* Princeton, NJ: Princeton University Press

Piaget, J. (1972). *Judgement and reasoning in the child.* Totowa, NJ: Littlefield, Adams & Co.

Rogers, C. (1951). *Client-centered therapy.* Cambridge, MA: The Riverside Press/Houghton Mifflin

Sarbin, T.R., Taft, R. and Bailey, D.E. (1960). *Clinical inference and cognitive theory.* New York: Holt, Rinehart & Winston

Schachter, S. and Singer, J.E. (1962). Cognitive, social and psychological determinants of emotional state. *Psychological Review, 69,* 379-99

Sharaf, M.R. (1960). *An approach to the theory and measure of intraception.* Unpublished doctoral dissertation, Harvard University

Singer, J. (1974). *Imagery and daydream methods in psychotherapy and behavior modification.* New York: Academic Press

3

The Process of Being Known and the Initiation of Change

Mark Aveline

PRIOR THEORY AND PRACTICE

The life of a psychotherapist may be likened to a journey without end. The way is shaped by where one starts from, who walked with you in the early stages, what persons, patients, friends and foes are encountered, and whether the terrain is harsh or easy going. Along the way there are many unforeseen twists and turns, doubling-backs and advances. Some divides in the path lead to dead ends, others to vantage points whence new vistas can be seen. Often, only in retrospect can one see why this path was chosen and not that. In a lifetime, only part of the great country of human life can be explored. To reach some point of rest is comfortable; to continue exploring is to know strange things and to be humble before the vastness of what is to be known. Quite soon, one discovers that others — therapists, poets, writers and philosophers — have explored the same domain and described what seems new. And yet, travellers' tales mean little till one has journeyed to the point where discovery lies. The psychotherapies that I describe in this chapter were two such journeys.

In 18 years as a psychotherapist, 7 of these as a trainee and 11 as a consultant, I have worked with many patients and read widely. Sometimes I feel that I have learnt a great deal, but often that I have hardly begun.

My path to psychotherapy has been unusually broad. I have been supervised by humanistic, Jungian and behavioural therapists and have been influenced by seeing the application of personal construct theory in therapy. I have worked on an intensive inpatient unit with a Freudian developmental perspective, and have learnt the skills of leadership of a closed group from an object-relations supervisor versed in the works of Fairbairn and Guntrip. Another perspective in my learning was opened up by personal experience in encounter groups and the use of creative therapies. Latterly, I have been impressed by the insights and the way of working developed in the Cultural, Interpersonal and Existential Schools. From all this comes a way of practising psychotherapy that is still evolving and a conclusion that there is no royal road in psychotherapy. All approaches illuminate aspects of any one condition; none is a total answer; each will appeal differentially to patient and therapist.

The unique feature of psychotherapy is the structured professional relationship between the therapist and one or more patients (the word 'patient' is used in the non-pejorative sense of meaning a person who suffers), who meet in a relationship which is genuine, equal in feeling but asymmetrical in disclosure (Hobson, 1985), and which is directed towards assisting the patient in making changes in personal functioning. In this relationship, though the declared need is with one, both may be changed — not shrunk but stretched! The good quality of the relationship restores hope and redevelops trust; it is both the means of change and the substrate for the risky business of developing new strategies for personally difficult situations. In a mechanistic and materialistic world, the deliberate focus on experience and the personal meaning placed upon it asserts the value of that realm of human life. In my therapy, the emphasis on personal responsibility and choice, on what the person can do today and tomorrow rather than on what was done in time gone by, points to change in that portion of the external world that is, or potentially is, under that person's control. The justification for psychotherapy lies in the help that it can provide with the problems that people have in living their lives and living with each other. In this, psychotherapy is a practical discipline and a creative art (Aveline, 1979).

My differential learning has given a special cast to my practice. In order to highlight changes in my practice from then to now and to contrast with other approaches described in this volume, I will summarise my practice points (p.p.) more dogmatically than is my wont. The importance of the process of being known and the personal history of the therapist, my last two practice points (8, 9), was highlighted for me by my key case.

p.p. 1. Countering demoralisation and enhancing hope

Most people seeking psychotherapeutic help are demoralised; their demoralisation results in distress and disability and stems from a sense of failure or of powerlessness to alter themselves and their environment. All types of successful psychotherapy have measures to restore self-confidence and to promote a sense of mastery through successful experiences (Frank, 1973; Aveline, 1984). I actively seek to counter the demoralisation and promote mastery.

p.p. 2. An interpersonal focus

I conceptualise personality as the meeting place of relationships, and all personal disturbance as occurring in or being a function of interpersonal processes. In this, I follow in the footsteps of Adler (1924), Horney (1945) and Sullivan (1953). For me, the individual is not an isolated, static unit but a person who can only properly be seen in the light of his actions and the reactions of his environment. While much of the work of psychotherapy is to do with elucidating intrapsychic processes, what happens between people is, in my view, the arena in which psychotherapy has most to offer. This arises naturally from the nature of psychotherapy which essentially is a personal remedy for problems of relationship.

p.p. 3. The present is accessible and relevant; the past is less knowable

All memories are distorted by active and passive forgetting, wishful thinking and the selective effect of the context in which they are being retold. In the dyad of patient and therapist, isolated as it usually is from the past and present external social systems, stories are told which can all too easily be assumed to be historically true rather than narratively true. A cosy blaming of faults on to others and especially parents may occur, thereby absolving the patient from his existential responsibility. What is more knowable and more relevant is what is happening now in the person's life. This is not to say that I am not interested in the past, but only as a prelude to the present and the future.

p.p. 4. Being and becoming

All of us who are psychologically alive are fundamentally involved in the process of being and becoming. We are our 'being in the world', the *Dasein* of Heidegger (1962) and Binswanger (1956), and this being is made up of acts. Acts are more than behaviours; they are intentional steps on paths that we map for ourselves. As a therapist, I am thus concerned with how the details of interactional sequences in current conflictual relationships both define that person's problematic 'being in the world' and lay down the benchmarks against which change can be determined and significant advances made. It is for difficulties in that world that the patient is seeking help, and it is by change in that world that I judge the success of our mutual endeavour. Hitherto change outside the therapy room was more important for me than change within the room.

p.p. 5. A corrective emotional experience

At some stage, in order to change, the patient has to face his personally most difficult situations and live through them to more fruitful ways of being. The skill of the therapist lies in his or her ability to assist the patient in writing a new end to an old, sad story. In this, it does not particularly matter whether the change occurs inside or outside the therapy situation, and indeed the direct benefit of the latter has obvious advantages (Alexander and French, 1946; Aveline, in preparation). Times of crisis in a person's life are particularly potent moments for change. As these cases taught me, continuing the therapy when all hangs in the balance is to take the path that leads to new learning.

In contrast to a purely psychoanalytic model, in my therapy the transferential elements have been background to the focus on current problematic actual relationships. Naturally and usefully, when the outside problematic pattern of interaction is recreated in the therapy relationship, I attend to this, but I do not primarily intend, as a psychoanalyst would, to create that pattern in a transferrence neurosis. My temperament is not suited to deep regressive work; my assessment of how therapy achieves its ends has not convinced me that it is generally necessary. Progression, not regression, is my motto.

p.p. 6. Significant acts

Each of us develops out of our experience an internal map of how the world is. Each map is different though the landscape is part of the common world; the perspective is determined by individual assumptions. The map enables us to predict our behaviour and that of others, and foresee the outcome of our actions. Frank (1973) aptly terms this the assumptive world. I find the concept straightforward and one that is easily accessible to me and the patient. Ultimately it is through acts, both the acts we do and the ones we do not do, that our assumptive world is reinforced or altered. In my practice, I place great emphasis on comprehending in detail the sequence of interpersonal events in any current problematic situation. I listen for metaphors or images which will form a personal shorthand for significant events or ways of perceiving self. This analysis informs the patient and me as to what is habitually done, and what would be significant acts of change. Such significant acts may appear relatively unimportant to an uninformed external assessor, but to us they have dynamic importance and, once succeeded in, represent the yielding of those dynamics.

p.p. 7. The indivisibility of the intrapsychic and the interpersonal

Often, psychotherapy writers have emphasised the intrapsychic or the interpersonal to the exclusion of the other and have likewise addressed their interventions to one and not the other. I see no special priority. The two are indivisible; each reflects and influences the other. When I intervene in the interpersonal world, my exploration takes me straight into the intrapsychic world of meaning. When I intervene in the intrapsychic world, I influence the interpersonal.

p.p. 8. Being known

A *sine qua non* of therapy that extends over time and explicates meaning and experience is a coming together of two explorers: patient and therapist. How they combine is a function of what they explore and who they are as people. Most often the union is not achieved easily. The growing closeness of the union activates in the exchange of therapy the conflicts that stymie the patient in his interpersonal life. The emphasis, here, is on the existential process of being known by another and less on the transference distortions

p.p. 9. The personal history of the therapist

In therapy we listen carefully to all that the patient says, but in attempting to make imaginative leaps into his world, to experience the other side (Buber, 1958), we often project on to him what we know best — our own determining myths and fantasies. Some might argue that it is impossible to do otherwise. Our own sensitivities enable us to respond to some hurts or outrages better than others. In this key case, aspects of my nature worked for and against the finding of the therapeutic way. I know myself to be tenacious, ambitious and seemingly self-contained; I enjoy creating. I believe myself to be trustworthy. I have a strong reparative element in my make-up and easily feel responsible and guilty. I dislike causing others humiliation or shame. I am acutely aware of anger, especially when it is directed towards me, and am sensitive to movements that others make towards and away from me.

DESCRIPTION OF THE KEY CASE

My basic training is in medicine and psychiatry. I work as a consultant psychotherapist in the National Health Service in Britain. My clinical practice is mostly with individual patients seen weekly for usually between 25 and 100 sessions. I also lead therapy groups and spend a small amount of time on marital and family work. I meet with individual patients in my personal office which is located in an informally furnished house. Patients have a choice of identical armchairs, and sessions are 40 minutes long at the same time each week.

I met with Mary 73 times over a 2½-year period, some time in the last six years. Some details of her biography have been altered to preserve confidentiality. In her early thirties, she was living alone and was in the first year of a three-year vocational training. Four years before, she had broken away from an unhappy marriage, and six months before I met her had suffered the major blow of her five-year-old daughter choosing to go from her to live with her former husband, himself resident 200 miles away.

In her pre-assessment interview goals in psychotherapy questionnaire, which all referrals to my Unit routinely complete (Aveline and Smith, in preparation), she identified as her chief problems depression, a past full of unsuccessful relationships and feelings of panic when she could no longer maintain a facade of normality. Her life felt futile and without purpose. She felt unable to do what she wanted and to assert her point of view without seeming aggressive. She was plagued by her need to justify herself and a tendency to feel guilty. Perhaps most important of all was her sense of being controlled by events rather than being in control of them and the way in which she had chosen loneliness as a means of self-protection. She wanted to be more positive about life and to overcome her fear of getting close to others and of letting them get close to her.

In working with her, these issues were our focus in considering her outside life, but also became the substance of our exchange within the sessions. On looking back at the therapy, I feel again her sadness, the sudden days and weeks of uplifting hope, and then of bitter disappointment. I remember hesitant approaches to one another and my uncomfortable feelings of being not the person that she required and of having injured her, and then having to repair the damage by making peace. Later the strength was found to overcome these hesitancies, truths were spoken, and the process of change was initiated.

The bare bones of her history as related at the assessment interview with a colleague were of growing up in a family where individuality and the open expression of feeling were not encouraged, especially not by her mother. Her single sibling, a brother four years older, conformed and was approved; she did not and was not. Having failed to get into university through not passing one of her 'A' levels, she followed her mother's choice of what was suitable for a girl by taking secretarial training and, then, quickly marrying. She had little in common with her husband and, despite trying to cement the relationship by having a child, they drifted apart. She emerged from the marriage and — to her great credit — had for two or three years before she came into therapy held down a demanding job and maintained herself and her daughter. She then took her individuation one step further by beginning post-vocational training; in her class she found herself a decade older than most of her fellow students.

Beginning

The first few sessions contained the key themes, though their significance was not fully apparent to me then. At the first session she observed me with care if not with caution, was forceful in wanting me to tell her what to focus on, and at the same time conveyed the high standard she had for herself and by implication had for others. The loss of her daughter to her former husband was a 'kick in the teeth' but not something that she could be angry about as it was one of her principles in life that everyone should make their own decisions; furthermore it was improper for one person to hold on to another. She was hesitant about committing herself to therapy but wanted the weekly sessions to begin sooner than I could offer.

She felt bitterly alone. Her life was her responsibility, but yet it seemed pointless and empty. Two years before, one important boyfriend, Terry, had wanted her but not her daughter; another, Martin, had wanted her on any terms but she had recoiled from his dependence, which she saw as weakness. To her detriment, she was over-ready to see the point of view of others and to be giving; others, therefore, only saw her competent self. She angrily reacted against my suggestion that this competent self was not just imposed by others but also by herself as a way of avoiding being hurt. She was, she argued, society's victim through its taboo on the expression of sadness and needs. Later, she was to say 'smile and the world laughs with you; cry and you cry alone.'

Sessions four to nine illustrate aspects of our relationship which were to be writ large later on. Mary had spoken with distaste of her parents' repeated message that they had only stayed together for the children. But facing them with her anger would not be fair and would kill them. I fed back my impression of her being fair on the outside, valuing integrity, and angry and critical inside. My words were an invitation to bring our paths closer together, and for a moment she accepted. She described herself as the 'cuckoo in the family nest', the only one who was different, the one who would not conform to the traditional female role. With approval in my voice, I emphasised that for her being different was life saving, but that she had paid and was paying the price of hostility and misunderstanding by others. She picked up my encouragement to take risks, to try relationships again, and retreated — perhaps I had been coercive — crying that she did not want to be hurt again. I criticised myself for running ahead.

A black cloud had descended by the next week and I deserved her anger for suggesting that her state was related to the week before. In addition, in her eyes, I was inhuman, cool and detached while she was human and full of feelings; to show these to me would be humiliating. Suicide was one solution, better than her previous escape routes of alcohol or anyone's bed. She willingly accepted my offer of an extra session. At session six she was coping better, having deployed her two defences of 'battening the hatches down' and 'filling the day with activity'.

An exam success in which she had used all of her academic ability, successful confrontations with noisy library users and a neighbour, and the experience of being held like a child by a girlfriend accounted for her exuberant state the following week. She was more open to my image of her as someone who takes a strong motherly role and yet who wants to be mothered.

I arrived late for session eight. Understandably Mary was angry. She was, also, downcast and silent. Reluctantly and in tears she accused me of taking a sadistic delight in having broken her shell and exposed her dependency. 'Now you've got me squirming — I suppose it's part of therapy.' I spoke of the need to integrate her valued independent and hated dependent self that she so wished to dispense with. She agreed that she was 'a person of extremes'. A contextual factor emerged: the end of the academic term and the impending loss of her life-structuring role as a student.

Easier ground had been reached in session nine. A key factor was a new man in her life, a gentle divorcee with whom she had in common the fact that he was a single parent. Mary was frightened by her attraction to him. She feared being swept away and getting hurt; it was safer to stay at one of her extremes: the extreme of isolation. I found myself urging her to go slowly; a justifiable caution but also a reflection of my over-protective almost possessive feelings.

Looking back on these sessions, many new understandings occur to me. At the time, I attended to and emphasised Mary's way of being (p.p. 4) in her reported world, that is, in the world of current relationships external to the therapy room (p.p. 2 and 4). Conversely my awareness of how caught up I was in a similar pattern within the room was at a preconscious level. The spotlight of my attention had not fully illuminated it; I did not see how my coming to know her was activating the pattern (p.p. 8). I noticed to be sure that sometimes my psychological movements towards her were comforting and sometimes frightening, and deduced from this the conflict between her isolated, lonely self and her dependent hurtable self. I had confidence that the experience of better relationships would be the corrective one which would reconcile her two extremes, and that this new 'being' would primarily occur in the external world (p.p. 1, 4 and 5). My focus was outwards-directed towards, for example, exploring the conflictual relationship with her daughter. Here, her difficulty in facing her resentment over the decision of her child of five to live with her former husband made sense when viewed against Mary's imperative not to be possessive and controlling like her mother (p.p. 3). I did not attend to my strong engagement in the repeated patterns of her story (p.p. 6). I was inclined to minimise the tension that flared up between us, and when I did address it, my framework was historical.

The second phase

Her daughter visited during the vacation. This brought to the surface resentful feelings that her life-space was being invaded. Life, once more, seemed out of Mary's control. She had little money, which reduced her independence and hurt her pride. She had to provide for her daughter, and the new man in her life was not proving as efficient as he had first appeared. Memories from her childhood flooded up to be discussed and pushed down again. She recalled two formative experiences; first, her mother stigmatising her for being partially deaf and, secondly, feeling very much alone when she was admitted to hospital at the age of five.

I gradually became aware that certain of my comments were received as insensitive assaults. My intended message was of benevolent interest in exploring her puzzling feelings, but the reception, for example, of anything I said about Terry, the well regarded boyfriend of two years before who wanted Mary but not her daughter, was quite different. He understood her and made her sit down when she was upset and say what she was really feeling. However, he, also, wanted his freedom to come and go as he pleased on the spur of the moment. I questioned her portrayal of him as 'sensitive and concerned'. Was he not a little selfish and had it not been insensitive to reply laconically to her lonely letter six months before that he might see her in a couple of years should his work bring him to her town? This communication was rejected out of hand. My response was to rephrase it in ever more tactful ways as it seemed that there was a truth to be faced or at the very least considered. This modification also failed, and it was clear to me that there was something that my way of practice was not taking into account.

The next session began stickily. Mary was silent and could only think negatively about herself. Her gloom was not lightened by my suggestion that she had been taught by someone to expect the worst. She replied that she could remember nothing before the age of ten.

At length, her irritation surfaced. What was the point of her seeing me when her views were not accepted. I was telling her what to think and threatening to take away her precious memories of Terry. To myself, I thought that those who threaten another's idols do so at their peril. To Mary, I suggested that a central concern for her was not to be influenced. In a more accepting tone, she remembered at the age of eight deciding to go her own way and not conform to her mother's wishes. I related this reaction against her mother's pressure to the inhibition that Mary felt about voicing her opposition when her daughter decided to move away. This seemed a likely direction and we wandered off down this path, temptingly smooth with room for two, and, perhaps, both a little relieved that we were on the easier ground of past relationships. With hindsight, I would have handled the situation differently and recognised that the jagged uncomfortable way was the main way, the road of central importance and change. I should have stayed with her feelings of outrage when I threatened to control her.

The pattern becomes clearer

Her lability of outlook and vulnerability to setbacks and her sensitivity to my presumed view of her were increasingly evident as each week went by. On return to college she regained her student role. The stream of study carried her on, but she hit against the rocks of isolation and being different. Some younger women cast her in the role of mother and protector, and confided to her their independent promiscuous lives. The tension in the room rose when Mary asked me what I thought of this promiscuity. I replied neutrally that on the one hand it could be a natural phase and the other a driven need. I turned the conversation away from what I thought to what she thought of her promiscuous phase, her search for comfort.

Mary was irritated by the suggestion that she had a dependent self. She spoke of her difficult relationships with men. Some depended on her and she despised them for this (the unacceptable part of herself); these men suffocated her by wanting to control her (I wondered if this was a warning to me). Others were independent spirits and these she liked best; but with them, a time would come — often the time of ending — when she would want them to bend to her in some visible way. For Mary, for them to bend would signify her great value to them. But, of course, men chosen for their independent style continued in this way and Mary would be cast down into depression (p.p. 2, 4, 6). The dilemma of her inner extremes was played out in her intimate choices.

At our next meeting she was consumed with self-hate. I interpreted that she was only listening to the criticism from her mother that she had internalised. For a moment she could take in my words and feel unpersecuted enough to tell me how her mother was still saying that she was bad and still implying to her that life without a man was awful. Then, the moment was lost, and her anger flared. She accused me of pushing her back into the marriage slot in society. Feeling sinisterly transformed, I replied that this was her interpretation and that I did not recognise any such intent on my part. I made sense of what had happened by postulating that she had an inner murderous hate for her mother which she generally turned against herself and which surfaced when she felt others treated her in a hateful way. Mary was horrified. She had never thought that before and anyway such thoughts could not be entertained as her parents were 'poor old people'. We ended on a subdued note.

Paradox, again, entered into our next meeting. Mary felt sad and pessimistic. If she died no-one would notice; no gap would be left. 'I would be sad', I truthfully replied. Mary grew angry. Out of this truthful, passionate exchange, layers of her being gave up their secrets. Being cared about provoked anger in her — anger at not having been loved by her parents as a child — and, also, a frightened longing for love now.

At our twentieth meeting, Mary was brighter. She had been thinking that as a child she had developed a false self (Laing, 1959) to please her parents and was only now bringing into view her inner self. Her parents relied upon her and assumed that they could continue so doing, which she resented. I wondered if she could not be more direct (p.p. 6) and gradually undermine their illusion, but Mary was apprehensive that any confrontation would destroy them — they remained upset for months after any criticism. However, we both laughed when I joked that there might be poison in the cake that she was baking in preparation for a visit home.

The following week's session was hesitant, with Mary in low spirits and seeming to hang on to my words. My comment that her state might be a reaction to the sense of power to challenge her parents that she had toyed with the week before was not understood and Mary started to talk in a small voice, crying and being critical of herself for not understanding my words. Again I felt that they were heard in a very different way than I intended, and I interpreted the transference by linking her present way of talking with how she had spoken with her parents as a child (Malan, 1979). Childhood memories emerged, and the next week she had a fantasy which was both distressing and curiously relieving that she and her brother might be illegitimate and not really of the same blood as her parents.

Significant acts

In the middle and final thirds of therapy, Mary's relationships with men and friends offered many opportunities for significant acts of change (p.p. 6). An early opportunity came with a move into a shared house with two fellow lodgers, one a man in his fifties and the other a single man of the same age as herself. The older man treated her like a young daughter and wanted to know the wheres and whats of her social life. The girlfriend of the younger man took a traditional female role and, much to Mary's annoyance, washed his shirts and spent hours in the kitchen cooking his meals. Mary felt trapped, her independence gone and her concept of her own femaleness threatened. She and I recognised that she was facing a recreation of some disliked aspects of her childhood, and we discussed how she might redress the balance by setting limits to what she would answer and negotiating times for use of the kitchen. Our co-operative agreement was tinged with ambivalence on her part as she felt scared when I had noticed without her telling me how frightened she was. Were her defences so easily breached so that others could see into her? As it turned out, *Kairos* (Kelman, 1969), the auspicious moment, had not arrived for successful significant acts and she moved back to her flat. She did, however, succeed in refusing to help her parents move house when they had already enlisted the aid of her brother and friends. A few weeks later she was to resist her mother babying her, and was able to hold her position despite her mother blackmailing her with tears; to her pleasant surprise, her father emerged from his background role to support her.

Two short-lived affairs brought all her fears to the surface. She went to a 'marvellous party' with one man, a recent divorcee, but was devastated when he would not meet her the next day. The hint of rejection was enough to make her literally run away in distress. The knowledge that he had a girlfriend and might adversely compare Mary sexually with her compounded the situation. She wanted to feel that he was committed to her. For me to suggest that caution might be prudent early in a relationship was to criticise her and take advantage of her vulnerability. This man drew back from Mary saying that he could not cope with her sudden 'cutting-off' from him. (I found Mary's cutting-off from me at moments of understanding and concern equally disconcerting.) Another man seemed very promising but stunned her with the news that he was going to work in another town. It seemed clear to me that she was choosing men who were as apprehensive about commitment as herself; she endowed them with an idealised image, ignored the warning signs, and then was devastated when the end came. In contrast to the conditional love from her mother, she wanted to be prized as she was, but her longing for this and her fear when it began to happen confused her men and ultimately drove them away.

In the final seven months, the same pattern recurred with an important new boyfriend, Stephen, but she was able to recognise the pattern, discuss with me what was going wrong and continue in the relationship while finding new solutions to old situations. How we passed from me being critic and attacker to collaborator and guide at moments of crisis is detailed in the next section. With Stephen, she learned to be more open, and, for example, to risk alienating him by asking him to stay away when she wanted to be alone. She was no longer panicked into flight by the apparent breakdown in the relationship and was able to hold her ground and work through the innocent misunderstandings. Most significant of all was the fact that the relationship lasted, and when she finished therapy it was set to prosper.

Being known and the initiation of change

With Mary I walked a narrow, changing path. The way ahead was often black, and one or both of us were at fault for that. She revelled in the sun when it shone as it rarely did, but expected it not to last. At times of despair she railed against the inequality of therapy; it would be much easier if we met as friends, as equals; then, it would be less humiliating and frightening to show her hurt, needy self. One wrong word from me and I would be transformed into a repressive critic, a role that I found uncomfortable. My sensitivities had the beneficial effect of easily allowing me to understand her reactions, but worked against an early confrontation of the pattern when I saw how pained she was by disappointment (p.p. 9). In terms of transference, I alternated between idealised friend and critical mother. Sullivan's (1970) concept of parataxic distortion captured how I felt; there would be dialogue between Mary and me — and then between Mary and a third, hateful person whom she regarded as being me. This sinister transformation happened again and again. I attempted to resist it by not accepting the new role or backing off and gently seeking to re-establish the collaborative relationship. However, the nicer I was, the more her underlying disappointment surfaced and the angrier and the more suspicious she became.

I came to see that these transformations were more than enactments of probable aspects of her relationship with her mother but were manifestations of what went wrong with others and what was happening between us. It was me as a person coming to know her as a person that was central. This knowing aroused all her fears and angry disappointments, which in turn called a halt to progress. Realising this allowed me to fight to be the person I am — not just the protective caring polarity that was encouraged by her idealisation and which she ultimately needed — but to use the anger that I felt at being halted and transformed and to share with her the impact of her attacks.

Two examples may illustrate this change. At the mid-point of therapy her appointment was cancelled one week as I had a teaching commitment. She rang asking for an appointment that week. As the teaching event had been cancelled, I offered her through my secretary her usual time. Mary refused the offer. When we met the next week she was withdrawn, subdued and apologetic. She was reluctant to examine the recent happenings but eventually said how disappointed she had been; she had been refused, the refusal was absolute and her need had been urgent. Angered at being once more cast in an insensitive role, I pointed out that she had rights and that I would have made time if she had made clear the gravity of her need. Despite her disbelief, I insisted that this was true. Consequently, we both broke the repetitive, ultimately sterile pattern that we had formed. She neither withdrew feeling let down nor flared up like a child criticised, and I did not sit on the edge of my chair feeling that I had failed, had harmed and, now, must put right. A productive exchange followed in which the great significance to her of asking for extra was explored as was the way in which she had invited disappointment by not being sufficiently direct. A few weeks later she was to test my 'good faith' by asking for and getting an extra session. Change had been initiated and the sequence of consolidation began.

It became progressively easier for us to recognise the pattern when it occurred between us and to address it without resorting to defensive manoeuvres. There were still times when she felt controlled by me and experienced my drawing attention to the fear and anger she felt during holiday breaks from therapy as 'grinding her in the dirt', or reacted with resigned hostility when my perception of events differed from hers, but these grew less frequent. The last was another re-creation of her childhood relationship with her parents when it had been pointless for her to ask for what she wanted as it would have been refused or she would be told that she did not mean what she had said. She became more direct and was able to determine the issues that she wished to address in a session. Her new decisiveness was reflected in similar actions outside therapy.

Some sessions later Mary felt sad and hurt when I did not understand something that she had said. She spoke of her resentment towards her parents and a fear that her anger if expressed would destroy them. She wanted to know what impact it had on me. I answered that it pinned me back into my chair, made me want to go away and left me feeling guilty over having been so clumsy or thoughtless. Then and now I think it was important to have answered directly. Answering as I did *and* at the right moment changed the relationship and freed us to explore together another area in our exchange and opened up a fruitful examination of the same awkward moments with those in her external life to whom she drew close. It helped her gauge her impact and countered both her apprehension that she could destroy and, more importantly, that she was without influence.

Other guides

Within the narrow confines of the consulting room, it is all too easy for the therapist to over-value his centrality in the patient's life. It was thus salutary for me to learn in the second year of Mary's equally long-standing relationship with a fellow student, a widower in his sixties. In their friendship, she was daughter, friend and in fantasy perhaps lover. With him she found she could share her inner feelings, have her confidences respected and be accepted and be prized for what she offered (p.p. 5). He was a guide to the high ground of good personal relationships. Her grief was great when he died of cancer. However, the good quality of that relationship paved the way for the sustained intimacy with her boyfriend Stephen.

The parting of the ways

The consideration of personal imagery and significant acts are important components of my approach. I thus took great pleasure in the painting Mary brought me some weeks before termination. She had pictured herself as a tree with stunted roots and a brittle trunk. However, above, a few leaves sprouted which she linked to commencing therapy and then coloured branches, expanding, full of life and spreading off the sheet.

She went her way. She had graduated, she was looking for a post and hoped to share a home with Stephen. Six months later she sent me a Christmas card with her best wishes.

EMERGENT NEW DEVELOPMENTS

The developments in my work as the result of this key case are extensions of my last two practice points: being known (p.p. 8) and the personal history of the therapist (p.p. 9). I continue to work practically with the interpersonal difficulties in the external world, but am much more aware of and comfortable in working in a personal way with these same difficulties when they occur between me and the patient. In this I emphasise more the personal and less the abstract historical aspects of the transference. My commitment to assisting with change in problematic relationship patterns in the patient's current life remains the same, but I now more fully appreciate the locus for change that exists within the therapy hour in the reality that patient and therapist create. Clearly this has historical antecedents on both sides, but it is in exploring the present experience of each other that much potential for change exists. I bring out my new learning in four further practice points illustrated by work with a subsequent case.

p.p. 10. Moments for change occur at times of tension within the therapeutic relationship

As I know keenly from my work with Mary, there will be moments in therapy when the therapeutic alliance, the 'non-neurotic, rational, reasonable rapport which the patient has with his analyst and which enables him to work purposefully in the analytic situation' (Greenson and Wexler, 1969) is disrupted by tension; this is generally the product of negative feelings and inclines the patient or therapist or both to withdraw. Advancing into the jagged awkwardness of the tension is difficult but illuminating. It is in this moment that one potential for a corrective emotional experience (p.p. 5) and initiation of change lies. Withdrawing is understandable but usually represents a lost opportunity. With Mary, it was only when I stopped pretending that we were at one that it was possible to examine how we had reached the brink of disaster — the breakdown of the relationship — and what the pattern of our interaction signified dynamically.

p.p. 11. Attend closely to the process of the sessions

Content and process are related elements in the sequence of the therapy sessions. Content is the subject matter which forms the readily apparent surface of the session. Process is the underlying, less than conscious, current that directs the content from moment to moment and session to session. The therapist who has a longitudinal perspective can decipher hidden important communications in the sequence of the content; he will be alert to messages about the therapy relationship conveyed in the form of stories told about external events or from alterations in emotional states or sudden changes in topic that are reactions to what has gone before. Subtle changes in emotional tone signal crucial interactions. As indicated (p.p. 10), it is the awkward moments that are often the most illuminating; they arise out of assumptions (p.p. 6) on either side somehow not being met. For the therapist, the feeling within the session is like running one's finger unexpectedly on a thorn or suddenly discovering that one has been cast in a drama quite different from the official play. My transformation with Mary from friend to repressive critic is one example; the alteration was triggered by minor failings to take the idealised role that she wished me to have with her.

p.p. 12. Consider how patient and therapist combine

How the therapist and patient combine in the exchange of therapy is a function of who they are as people. To the combination, the therapist contributes a certain role model learned in training, but of greater importance are his or her personal qualities and the engagement of interests and vulnerabilities by the patient's actions. The interface is formed by the interaction between the two psychological worlds of patient and therapist; both react out of their public and private selves, and *both* are involved in processes of appraising and confirming, valuing and rejecting, freeing and constraining. Understanding the different levels on which the therapist is engaged and having the confidence to use the reactions productively at the right time may convert negative aspects of the fit into positive ones.

With Mary, my protective tendency was enhanced by not wanting to see her hurt and not wanting to be the originator of that hurt. The relationship felt off balance, and we were often close to falling. At the right time, that is, once sufficient trust had been built up through our repeated struggles, a rigorous appraisal of what was happening between us led to the more equal and mature relationship that Mary had desired.

p.p. 13. Be open to being moved by the patient

For many good and less than good reasons, the therapy relationship is fundamentally unequal in power (Heller, 1985). This may compound the patient's sense of powerlessness (p.p. 1). Furthermore, the patient may doubt that he, his dilemmas and feelings have any impact on others, and if they have any impact, he may be unsure of its form. I have always conceptualised the therapeutic relationship as a dialectic where both may be changed; certainly both are moved by what passes between them. Now, I am more open in showing how I am moved.

In my second case, the way in which I showed my frailty illustrates this point and the other developments in practice.

A SECOND CASE

I had been working for several months with a highly intelligent, schizoid young man. He had no friends and affected not to need any. Nevertheless an acquaintance becoming less friendly and thus psychologically moving away from him had precipitated an overdose. His father was an intensely critical, high-achieving man who wanted his children to achieve but who could not cope with their worries. As a child, the patient had learnt to defend by attack and felt more secure when, then and now, he penetrated the defences of others with rapier-like thrusts. His problematic pattern of relationships and its likely origin were clear to me, but he was reluctant to accept my formulation. With me, he undermined my confidence by constantly denigrating the rationale and practice of therapy and manoeuvring me into the position of being the one to sort out his problems as if they had nothing to do with him. The more I strove to understand him, the more he denigrated my acts (p.p. 11). In terms of process, being understood was for him the same as being vulnerable.

I began by interpreting the re-creation of his family dynamics with myself in the role of dangerous father who must be rendered helpless, but to no avail. The interpretation was almost certainly historically correct, but it did not address what was happening in a way that permitted change. His thrusts continued; they penetrated my being and achieved their purpose. I was ready to give up. My omnipotent need led me, in my public self, to be calm and unperturbed but this wore thin as the weeks went by (p.p. 10, 12). At length, I sued for peace. I said 'You can go on using your rapiers against me, and you are so good at it that you will defeat me and I will give up. I don't want that, but is that what you want?' (p.p. 13). Initially he was outraged; I had no right to be upset and should be able to take anything. Later he became less attacking; he was even able to speak of his 'destitute' inner self. My unperturbed defence against being rendered helpless by his attacks had the effect of redoubling their ferocity (p.p. 10, 12). Revealing my fraility, while it appalled him, made me less dangerous and opened the way to productive work (p.p. 13).

IMPLICATIONS FOR OTHER THERAPISTS

It would be self-deceiving to suggest that the forward steps that I have taken have not been taken by other therapists. However, in the therapeutic landscape some are already on what seems to be a promising path and others could beneficially draw closer. It could also be that other guides have found equally good paths to the high ground of good relationships.

The implications of my learning are sixfold: (1) the advantages of synthesis; (2) the importance of the assumptive metaphor that we each have for our kind of therapy; (3) dialogue and authenticity as fundamental elements in the encounter of therapy; (4) the importance of adopting a structural approach to understanding the interactive product of the therapist and patient; (5) the value in promoting change of addressing the present rather than the historical aspects of the transference; and (6) a suggested model for identifying the relationship patterns that are difficult for the patient and which will be problematic in therapy.

Synthesis

Earlier I have stated my view that the intrapsychic and the interpersonal are indivisible (p.p. 7). At least in their writings, many authors act as if this was not so and maintain that there is some primary good in concentrating on what seems to me to be one side of the same coin or, if you will, one end of a continuum. Kleinians consider all their patients' utterances as manifestations of transference, and turn away from considering the detail of the external world. Skinnerians deny the importance of inner experience and conceptualise individual actions as behaviours dictated by stimulus and reinforcement just as the puppet moves to pulls of the strings. I accept, of course, that in practice there is a gap between what therapists say they do and what they actually do; successful therapists are much more similar than different. However, these extreme positions are unreasonable. The twin focus of my approach is a strength. I consider equally the significant acts in the external world that a person makes and wishes to be able to make and the inner world of meaning and dynamic origin. Adopting my position would circumvent much of the continuing sterile debate in which analysts criticise behaviourists for being superficial and behaviourists regard analysts as impractical fantasists. The way might then be open for each to learn from the other.

My work has a pragmatic contemporary emphasis on interpersonal problems and solutions. My two cases fit easily into my model, but then their interpersonal concerns are the concerns of our time. As Levinson (1972) has observed, patients change as the culture alters. The conversion hysterias that Freud saw are rare now. The existential *Angst* that dominated the 1960s and early 1970s has been superseded by concern with the quality of personal relationships.

Images of therapy

In this chapter I have proposed the image of therapy as a landscape which is explored and travelled through by patient and therapist; the journey is important for both. In a similar vein, Schafer (1983) describes the therapist as a seasoned, hardy guide to difficult places. Elsewhere (Aveline, 1980), I have explored the metaphor of the therapist as a good servant who puts his master's needs before his own and safeguards his best interest. Images are important. Hobson's (1985) concept of therapy as conversation and Mair's (1977) of promoting dialogue with and among the patient's inner community of selves are implying a totally different relationship to that predicated on seeing the mind as a black box or supercomputer, or mankind as fallen angels. It behoves therapists to become aware of their assumptive metaphors and the roles that these prescribe. Freud (1938) saw the analyst as an archeologist exploring into the patient's past and making constructions of what had existed before. This backward stance was in line with his view that one function of analysis was as a system of scientific enquiry; it paid relatively little attention to the present and the future.

Langs (1973) proposed the therapist as expert and healer and cautioned against stepping out of that role. He counsels the therapist to maintain proper boundaries and be an effective, healthy, non-corrupt model for the patient; in this, he will guard himself against being seductive or hostile. I agree entirely with this intention: my highest ethical rule is 'Thou shalt not exploit the power relationship of therapy' — but I doubt the means. Overall, I find the image aseptic and cold, safe but unmoving.

Storr (1968) uses the image of an enigma.

> By keeping his own personality in the background and revealing as little of himself as possible, the analyst presents the patient with an enigma. The less the patient knows, the more will his picture of the analyst be coloured by his experience of people in the past; and the clearer will be the analyst's and the patient's perception of what has gone amiss with his previous relationships (p. 78).

I suggest that one can be enigmatic but not an enigma. Everything that one does, what one says, how one sits and the way in which the room is set out, reveals aspects of one's being which are the object of close, legitimate scrutiny by the patient. Indeed, as I have demonstrated in my examples, there is advantage in being, as Guntrip (1968) put it, 'a sufficiently real person to the patient to give him a chance of being a real person himself and not an assembly of defences, or a role, or a conforming mask, or a mass of unresolved tension' (p. 351). Guntrip predicated change on the patient meeting with personal reality in the therapist — a demanding task indeed!

Dialogue and authenticity

The line that I am developing is similar to that taken by Lomas (1981), though I cannot equal his openness as a therapist. Coming from psychoanalysis, he stresses in his work the value of ordinary responses to troubled people as well as the special knowledge unique to psychotherapy. Friendship is his paradigm for therapy rather than the application of scientific theory.

> The commonplace attitudes which are relevant to healing lie in the direction of warmth rather than coldness, trust rather than cynicism, closeness rather than distance, encouragement rather than discouragement, spontaneity rather than calculation. (Lomas, 1981, p. 6).

Above all, he is humble and respectful; the same point is made by Greben (1981). Humanist existential writers, such as Rogers (1961), Buber (1958), May, Angel and Ellenberger (1958) and Yalom (1980), use the language of meeting and encounter. They point towards an authentic meeting, an exploration of the 'in-between' and an experiencing of the other side. Jung saw therapy as a dialectical process between two involved persons in which both were open to the other's influence, both were engaged in enquiry and both contributed to the joint experience (Fordham, 1979). In other words, Jung moved and was moved by his patients. How much do other therapists allow this vital movement?

A structural approach to the dynamics of the patient-therapist relationship

All therapists need to consider their contribution to the pattern that emerges between them and their patient. The therapist is never a neutral figure, however much his theory encourages the belief in consistent scientific techniques (interventions and interpretations) with the prime variability residing in the patient. Sullivan's (1953) term, the 'participant-observer', underlines this point. Long before, James (1950) described the multiple social selves each of us has, and which are differentially encouraged by certain people. Levinson (1972) argues convincingly for a structural approach in which we can only understand what is happening by considering how the systems of patient, therapist, family and society are mutually engaged. Each patient has a private myth which transforms the therapist on contact and in which the therapist is inevitably caught up. An authentic responsible recognition of what is happening may break the pattern and be a corrective experience.

In my second case, there was a struggle for survival in which for a while only one of us seemed likely to survive. I was cast in the role of attacker, and needed for my sake to defend my existence. I did indeed represent many of the values of the patient's father's generation. To attempt to win through by exposing the patient's vulnerability was to be an attacker. To abandon that role was to give him true power to decide his own disclosures.

Transference and counter-transference

With the concepts of transference and countertransference, Freud made a most fundamental contribution to our thinking. In the examples that I have cited, I recognise the importance of past perceived experience for present reactions and show how much my perception has been shaped by the frame of transference. Indeed, paradoxically, these two cases forcibly reminded me how much present patterns of interactions are facsimiles of past relationships with important others. The traveller's tale of the psychoanalyst made more sense to me than ever before. However, only when, in a very ordinary way, the current reality was addressed rather than the historical antecedents did the pattern change. History provides us with understanding, but insight is not synonymous with personal change.

Transference is a useful way of ordering what happens, but may be seized upon by the therapist to distance him- or herself from the awkward moments I have described. In the same way, the person as a person may be lost in the higher order constructs of psychopathology. For the therapist and patient alike, the awkwardness of being known may be attributed to there-and-then relationships with parents that are safely past rather than to something that is happening now. In contrast, addressing the emotional reality of the here-and-now is therapeutically influential. Further ways of advancing towards the important goal of a transference-free relationship in therapy can be achieved by supporting the patient's observing ego through accepting correct perceptions, especially of therapist deficiencies, openly admitting errors, avoiding arrogance and explaining the rationale of procedures (Greenson and Wexler, 1969).

Identifying likely problematic relationship patterns within therapy

Many combinations of therapist and patient fail. Negative patterns develop and are not resolved. Attempts to ignore what is happening, or merely to interpret the historical antecedents, frequently — as in my two cases — fail to resolve the impending impasse. But, it is often difficult to perceive the pattern in which one is or will be caught up.

In an exciting innovation, Strupp and Binder (1984) have found a way of describing in narrative form what happens characteristically between a patient and others. These interpersonal transactions are historically significant and sources of current difficulty. Using the patient's words, the therapist constructs that person's characteristic interpersonal narrative. The narrative begins with interpersonal acts committed by the patient. In the second place the expectations that that person has about the reactions of others to him are documented. Third, the consequently observed actions of others are noted, as is how the patient then acts towards himself. Such a model would have been very useful to me in my work with Mary. Its atheoretical approach may prove very useful to therapists of many persuasions, and especially to those interested in the vicissitudes of interpersonal processes.

When the relationship is in trouble, directly addressing the problematic feelings that the patient has about the therapist can be helpful (Foreman and Marmar, 1985). This may be enough to join the paths once more. What has to be recognised is the nature of the psychotherapy undertaking. In this endeavour, in the final analysis, patient and therapist are ordinary mortals. The patient is engaged in a process of being known, and will defend against this by enlisting the therapist in the service of his private myths. Working with the reality that exists between them is a way of change.

REFERENCES

Adler, A. (1924). *The practice and theory of individual psychology*. Transl. P. Radin. London: Kegan Paul
Alexander, F. and French, T. (1946). *Psychoanalytic therapy: principles and applications*. New York: Ronald Press
Aveline, M.O. (1979). Towards a conceptual framework of psychotherapy: a personal view. *British Journal of Medical Psychology, 52,* 271–5
Aveline, M.O. (1980). The therapist as the servant of the patient. Paper

read to Psychotherapy Societies in Adelaide and Sydney

Aveline, M.O. (1984). Books reconsidered: persuasion and healing: J.D. Frank *British Journal of Psychiatry, 145,* 207–11

Aveline, M.O. (In preparation). The corrective emotional experience in psychotherapy: a fundamental unifying concept

Aveline, M.O. and Smith, J. (In preparation). Psychotherapy pre-assessment interview questionnaires: form, content and therapeutic impact

Binswanger, L. (1956). Existential analysis and psychotherapy In F. Fromm-Reichmann and J. Moreno (Eds), *Progress in psychotherapy.* New York: Grune & Stratton

Buber, M. (1958). *I and thou,* 2nd Ed. New York: Charles Scribner

Fordham, M. (1979). Analytic psychology and counter-transference. In L. Epstein and A.H. Feiner (Eds), *Counter-transference: the therapist's contribution to the therapeutic situation.* New York: Jason Aronson

Foreman, S.A. and Marmar, C.R. (1985). Therapists' actions that address initially poor therapeutic alliances in psychotherapy. *American Journal of Psychiatry, 142,* 922–6

Frank, J.D. (1973). *Persuasion and healing,* 2nd edn. New York: Schocken Books

Freud, S. (1938). Construction in analysis. *International Journal of Psychoanalysis, 19,* 377–87

Greben, S.E. (1981). The essence of psychotherapy. *British Journal of Psychiatry, 138,* 449–55

Greenson, R.R. and Wexler, M. (1969). The non-transference relationship in the psychoanalytic situation. *International Journal of Psychoanalysis, 50,* 27–39

Guntrip, H. (1968). *Schizoid phenomena, object relations and self.* London: Hogarth Press

Heidegger, M. (1962). *Being and time.* Transl. J. Macquarre and E. Robinson. New York: Harper & Row

Heller, D. (1985). *Power in psychotherapeutic practice.* New York: Human Sciences Press

Hobson, R.F. (1985). *Forms of feeling: the heart of psychotherapy.* London: Tavistock

Horney, K. (1945). *Our inner conflicts.* New York: W.W. Norton

James, W. (1950). *The principles of psychology,* vol. 1. New York: Dover Publications

Kelman, H. (1969). Kairos: the auspicious moment. *American Journal of Psychoanalysis, 29,* 59–83

Laing, R.D. (1959). *The divided self.* London: Tavistock

Langs, R. (1973). *The technique of psychoanalytic psychotherapy,* vol, I. New York: Jason Aronson

Levinson, E.A. (1972). *The fallacy of understanding.* New York: Basic Books

Lomas, P. (1981). *The case for a personal psychotherapy.* Oxford and New York: Oxford University Press

Mair, M. (1977). The community of self. In D. Bannister (Ed.), *New perspectives in personal construct theory.* New York and London: Academic Press

Malan, D.H. (1979). *Individual psychotherapy and the science of*

psychodynamics. London: Butterworths
May, R., Angel, E. and Ellenberger, H.E. (1958). *Existence: a new dimension in psychiatry and psychology.* New York: Basic Books
Rogers, C.R. (1961). *On becoming a person.* London: Constable
Schafer, R. (1983). *The analytic attitude.* London: Hogarth Press
Storr, A. (1968). The concept of care. In C. Rycroft (Ed.), *Psychoanalysis observed.* London: Pelican Books
Strupp, H.H. and Binder, J.L. (1984). *Psychotherapy in a new key.* New York: Basic Books
Sullivan, H.S. (1953). *The interpersonal theory of psychiatry.* New York: Basic Books
Sullivan, H.S. (1970). *The psychiatric interview.* New York: W.W. Norton
Yalom, I.D. (1980). *Existential psychotherapy.* New York: Basic Books

4

Beyond the Core Conditions

Brian Thorne

PRIOR THEORY AND PRACTICE

In 1980 I had been working as a person-centred therapist for more than twelve years. I was, and still am, fully convinced that the quality of the relationship I can form with my client is the crucial factor in therapeutic effectiveness. For me the creation of a psychological climate conducive to therapeutic movement is the primary goal, and I believe that by 1980 my ability to offer the core conditions of acceptance, empathy and genuineness in a relationship was reasonably well developed. Repeated experience, too, had convinced me that if I was capable of accepting my client, of developing and communicating an empathic understanding of my client's world and of remaining authentic in the relationship, then indeed something productive would almost invariably occur. In other words, the core conditions as described and researched by Carl Rogers and his associates were usually the necessary *and* sufficient ingredients for bringing about positive change (Rogers and Dymond, 1954).

In the years that followed my first encounter with Sally (at the end of 1979), I did not come to question these basic beliefs nor to doubt the essentially optimistic view of human personality which underpins the person-centred point of view. My understanding of the core conditions, however, was broadened immeasurably, and my actual behaviour as a therapist underwent a significant transformation.

My approach prior to 1980 was characterised by a marked emphasis on remaining in the present. This did not mean that I was oblivious of the importance of past experience, but I possessed a strong conviction that human beings have the ability to escape from past conditioning and to make choices about the direction of their lives. I had discovered that if I was prepared to invest energy in the relationship with my client and to offer him or her my attentive and accepting presence, then the contact and communication between us was often sufficient to establish a new basis for hope and change. This is not to suggest that my work lacked profundity. On the contrary, the practice of empathy often leads to a level of communication which is unique in the client's experience and involves a confrontation with feelings at the deepest level. The intensity, however, was usually of the moment and sprang essentially from the client's simultaneous experience of being in touch with deep feelings and of being understood and accepted by me. In person-centred terminology this could be expressed as the direct and immediate sensing of the complex interrelationship between congruence, empathy and unconditional positive regard as they are lived out in the context of a therapeutic alliance. The following interaction, typical of my work, illustrates the point:

> *Client* When she said that sort of thing to me as a child I felt cornered, trapped.
> *Therapist* She had you in her power; you were her prisoner.
> *Client* She was always so powerful. I hated her for that and yet I desperately wanted to please her.
> *Therapist* The person whose approval you needed was a kind of hateful gaoler.
> *Client:* She never wanted me to be free . . . she couldn't bear to let me out of her cage . . . (weeps).

The intensity of this dialogue is immediately apparent. Clearly at a certain level it is about the past and the client is undoubtedly in touch with past feelings. And yet the intensity springs not so much from the reliving of the past as from the present experience of having the past (and continuing) feelings understood, accepted and shared by the therapist. The past provides the content of the dialogue but the intensity springs from the way that content is received by the therapist in the present.

This brief extract also demonstrates my considerable reliance prior to 1980 on verbal exchange. I am an articulate person and much of my early training was in language and literature. I am fascinated by words and am always sensitive to the moments in therapy when prose gives way to poetry. The interaction above can be seen as the elaboration of a metaphor which finally reaches an intolerable climax: cornered, trapped, power, prisoner, hate, gaoler, freedom, cage. It is when the client herself juxtaposes her longing for freedom with the experience of her mother's cage that the moment of insupportable tension arrives and the tears begin to flow. I believe that such exchanges were frequent occurrences in my work and they have indeed remained so. Empathy and its expression often leads into a world where language becomes ever more richly expressive and where the practice of therapy assumes the characteristics of an art form.

My Christianity was, I believe, well known in professional circles long before 1980. I had never made any attempt to conceal my religious allegiance to the Anglican Church and was even occasionally asked to address religious conferences or to preach sermons. I was always at pains, however, to ensure that my religious convictions did not in any way intrude overtly into my therapeutic work. Looking back on it I believe that this scrupulous avoidance of any possible slip into unintentional evangelism had the strange effect of making me excessively wary of responding to those clients whose primary preoccupation lay in the area of the spiritual and transcendental. It was as if my fear of being perceived as a proselytiser prevented me from fully accompanying those clients who wished to move into the very areas which I knew to be of the deepest significance. Perhaps, too, it was another kind of fear which lay behind my reticence. My long internal debates on guilt and original sin had, I suspect, left me wondering if a Christian could ever aspire to offer unconditional acceptance to a fellow human being. And yet I knew that despite the enormity of the task it was precisely unconditional acceptance that I wished to offer to my clients. Better, then, to put my Christianity to one side just in case an imperfect theology rendered an already supremely difficult task well-nigh impossible.

My ability to offer unconditional acceptance to a client was also influenced by the fact that until 1980 I was working almost exclusively in an institutional setting. As a therapist in a university I was constantly confronted by the constraints of an academic environment. These made themselves felt in a number of ways. In the first place, most of my clients were young — some in late adolescence and many in early adulthood. There is, of course, something highly refreshing about such a clientele, for change is often rapid and demonstrable. Such a period in life frequently offers a second chance for accomplishing some of the key tasks of human development, and many young people are quick to seize the opportunity offered by an effective counselling service. For the therapist, however, there is the danger that the presence of highly motivated clients can make the stuck or recalcitrant individual particularly difficult to tolerate. Secondly, a university exerts its own pressures and establishes its own norms for behaviour. As a therapist it is virtually impossible to remain unaffected by these and I am sure that there were often times when I found it challenging to say the least to offer an unconditional acceptance to a student who seemed intent on denigrating the university and all its works, or was unwilling or unable to attend a single seminar or lecture throughout an entire term. Furthermore, however much a university counsellor may believe himself to be dedicated to the well-being of his individual clients, there is no doubt that the institution asserts its own irresistible claims on his loyalty, often in ways that are not immediately apparent either to him or to others. In short, as a university counsellor there were times when I had to struggle hard to offer the kind of acceptance to my clients which I know is desirable. It is all too easy to become impatient or to become contaminated by an institution's values and criteria, and as a result to see stuckness or recalcitrance as evidence of a thinly veiled bloody-mindedness rather than as signs of desperation or fear.

When, in 1980, I established a small private practice it was not only the release from obvious institutional pressures which I experienced but the gradual recognition that I had allowed myself previously to be trapped in a false sense of responsibility. When I first began working in universities the paternalistic ethos of the days when most students were legally still minors and *in statu pupillari* was still around. In subtle ways the message was conveyed that the university was responsible for its students, which meant, according to the situation, that students could not be trusted or that they had to be protected. For a therapist the hazards of such an environment were equally subtle. I realise now that for all my protestations about the trustworthiness of the human organism and its capacity for self-actualisation I was often ensnared either by my youthful clients' desire to put me in a parental role or by my own vague anxiety about the institution's expectations of its salaried counsellors. This latter anxiety was all the more difficult to combat because the expectations were never clearly articulated, and doubtless varied considerably in any case among the senior members of the academic community.

In practice I believe now that the prevailing youthfulness of my clientele and the ambience of a university setting meant that I frequently fell into the trap of being responsible *for* my clients rather than *to* them. The implications of this are considerable for any therapist, but for someone working in the person-centred tradition they are profoundly significant. They strike at the very heart of the egalitarian relationship and leave the therapist in the superior position however carefully this dynamic is concealed or obscured.

The ability or failure to achieve true mutuality or parity of esteem in a therapeutic relationship inevitably determines to a large extent the level of risk-taking that can take place. I sense now that for much of the time prior to 1980 I was unwilling to offer my clients the depth of acceptance which is required if radical shifts in feeling or behaviour are to take place. Furthermore my own exaggerated sense of responsibility meant that I could seldom permit myself to face and acknowledge my own vulnerability or powerlessness. In short, by maintaining a superior and overly responsible stance I was failing much of the time to offer the core conditions at the deepest level. I was neither fully accepting nor fully genuine because I was too insecure to risk the fantasised displeasure of the institutional hierarchy if clients went dramatically off the rails, and too caught up in the responsible quasi-parental role to reveal my own vulnerability or confusion.

This is not to say that I was unsuccessful in my work. On the contrary, for many young people the discovery of a 'good parent' releases them to test out their autonomy and to take risks which for them may seem enormous but which, objectively, are not particularly earth-shattering. This was often true for clients who had previously experienced grave difficulty in making decisions because of the fear of adverse judgement or rejection. Such people found it possible with me to explore and to face their own thoughts and feelings, perhaps for the first time, and with my continuing support to act on their discovery. For an intellectually gifted student, for example, the decision to leave the university before graduating could well be momentous and require the greatest courage. For me, however, as the therapist, the student's struggles, while calling for a high level of empathy and much acceptance, did not threaten my own inner strength or incite me to take over control. I could remain comfortably and effectively in the role of the good and loving parent who could rejoice in the growing autonomy of my client-child.

Self-destructive clients were an altogether different matter. My fear of a student committing suicide was such that I could seldom stay in a relationship with such a client without quickly drawing in other 'experts' and setting up safety nets. In retrospect, I believe that my own inner 'wobbliness' and my sense of responsibility for the other person made it virtually impossible for me to engage with suicidal clients at a level where a real meeting could take place. Between 1967 and 1979 three clients of mine did, in fact, kill themselves. All three had seen a psychiatrist within a few days of their deaths and one died the morning he was due to enter a therapeutic community hospital. Of course, perhaps nothing could have prevented these sad outcomes, but I cannot help wondering what would have happened if I had been more able to accept my own weakness and apparent lack of resourcefulness and if I had not felt so very responsible for the individuals in question that I had to call in the psychiatric 'big guns'.

One other aspect of my therapeutic practice before 1980 is worth noting. I was very much preoccupied with boundaries.[1] In my previous career as a schoolteacher in a boarding community I had experienced what it was like to be inundated by the needs and apparently insatiable demands of emotionally deprived youngsters. I had only just survived the experience of being 'on tap' 24 hours a day, and as a therapist I was concerned to keep to the 50-minute-hour and the once- or twice-weekly session. Of course, there were crisis times when I broke my own rules, and there was the occasional client whose need was such that more frequent meetings were required, but I was in no doubt that for most clients most of the time I was all in favour of once a week for 50 minutes.

DESCRIPTION OF THE KEY CASE

Sally originally came to see me with her husband, Kenneth. The couple had been experiencing sexual difficulties throughout the entire sixteen years of their married life and had made various attempts to seek help from GPs, psychiatrists and others. The chief manifestation of the problem appeared to be Sally's inability to feel any sexual desire for Kenneth although in other ways she gave evidence of a deep love for him. What was more she felt abhorrence of sexual intercourse and was intensely afraid of it. When the pair came to see me, Kenneth was near desperation point and Sally was lost in a tangle of guilt and crippling fears which remained inexplicable to her. She continually described herself as 'stupid' and saw herself as impossibly obtuse. And yet she was totally unable to overcome her terror and sexual paralysis.

I had known the pair for some time on a social basis. Kenneth was a well-respected priest in the city and Sally was herself a volunteer worker with a local charity. Both were Christians, and Kenneth, of course, was deeply involved in Church affairs. It rapidly became clear that the decision to seek my help was the result of much careful thought, and that my Christianity was a crucial factor in the decision. In the past the couple had come to a puzzled impasse with each therapist they had worked with; slight improvements had evaporated without trace and the totality of the stuckness which gripped Sally seemed impossible to convey. She felt near despair and now believed that the only hope lay in working with someone with whom Kenneth felt at ease. It seemed therefore that I had been selected because they both knew me already and were aware of my Christian allegiance and because Kenneth felt he could trust me. Another important element was the fact that both of them had read the text of a lecture I had given on intimacy (Thorne, 1982), and had felt moved and impressed by it. Both this text and other things I had said in public had made Sally feel that I had an understanding of love which she considered to be of fundamental importance and which she had not previously been able to articulate. I believe it was also not irrelevant that the couple had met my wife and family and sensed that my own marriage was in reasonable order.

The initial sessions with the couple proceeded predictably enough. I listened to the story of their marriage and of their previous attempts to find help. I found it possible to empathise deeply with both of them and could sense the mounting fear and desperation with the passage of the years. It was also clear to me that they did indeed love each other and that their inability to make love in the way which they both desired was much more than a sexual difficulty. Within a month or so of our first meeting I realised that I was involved not in 'doing sex therapy' but in some kind of existential battle, the nature of which I could only dimly imagine. Strangely enough, I felt both ill-equipped and confident as if my lack of expertise in what I sensed to be an almost cosmic arena was actually more than compensated for by the couple's trust in me and my own trust in myself, or, as I might explain it to those who could accept the terminology, my trust in the God within me.

It was not altogether surprising when one evening shortly after our fourth meeting together Kenneth rang me to say that Sally was helplessly stuck and very afraid. Would it be possible for me to take her on for individual therapy? I agreed to this but on the understanding that from time to time we would continue to meet as a trio to review the process as we were experiencing it. I also made it clear that open communication should continue between the three of us at every stage from now on.

Sally at this time was almost blind with fear. As I strained to empathise with her state of being I became aware of her total lack of security as if she could experience no solid ground. At the same time there was a black annihilating fear which she described, when she could express it, as permeating every part of her being. Our sessions together were difficult in the extreme. I often felt at a loss how to proceed and admitted this. Gradually I came to realise, however, that I could trust Sally to find her own way as long as I did not panic and as long as I could accept the very stuckness which she herself found so unacceptable.

I was astonished by her courage in allowing herself to get in touch with a level of fear which at times seemed to threaten her sanity. Now and again she was able to speak of what she was experiencing and I would hang on to her metaphors which were usually to do with chaos, blackness, dense fog and suffocation. Betrayal, too, featured in her images. I believe now that if I had in some way sought to force the pace at this stage, she would never have come to trust me and would have had no chance of trusting herself and her own wisdom. She later told me that she came to feel during these early sessions that I was prepared to see her as a whole being and that I would not 'dissect' her in order to cure one part while leaving another part to fester.

As I think back on this initial phase of our therapeutic relationship, the major conflict which I experienced was undoubtedly to do with verbalisation. In the past my primary way of conveying acceptance was verbal, and my empathy and genuineness were similarly expressed for the most part through the sensitive use of the whole repertoire of language. With Sally I often felt perplexed about what to say and only gradually came to understand that words were frequently inappropriate to what was happening between us. As a result I found myself both doing and experiencing things which were new and at times unnerving.

In the first place, in the presence of Sally's physical anguish I found it increasingly important to know what was going on in my own body. I needed to ensure that my body was in receipt of my full attention and compassion if it were to be in a fit state to act as a companion to my often stuck and silent client. It was as if my physical being could empathise with hers without the need for language. It was vitally important, however, that my body did not *identify* with hers, for if it had done so we should both have ended up paralysed with terror!

Secondly, the more I succeeded in befriending my own body during our sessions, the more I sensed the richness of the potential repertoire of physical responses which was available to me as I attempted to accept and understand Sally. In my previous work with clients I had sometimes felt the appropriateness of the light touch on the hand or knee, the reassuring arm round the shoulder, even the occasional hug. With Sally, however, I began to move into a quite new and unexplored terrain. The discipline of remaining in touch with my own body resulted in a whole range of intuitive responses which, as I recall them, demanded all my courage to implement. I would find myself taking her hand, which was often cold and lifeless, and massaging it for minutes on end, sometimes silently, sometimes as we continued to talk. On other occasions I would catch her tears with my fingers and spread them across the whole surface of her face as if to cleanse her both from and with her own suffering. It seemed that these responses — and many others like them — could communicate at a level which was beyond words. It was as if she was choosing little by little to make herself vulnerable to me not through what she said but through her distressed and frightened body.

I was conscious both at this stage and later of the powerful sexual dimension in what was happening between us. Sally had brought to me her fear of sexual encounter and intercourse and yet she was apparently prepared to become increasingly vulnerable in my presence. She is commonly regarded as an attractive and even beautiful woman and it was therefore not surprising that I quickly became aware of my own sexual responsiveness. The situation was potentially fraught with danger and for a week or two I wondered if I could continue. With the help of my own supervisor, however, I began to see that perhaps Sally *needed* my total presence. There was no way in any case in which I could deny my own sexuality. To be congruent meant that I could offer her nothing less than my own wholeness, and this must include my physicality and my sexuality. The dilemma was whether I could do this in a way that could enable her to face and accept her own body and sexuality without guilt and without fear. It seemed a formidable task.

In the summer of 1980, as in previous years, I was to be a staff member at a week-long residential workshop organised by the British Centre of the Facilitator Development Institute of which I am a Co-Director. These annual events offer an opportunity to members of the helping professions and others to experience and explore the dynamics of large and small groups and to further their understanding of the person-centred approach in relation to their own personal and professional development (Mearns and Lambers, 1976).

I was somewhat surprised when Sally suddenly asked me one day if she might attend the workshop. My own feelings about this request were mixed but after much deliberation I supported her registration.

In the event, the summer workshop turned out to be a time of major development in Sally's therapy. Much occurred between us during the week but one central episode requires a detailed description. Towards the end of the week, after a particularly exhausting day, I suddenly remembered that I had tentatively arranged to meet her before the day was out and although it was now eleven o'clock at night the urge was strong to see her. My feelings were mixed: there was a sense both of duty and desire. Indeed, the latter feeling became at one moment so strong that I mistrusted myself, changed my mind and entered the lift to go to my own room on the sixth floor. No sooner had I done this than the sense of shirking my responsibility returned. By the time I had descended five floors again and was knocking on Sally's door I felt in a state of healthy if exhausted tension.

It was clear that Sally was both surprised and moved to see me. This was the first time in our relationship that I had gone to her, and it seemed that my arrival validated her in a way that immediately introduced a new element of equality into our intimacy. She could also see that I was exhausted and unusually vulnerable. I stayed with her for some four hours, and during that time we discovered much of the *prima materia* which was to occupy us for the next three years.

In the first place, there was a strong sense in both of us — to which we gave open and joking admission — that what we were doing could be perceived as illicit, disreputable, even sinful. I had come like a lover in the night, to rob a married woman of her virtue. She, for her part, was aware that she could be seen as the seductress. We both acknowledged the ambiguity of the situation and succeeded, more or less, in putting any incipient guilt to one side. We trusted our own goodness while acknowledging the power of self-deception. Secondly, as so often in our formal therapy sessions, our meeting was in some ways more a communication between bodies than an exchange of words. My own exhaustion heightened my physical empathy and I knew that whereas my body was dropping with fatigue hers was yearning to come to life after years of frozen and deathly sleep. It seemed, too, that her body was deeply ashamed of being present let alone of being seen. I am convinced in retrospect that if my own body had been its usual active and energetic self Sally's would have remained stuck in its isolated frozenness. As it was she painfully and courageously stayed in touch with her body, owned it and allowed her breasts to be exposed to my gaze.

Thirdly, I found myself allowing my own body to express its acceptance and understanding of Sally's. I gently massaged her stomach and stroked her back. Her tears flowed and from time to time she moaned. I felt sexually excited but at no time either then or later did I feel the slightest desire to have sexual intercourse with Sally. This fact proved to be of the utmost importance to her in all the work we did subsequently. If there had been the slightest chance of tipping over into adultery, nothing could have been achieved. I have no way of knowing, but I suspect that my feelings that night were akin to those of a mother for a newly born child, that is to say, strongly sexual but tenderly protective.

Fourthly, the whole episode triggered in Sally instant recall of an experience, previously blocked from full consciousness, which she had undergone some 18 years before during her courtship with Kenneth and which was to prove of immense significance. The pair had met in Vienna following a period of separation of some 19 months during which Kenneth had been completing his National Service in the Far East. They were to be alone together for four days, and on her way to Vienna she was not even sure that she still loved Kenneth. She felt numb and frightened. The initial encounter did little to restore her confidence. She was glad to see Kenneth but sensed no excitement in herself. In fact she became intolerably aware that for as long as she could remember she had been without the kind of emotional and sexual desire about which she had read in books. Only during the four months she had known him before he went abroad had she realised that her body had instincts of which the rest of her felt totally ignorant. After 12 hours of Kenneth's company in Vienna she was on the verge of despair about the relationship.

On the second day, her mood suddenly changed when, having got up early, she went into his room and saw him still asleep. Her numbness left her and she began to experience within herself physical sensations which were new to her and which made her tingle all over. She began to realise that she loved him deeply and could scarcely believe the vibrancy of her own body. The next afternoon she went to Kenneth's room. They began to embrace and cuddle and were soon, it seems, involved in heavy petting. For Sally the experience was utterly transforming. For the first time in her life she felt whole and fully alive as if channels of energy and power were now open in her which had been blocked not simply for years but from the beginning of her existence. She felt deep love for Kenneth and was transformed into a new creature. What is more she knew with complete certainty that she wished to give herself to Kenneth and desired full sexual union with him there and then. Her whole body became infused with yearning desire.

As the memories flooded back Sally wept in my presence at the realisation that in those moments there had been for her no consciousness of guilt, no sense of wrong-doing although she was usually fully acceptant of the moral standpoint implicit in the Christian teaching which forbids sexual union before marriage. She wept as she recalled her wholeness, her desire and her innocence.

Kenneth's Christian upbringing, it would seem, was less easily transcended. In the arms of the radiant and vibrant Sally he was overwhelmed with anxiety and guilt. His way out of the dilemma was to ask her to pray with him. Within the instant, unspeakable pain descended upon Sally and against the massed battalions of the Church she retreated into numbness, terror and guilt. It was some 15 months later before she and Kenneth eventually married. It was only then that Kenneth's spiritual mentors deemed it appropriate for them to enter into holy matrimony. By that time Sally was once more the frozen creature she had been all her life — except for a few precious hours during a Viennese spring.

For Sally the rest of the workshop after this eventful night was a time of peace and fulfilment. She participated in everything with increasing ease and took to walking around the gardens in bare feet. There were moments when she seemed radiantly happy, and despite my own exhaustion I was able to share her happiness and wonder at her progress. I was, however, under no illusions. I knew that she had won for herself an interlude and the taste of a possible future but that in reality our therapeutic work had only just begun.

During the following weeks I was once again thrown into serious confusion about my own therapeutic role. It was clear to both of us that the remarkable progress which had occurred at the workshop was to a large extent facilitated by the residential context and by my willingness at a crucial time to work directly on Sally's body. Both of us were well aware, however, that I had no special training (beyond some elementary massage techniques) in body work, and that if the way ahead for Sally lay in releasing memories and energies which were locked in her body structure, then I was scarcely equipped for the task. It seemed a natural step in the circumstances to refer Sally to a trusted colleague in the neighbourhood (a woman) who is a therapist of great experience and has an extensive training in bio-energetic analysis. After a joint session with Kenneth in which the situation was reviewed in depth, Sally was duly referred to this therapist while I promised to continue in a supportive role on a less frequent basis during the weeks ahead.

Although I believed that this referral was appropriate at the time, I am now convinced that Sally and I arrived at the decision in order to avoid a situation which at that stage was too fear-provoking. Neither she nor I could have found the courage at that time to face the work which ultimately we had to do together. When she 'returned' to me three months later after a number of helpful and illuminating sessions with my colleague, we were both less faint-hearted. I discovered subsequently that during their work together this wise and perceptive therapist had not once touched Sally's body!

The period following the referral 'interlude' was characterised by an intense and often painful exploration of moral and religious questions. Sally's rage against the Church often erupted in violent attacks upon its seemingly narrow-minded condemnation of what seemed to be truly loving sexuality. At the same time, however, she was fearful of falling into heresy and found much comfort in the writings of Julian of Norwich and of theologians like Harry Williams and Sebastian Moore to which I had no hesitation in directing her (Julian of Norwich, 1966; Williams, 1972, 1976; Moore, 1980, 1982). It seemed that she was assailed on all sides by censorious judges. The voices of parents, church authorities and even secular psychologists rivalled each other in causing her untold guilt. As a result it seemed to Sally that to love deeply was to be immoral. It was therefore of supreme importance that somehow I succeeded in conveying to her that precisely the opposite is true — that to love deeply and with integrity is the most truly moral activity that a human being can engage in. It was of crucial significance to her at this stage that I was both a Christian who believed in the reality of her immortal soul and also a therapist who had attempted to articulate a theology of sex which acknowledged psychological realities without discarding the essential heart of the Christian tradition (Thorne, 1982). As at so many other points in our work together, Sally needed to know that I was responding to the whole of her and not to just a part. It was as if she had to be quite certain that I treasured her soul before she could allow me once more to approach her body.

Gradually, however, we began to speak of physical sensations and more especially of the frozen feeling in her stomach and of the sense of blockage and choked-up energy. She felt her tentative hopes would be dissipated if the work were not continued intensively, and asked for homework between sessions in order to try to hold on to her sense of progress. At my suggestion she attempted a collage on nakedness during my absence for a brief period from the city. She also drew pictures depicting the 'black' areas in her body and the iron bands in her stomach. One afternoon in May 1981 she allowed me to place my hand gently on her stomach above the genital area. The tautness was unbelievable as if indeed there were actual iron bands binding together her intestines. The immediate reaction in her to my touch was of intense fear but she endured this and within a minute or two the terror seemed to have subsided somewhat. She asked me to keep my hand on her stomach for a further five minutes or so and then remove it. We discussed this incident at length and agreed that we were now embarked upon a path leading through country where neither of us knew the landmarks. We both felt, however, that we had no option but to proceed, and knew that we trusted each other to move with patience and the deepest possible respect.

Three days later Sally accepted, with much fear, my offer to massage her stomach. The effect of this was dramatic. She quickly experienced the most annihilating sense of shame, of unworthiness, of having no place in the world. Her misery was pitiable to witness but she clearly willed herself to endure it. For almost half an hour it was as if she suffered an overwhelming sense of rejection, abandonment and worthlessness. Gradually, however, the intensity of this hellish experience diminished and she was content to sit with her eyes closed — exhausted but at some kind of peace. For a minute or two, she said later, the sun came out but then it was quickly obscured by a whole cloud of censorious figures some of whose faces she could see distinctly.

I was now seeing Sally twice weekly, and the next session was to mark the beginning of a six-month period during which I found myself constantly revising and reviewing both the frequency and the length of our times together. For Sally this session saw a groping through the fog which finally resulted in the terror of removing most of her clothing. For me these minutes were among the most taxing I have ever experienced as a therapist. Within me a mixture of conflicting feelings raged. If I had ceased to trust my client at this point or if I had lost confidence in my own trustworthiness, then I believe all the work we had done would have been in jeopardy. What is more, if I had lost touch with my own body or failed to accept unconditionally the feelings of excitement within me, I believe I should have been plunged into a morass of inappropriate guilt which, for Sally, would have meant a macabre re-enactment of the Vienna episode with, I suspect, disastrous consequences. As it was, the feelings of fear, which were certainly strongly present within me, rapidly gave way to a sense of professional integrity which was buttressed by all that had preceded and, more particularly, by the hours of ethical and theological exploration which we had shared together and by the knowledge that all that happened between us would be communicated to Kenneth. The effort cost her so much that she was exhausted and was unable to leave at the end of her session. What is more she was convinced that she needed to go on and to capitalise rapidly on what she had accomplished. I arranged for her to rest for a while and then agreed to work with her for a further three hours that evening.

In the months that followed, the three-hour session featured quite frequently and I believe that this was both appropriate and necessary. The 'normal' one-hour sessions were usually devoted to a review and a reflection on what had happened in the lengthier meetings or to joint explorations with Kenneth of the process in which they were both now heavily involved. The three-hour sessions themselves were often almost wordless. They usually involved a most extraordinary process of regression of which I at times had only the most elementary understanding. Blindly but instinctively Sally seemed to know what she had to do although often she required my encouragement to trust her own wisdom. Strangely enough I, too, sensed what was required of me and came almost to expect that Sally would accept and validate my interventions, although I did not once, I believe, fail to check out with her the appropriateness of my responses when they were of a non-verbal kind. During most of these lengthy sessions there came a point when Sally summoned up the courage to remove some of her clothing and on a few occasions she chose to be completely naked for periods of time. This exposure of her physical being never became easy for her but as the weeks passed there were certainly times when it seemed she was able to accept herself and to relax completely in my presence. This was the prelude to astounding journeys into her past which she made wordlessly but often with great emotion. For my part I discovered, with her help, that my principal task was to massage with great gentleness her stomach, her shoulders and sometimes her buttocks. It was also important for her to be held, sometimes for long periods. Later it was necessary that this holding occurred in such a way that she could clearly hear my heart beating. This it seemed gave her enough security to make her journeys back to adolescence, childhood, infancy and even to life in the womb.

Sally, it seemed, needed my companionship in a journey and I did my best to stay alongside her and to take my lead from her. She had at least the courage to set out and I could in no sense be a guide. But it was vital that she did not lose contact with me. If she had done so, fear would have overwhelmed her and I doubt if she could have borne the suffering and the pain which she encountered and which often made her howl or weep silently for hours. To her it seemed that she returned to the very beginning of her existence and that she lived again in her mother's womb. Among much else she endured the full weight of her mother's grief at the death of a beloved brother (it was war time) and was amazed and bewildered to feel her body locked in grief for a man whom she had never known. She experienced, too, her mother's deep ambivalence about the child she was carrying and in one awful moment the sense of her mother's desire to abort her. At the moment of birth she was thus permeated by grief, alienation and the desire to die. Such was her inheritance and she had carried it with her to the present time. Only in Vienna had she momentarily been free to be herself, and at the summer workshop she had sensed again the possibility of that freedom.

I have described in a few words some of the major insights which flowed from many hours of work, some of it reflective but most of it wordless and physical. Where possible the knowledge which came to Sally as she 'managed' her own regression was checked out with members of her family and others. In every instance, to her deep shock and awe, it appeared to tally with the 'objective' facts as others recalled them. As she gradually freed herself, first from the grief and desolation which had afflicted her in the womb and then from the guilt and the burden of moral responsibility which had resulted from her family and religious upbringing, so she was able to begin relating to her parents in new ways. She stopped her mother visiting for many months and then wrote letters which elicited a new level of communication. She arranged to spend an evening in London alone with her father, something that had never happened before. With Kenneth and with her own children there was a new depth and a new openness. At one particularly gruelling period for her I spoke with the assembled children and with Kenneth in order to alleviate their distress and to increase their support for Sally. It was as if Sally's therapy at this time became a family project and I shall never know how much she owed to their love and patience despite their own frequent confusion and anxiety.

It was to be another two years after this intensive 'regression' period before Sally's therapy came to an end. The extent of the changes in her can to some extent be gauged by the dramatic content of a session which occurred in the final month of our work together.

On 18 October 1983 she arrived in a state of high agitation. She was caught up in a frenzy of energy and vitality which she felt powerless to control. Her need to discover boundaries and to find security was pre-eminent. In response to that need I knew instinctively that words would be useless. At the same time I was flooded with an awesome sense of the trust she had placed in me and of the indescribable risks she had taken in my presence during the previous four years. I was also poignantly aware of the fact that during that time we had often experienced together a level of communication which had about it a quality of the transcendental. It was, I believe, my faith that ultimately God was in control that enabled me at this final stage to respond to Sally's needs in a way which would otherwise have been unthinkable. It seemed to me that she was facing an immense crisis of trust in herself. She was physically and sexually vibrant and she was full of yearning. At the same time she was terrified of being carried away by a desire so enormous that it could never find its satisfaction in the love of her husband. In short, she feared becoming the personification of lust and corruption and yet was straining to break iron bands which, if they gave way, might leave the path open to just such a corruption. No amount of talk could have allayed so enormous a dilemma. I knew what I had to do and yet my cowardice (and the fear for my reputation!) almost prevented me from acting. I had to trust my own body, my own sexuality, my own love of God, my love for Sally and my regard for the sanctity of marriage. I had to put the whole of myself to the test for nothing less would do. This time there was no question of checking out with Sally for it was only I who could give permission to myself. I sensed that Sally would only learn that her body would not betray her if she could experience directly and profoundly that I could trust my own body and not be afraid. With this perception my own cowardice evaporated and minutes later it was possible for us both to be naked and vulnerable before each other and to discover that our bodies and our sexuality were trustworthy and that our desiring was in harmony and not in conflict with our ethical selves. Sally allowed herself to be held closely and tenderly and learned that it is possible to be very loving without self-betrayal and without betraying others.

That night she wrote to me:

Dear Brian,
We accomplished a revolution — we accomplished a complete cycle in the way forward, and we accomplished a coup d'état . . .
Now I am reminded of the very deep peace which I found with

you at S . . . and I am remembering again. And it is something to do with your belief, your belief in God, your belief in you and, of course, your absolute belief in me. And maybe a little bit to do with my belief too: but I don't think I would dare to believe in this revolutionary trust without you.

Kenneth is very happy too.
With very much love,
Sally.

When two years later, she and Kenneth left the city for another part of the country, she was able to have sexual intercourse without fear overwhelming her, she was no longer burdened with a sense of guilt or moral responsibility, and, in the battle for her soul, her judgemental God had been replaced by the God of Love.

EMERGENT NEW DEVELOPMENTS

In some ways I have come to think that it was with Sally that I had the courage for the first time to test out the person-centred approach to the furthest limits. For more than a decade I had attempted to be accepting, empathic and genuine with my clients. I had also tried to trust their innate wisdom and to have faith in their capacity, given the right climate, to find their own way forward. Never before, however, had I found the courage and ability to experience and express those attitudes and beliefs so consistently over such a lengthy period of time.

I believe now that the fact that Sally and Kenneth had come to me as someone they already knew was both liberating and challenging. I was free to be Brian Thorne but at the same time I was challenged to face myself anew. It was as if I had to 'come clean' with myself on an almost daily basis. With Sally I could not dodge the implications of believing that I am an eternal soul, that the source of all being is infinite love, that the body is the temple of the divine, that sexuality and spirituality are indivisible, that prayer is a route into the invisible world. To be genuine with Sally meant living out those beliefs in the moment-to-moment relationship with her. Talking about them was at times important and necessary, but far more fundamental was the way in which those beliefs coloured and permeated my acceptance, not only of her, but also of myself. I had to take my own soul and body seriously and to cherish them as much as I cherished hers. To be empathic also assumed new dimensions. Souls and bodies, I discovered, can receive and understand each other as well as minds. Touch, massage, holding, hugging, fighting became the channels for a form of empathy which was beyond words. In the sanctuary of silence our souls met and acknowledged their common inheritance. In case all this sounds unduly solemn I should also add that there were times when we were both rendered helpless with laughter. With Sally I dared to be whole because nothing less would do, and in the process I discovered levels of genuineness, acceptance and empathy which gave access to a transcendent world where healing occurs because the understanding is complete. In short, thanks to my work with Sally, I have come to acknowledge and to affirm that for me the practice of person-centred therapy cannot be divorced from my journey as an eternal soul. This does not mean that my therapeutic work has taken on an overtly religious aura. It does, however, enable me to be fully present to my clients in a way which was not possible before, and to be in touch with a whole range of experience which was previously excluded from most of my therapeutic relationships.

I now believe that most existing theories of personality and personality development sell the human species short. With Sally I came to recognise the essential mysteriousness of personality and found in this a refreshing change from theories which attempt to offer an almost complete understanding. Much the same can be said of my view of human relationships. With Sally I found myself responding to another individual in ways which were new and uncharted, and I have come to think that, as therapists, we do ourselves and our clients a great disservice if we remain fixed in certain modes of relating in the mistaken belief that these alone are 'therapeutic'.

Undoubtedly the sense of mystery was much augmented by the journeys which Sally and I made together into pre-natal experience and into the altered state of consciousness which I have labelled 'transcendental'. In an important sense these excursions came about 'by accident'. We did not set out with the *intention* of exploring intra-uterine experience or of taking heaven by storm. We arrived in these somewhat unexpected domains because of the nature of our relationship, which differed in significant ways from what I had experienced in my previous therapeutic work. There was first of all a shared understanding of reality which incorporated a belief in God, the invisible world and the power of love. I was thus released from any latent fear of slipping into the role of the unwitting evangelist or of imposing my belief system on another human being. Secondly, the knowledge that other therapists, including experienced psychiatrists, had tried and failed to alleviate Sally's distress, the absence of institutional constraints (Sally was a 'private' client) and the total support and commitment of Kenneth meant that we were free to explore the many dimensions of our relationship. There was nothing to lose. From my point of view I was also conscious from the beginning of an almost complete absence of anxiety about the outcome of the therapy. I did not feel responsible *for* Sally but my responsibility *to* her was reflected in my preparedness to work hard at the relationship and to be open to myself in ways which often felt risky. There were, of course, times when I faltered in my resolve and lacked courage. The most striking example of this occurred when Sally expressed the desire to go to the FDI summer workshop. For a time I was overwhelmed at the thought of the immense amount of work which her presence at the workshop might cause me — in a situation which demanded much energy and commitment anyway. In the event I did have to work very hard — to the point of exhaustion — but I experienced no resentment because I was caught up in the excitement of new learning which embraced us both and which sprang from our faith in ourselves and each other. It is no exaggeration to say that I was constantly awed by what happened between us and by the astonishing power of a therapeutic relationship where mutuality was a basic assumption.

In such a relationship both my client and I were able to discover that our most valuable resources lay in those very areas which often seem to present serious stumbling-blocks to effective therapy. For Sally her stuckness became supportable and eventually productive as she experienced my acceptance of it. For me my inability to find appropriate words and my tentative ventures into new forms of physical communication became richly rewarding as I experienced Sally's total acceptance of my apparent incompetence and ignorance. Because it was all right to be powerless and perplexed I was able to stay with these feelings and engage with them instead of denying them or rushing into 'strategies' or 'techniques'. The way forward proved to lie in and through stuckness and silence and in our willingness to trust such unlikely points of departure.

In summary, my work with Sally convinces me that if two people believe that love is the governing power in the universe, and that we have not yet penetrated more than a fraction of the mystery of human personality or human relating, then they may be prepared to accept and to share their weakness, vulnerability, embarrassment and ineptitude and find that it is in this apparent poverty that riches are concealed.

Undoubtedly my work with Sally enabled me to discover the reliability of intuition. This is a slippery word and needs explanation. By intuition I mean that kind of organic wisdom which has elements of thinking and feeling but is qualitatively different from either. Almost always such intuition brings new knowledge or prompts fresh action. The knowledge or the action can often appear to have little rational basis and at times may seem somewhat crazy or bizarre. Accepting the knowledge and implementing the action inevitably requires a degree of risk-taking, and there is always the possibility of being regarded as foolish or misguided with the accompanying threat of rejection. With Sally I discovered that intuitive wisdom seldom comes as a flash of inspiration. Indeed, I distrust so-called moments of illumination which in my experience can as easily be harbingers of confusion as of light. Intuition as I came to recognise it working with Sally is at its most trustworthy when it makes itself heard in the context of a patient acceptance of not knowing what to do, an admission of a lack of clarity or expertise, a willingness to rest in a relationship with love but without expectation. Often such times were characteristed by lengthy periods of silence, and the intuitive prompting would come gradually, almost hesitantly, as if it could only dare to make itself known when we had both accepted and acknowledged our joint incapacity to find a way forward but were nevertheless content to wait.

It was at such times that we found ourselves able to initiate behaviours which had seldom or never featured in my practice before. These behaviours resulted from intuitive responses unique to our relationship and are clearly not transferable to other relationships. Nevertheless they may have some general significance in so far as they seem to fall into three quite distinct categories. First, there were those behaviours that actually ensued within the therapeutic session itself. Most often these were of a physical kind, and what astonishes me now is how outrageous some of them would have seemed to an outside observer. On the other hand it is perhaps not surprising that Sally's profound concern with her body and her sexuality should have resulted in her gradual determination to confront her own nakedness in my presence. More surprising, perhaps, was my own willingness to trust those intuitive promptings which enabled me to encourage Sally to undress or, on occasions, to initiate a particular form of physical contact, whether it was simply holding hands or, as in the final stage, joining in a naked embrace. Clearly it would be ridiculous to suggest that such behaviour could or should be repeated in other therapeutic encounters. The experience with

Sally does suggest, however, that the scope for and the relevance of physical responsiveness between therapist and client may be far greater than we usually permit ourselves to consider. The fear of sexual irresponsibility and the continuing taboo on tenderness in our society work powerfully against the proper exploration of physical and sexual communication in therapy, and hinder the study of the essential love and mutuality between client and therapist which are the prerequisites for such communication.

Intuition did not lead only to physical contact. There were times when it led, on my part, to a silent prayer or on rare occasions to an expressed desire for God's blessing on our work. Sally's own Christian faith made such behaviour acceptable and unembarrassing. I have little doubt that there were occasions when she, too, prayed silently for herself and for me during the session. There were other times when I found myself going to my bookcase in order to find a poem or an extract which had come into my mind during one of our lengthy silences and then reading it aloud to Sally. There were occasions when I grabbed pencil and paper in order to illustrate or clarify diagrammatically some particularly complex material with which we were struggling. I even recall drinking sherry together on one occasion, being conscious that this act somehow symbolised the merging of the secular and the sacred, the social and the intimate — a kind of ritualised therapeutic communion. Sharing dreams together had something of the same quality.

The second category of behaviour prompted by intuition involved activities on Sally's part which took place *outside* the therapy sessions. She would feel the need for 'homework' and would sometimes ask directly for guidance. Whenever she did so I was surprised how readily ideas came to my mind. It was as if she knew instinctively the moment to ask, and sensed when an answer was available. It was in this way that she came to draw pictures, write letters and read many books which later contributed much to the content of our times together. As far as I recall, these 'extra-curricular' activities always resulted from Sally's felt need for them, and I do not remember offering suggestions unless asked. When she wrote me letters — as she did frequently — it was only rarely that I replied but I seemed to recognise those occasions when a response was required.

The third area where our respective intuitions served us well was in the structures we evolved for our meetings. During the years we worked together we continually renegotiated the boundaries. There were periods when we met once a week for fifty minutes in the traditional manner. There were other times, however, when Sally wanted and asked for more frequent meetings and yet other occasions when I recognised her unspoken need and offered her more time. As I look back on it I am surprised that I was not monumentally inconvenienced by this changing pattern, especially when for a time the sessions were not for fifty minutes but for three hours! I recall no such inconvenience even if I was sometimes daunted by the prospect of the work ahead. I rather suspect that it is fear and laziness which makes us as therapists so keen to control the structures of therapeutic relationships. Fear is a legitimate reason as long as we acknowledge it, but it is difficult to establish much of a brief for laziness, a thought shared by Dr Scott Peck an American psychiatrist, who suggests in a powerful book that laziness is the 'original sin' and the enemy of all human growth (Peck, 1978).

My work with Sally has resulted in a somewhat changed attitude to past experience. With her I discovered that if I could be fully responsive to the experience of the moment, I was likely to be led, unexpectedly and unpredictably, deep into the past. The 'regressive' period in our relationship was for me frankly astonishing. I am well acquainted with the literature of rebirth and have witnessed some primal work. At no point in the therapy with Sally, however, did I feel that I was operating as a primal therapist, although there were stages when I found the writings of Frank Lake (1981) particularly illuminating. My astonishment sprang from the profundity of the experiences which Sally underwent and from her subsequent ability to make sense of them even when there had previously been no conscious knowledge of the data on which they were based. I conclude that while in the womb Sally was impregnated by her mother's psychological state of being: she literally took into herself her mother's grief, despair and longing for oblivion. Such a conclusion enables me to go some way towards understanding why there are people who seem to be afflicted with despair or terror for which there seems to be no adequate explanation in their own life's experience. In such cases I am now more than a little motivated to discover what was happening to the mother during the period of pregnancy. I have been startled to find that Sally's experience of blackness and suffocation is replicated in other cases, and that not infrequently a level of distress in the mother is revealed which at the time of her pregnancy engendered deep despair or an intolerable sense of guilt and unworthiness. For three clients with whom I have worked in the past 18 months the simple uncovering of this fact (through discussion with the mother or other close relatives) has been sufficient for them literally to disown their misery. They have come to realise that their intense feeling of not being worthy of life does not belong to them although it has been part of their consciousness for as long as they can recall. It would seem therefore that these crippling intra-uterine experiences can be deprived of their power if they are re-experienced or in some cases simply investigated in the context of a loving relationship. I have become more convinced that the person-centred emphasis on the creation of a psychological climate conducive to growth is fundamental to all therapy, and that if this climate can be consistently and generously offered, past pain can be relieved and transformed no matter how far back it is lodged in the client's history.

My relationship with Sally has had another highly significant effect on my professional life. I am now keen to write about my work and to speak about it in detail. Part of the motivation for this is assuredly a natural desire for fame, but I believe that, at a deeper level, I wish to be known for what I am and that I am prepared to risk myself and my work to the public scrutiny of others so that I can be clearly seen by those who might be able to derive some benefit from my own attempts to be a therapist. Sally knew me before we started on our therapeutic work together. If she had not, I doubt if we could have travelled so far.

IMPLICATIONS FOR OTHER THERAPISTS

Sally's uncompromising faith in me forced me to face myself in two fundamental ways. First, she made me question how much I really valued the particular approach to therapy which I professed to practise. In effect, she incited in me a commitment to the basic tenets of person-centred therapy which surpassed in depth and tenacity any previous allegiance on my part. Secondly, she demanded my integrity. I was compelled to face the complete range of my beliefs and feelings about myself, the world and the human race, and when I discovered apparent contradictions to search for some kind of resolution. Whatever safety I might have had in the therapist role was ruthlessly stripped away by Sally's consuming faith in my genuineness. She compelled me to be honest. I suggest that it might be no bad thing if every therapist asked two questions of himself or herself every year or so: (i) What would it mean if I *really* practised the therapy I profess? (ii) What do I believe about my own nature, the human race of which I am a part and the world in which I live?

And then, in the light of the answers, to re-examine his or her professional activities.

Sally also made me focus on areas which are often neglected in therapist training. With her I gradually developed the ability to move between the worlds of the physical, the emotional, the cognitive and the mystical without strain, an ability which I have subsequently come to recognise as fundamental to the expression of tenderness (Thorne, 1985). I do not believe that such tenderness is likely to be found in someone who has failed to take with the utmost seriousness the process of human birth and the significance of death. It follows therefore that as therapists we should be encouraged to find out all we can about the external factors surrounding our own conception, our time *in utero* and our birth. I believe, too, that we should be required to face the fact of death and of our own death in particular and to discover what we understand and feel about our mortality. Such self-exploration could be followed by the opportunity to relate in some depth to a pregnant woman, both before and immediately after the birth of her child. Such an experience would be a particularly valuable part of a therapist's training and an especially rare privilege for many young male trainees. We might also welcome opportunities for relating to terminally ill people and for sharing with them the last stages of the movement towards death. For me it has now become faintly incredible that therapists so seldom, it seems, apply themselves at the experimental level to a thorough-going exploration of these two fundamental 'givens' of the human condition.

The person-centred approach is based on the belief that the human organism is trustworthy and that we have within us the necessary wisdom and resources for our development to full humanness. And yet how difficult it seems to be for those of us who are therapists to trust the truth of this assertion when we ourselves are the organism in question and when what that organism is prompting in us is a loving and spontaneous response to another person. Clearly it is right and proper that we should be cautious for we know that our capacity for self-deception is great. On the other hand, if I have done my best to accept and empathise with my client and if I have worked assiduously at staying in touch with the flow of my own experiencing — if I have done all that, and then find that from deep within me there comes the impulse to stretch out to my client in a new and perhaps unexpected way, should I not trust that impulse and act upon it? And yet it seems that so often we do *not* trust these impulses because at the deepest level we do *not* trust our organism, we do *not* believe in the spontaneous goodness of ourselves and we do *not* believe that our deepest and often most ecstatic desire is to enable another person to become whole. Or, to put it another way, at such moments we can become paralysed as we find ourselves caught in the conflict between desire and control.

Such paralysis, I am now convinced, is often the result of our failure to befriend our bodies and our sexuality with a consequent lack of integration of these aspects of the self into our self-concept and into our self-loving. Given the history of our culture this is scarcely surprising. In many overt and in countless other hidden ways we are taught to distrust our carnal and sexual selves so that they are forced into the role of internal enemies whose main intent is to bring about our downfall. We come to fear and distrust the body which is the temple of the spirit and our sexuality which is the primary source of our loving and our yearnings. The price we pay for such fear and distrust is immense. We are locked out of the Garden. As therapists we fail to be the healers we have it in us to be because it becomes too risky to practise what we profess to believe. To trust the integrity of our being in this deepest sense seems to put us in dire jeopardy, and we lack the courage to take the leap.

The implication of all this for therapists is obvious. We need to discover ways of enabling ourselves to befriend our bodies and our sexuality so that we can become increasingly responsive to the impulses of tenderness which well up at those moments of sublime recognition when inner spirit meets inner spirit. My practical suggestions for encouraging such a befriending of body and sexuality are radical and demanding. I believe we need to create opportunities where therapists can become comfortable with their own physicality and with the physicality of others, and where they can learn to cherish and respect themselves and others as physical beings without shame or inhibition. It may be that massage workshops should be an essential part of all therapist training, but even these will fail to offer the opportunity I am proposing if the focus is on technique rather than on responsiveness to and prizing of the physical being of oneself and others. From a comfortableness with physicality and nakedness there can come a progressive decrease in the sense of awkwardness between the sexes. Much of this awkwardness springs in our culture from the conditioned notion that a man and a woman, if they are naked together, or a man and a man, or a woman and a woman for that matter, can only have one objective in mind — namely to have sexual intercourse. This obsessional preoccupation with having sex is the greatest obstacle to the befriending of our sexuality. Our sexuality becomes trapped in the genitals and cannot therefore radiate through our physical being and become the essential ingredient of all our loving and creativity. What is more the obsession with having sex makes it well-nigh impossible for us to own our *sensual* needs and capacities. Sensuality flows from and is nourished by a sexuality which is free to infuse the total being and is not fixated on and imprisoned by the obsession with and the compulsive need for intercourse. It is appallingly tragic that countless human beings in our culture are forced into sexual relationships because this is the only context in which they can satisfy their longing for holding and for physical touch or embrace. Many clients who come into therapy are asking for touch for they know that their healing is dependent upon such physical responsiveness. It is a double irony if the therapist, because of his inability to befriend his own body and sexuality, is unable to trust his instinctive desire to offer such a physical ministry because he fears for his reputation or is terrified that he may abuse his client.

I am well aware that much of what I have said in this concluding section could be open to the most perverse interpretation. I am aware, too, that there have been and presumably are, therapists who have sought to defend or justify physical or sexual behaviour with clients which I find abhorrent and totally unethical. I cannot myself imagine, for example, any situation where I would find it appropriate or justifiable to have sexual intercourse with a client in the process of therapy. Nor can I believe that it would ever be acceptable to begin a therapeutic relationship with the aim or intention, however covert, to induce or persuade a client to enter into physical contact of any kind, let alone to encourage nakedness or the removal of clothing. In choosing to describe my work with Sally my intention is to focus on what proved to be the implications of offering the core conditions of acceptance, empathy and congruence to a particular woman with grave sexual problems who was alienated from her physical being and yet had a profound belief in the power of love to heal and to make whole. Furthermore her concept of wholeness embraced the spiritual as well as the physical, emotional and cognitive, and her concept of love involved a belief in the divine origin of all love.

Inevitably, therefore, the final focus of this discussion must be on the word 'love' and its implications for therapists. It is notable that in the vast corpus of professional literature which now exists on counselling and psychotherapy there is scant reference to the issue of love. And yet I have known for many years that for me offering the core conditions, if I do so consistently and honestly, means a willingness to love my clients and the likelihood that I shall end up doing so. My work with Sally has convinced me that it is, in fact, essential for me to love my clients if genuine healing is to occur, and that the deeper the wound or the graver the deficiency the more likely it is that I shall have to extend myself in love to a degree which is costly in effort and commitment. There is part of me which does not like that conclusion. There are times when I would prefer my success as a therapist to depend on my knowledge, my therapeutic skills or techniques, my experience, my years of self-exploration. But I know that I should be deluding myself to believe that. Little in my experience had prepared me for my encounter with Sally or for the kind of work on which we eventually embarked. I knew little of 'body therapy' and my experience of primal work was minimal. I am no great expert on prayer and I had never before entered into complex theological dialogue with a client. The terrain was largely unfamiliar to me, but at least I knew after a very short time that I loved Sally and, as we began to take the first steps together, I felt that love returned. It is in Peck's (1978) book to which I have already referred that I found the chief characteristic of our mutual love most beautifully and concisely expressed. He defines love as 'the will to extend one's self for the purpose of nurturing one's own or another's spiritual growth' (Peck, 1978, p. 199). This definition captures exactly the essence of my love for Sally, and I conclude that it was my trust in the nature of my loving which enabled me, first, to work so hard without resentment, and, secondly, to allow my love to grow. Instead of 'cooling it' or taking fright at my feelings I permitted myself to develop a strong sexual attraction to Sally and to cherish her physical being with all the tenderness I could muster. She, in turn, allowed herself to love me with increasing confidence and lack of inhibition. At no time, however, except in the first bewildering stages, was there a danger of us falling in love. To do so would have meant a collapse of the boundaries between us and a loss of the separateness which is crucial for maintaining and enhancing the autonomy of the individual. Love which is expressed in 'the will to extend one's self for the purpose of nurturing one's own or another's spiritual growth' cannot permit such fusion if it is to remain true to its nature. Such love, however, is very demanding in the discipline it imposes and it is difficult to see why a therapist without a belief in the potential divinisation of humanity and therefore in a divine source of power should submit himself or herself to such a discipline. It may be, however, that what I have described as the longing for the spiritual growth of another can be experienced as a profound and unselfish desire for a fellow human being to become fully human. For me this amounts to the same thing but I can readily appreciate that for many therapists the change in language is important. I am persuaded, too, but less readily, that a deep and unshakeable yearning for the fulfilment of another's humanity need not be linked to a belief in God or indeed to any 'religious' interpretation of reality.

A final word of clarification needs to be added before I am accused by theological readers of a heresy first perpetrated by the fourth-century British monk, Pelagius, who taught that man's free will is sufficient to attain salvation and that there is no original sin. It will be evident from my work with Sally that there were moments when we attained a level of communication which could certainly be described in terms of an altered state of consciousness or as a breakthrough into the transcendental. I am suggesting that such moments bring about the release of healing forces of great potency and that they are more likely to occur if therapists attend to the issues I have outlined in this final section. I am not claiming, however, that such moments will then *inevitably* occur. To make such a claim would be to suggest that imperfect human beings have within them the ability to become God by *their own efforts*. My contention in this chapter is that therapists have a particular obligation to ensure that they prepare themselves with the utmost discipline for the task of creating a climate where both they and their clients can be fully open to the mysterious power in which they share but which is greater than they.

NOTE

1. See my interview with Windy Dryden (1985) for a further exploration of this issue.

REFERENCES

Dryden, W. (1985). *Therapists' Dilemmas*. London: Harper & Row

Julian of Norwich (1966). *Revelations of divine love* (tranl. Clifton Wolters). London: Penguin Books

Lake, F. (1981). *Tight corners in pastoral counselling*. London: Darton, Longman & Todd

Mearns, D. and Lambers, E. (1976). Facilitator Development Institute. *Self and Society,* 4(12), 9–12
Moore, S. (1980). *The fire and the rose are one.* London: Darton, Longman & Todd
Moore, S. (1982). *The inner loneliness.* London: Darton, Longman & Todd
Peck, M.S. (1978). *The road less travelled.* London: Hutchinson
Rogers, C.R. and Dymond, R.F. (Eds) (1954). *Psychotherapy and personality change.* Chicago: University of Chicago Press
Thorne, B.J. (1982). *Intimacy.* Norwich: Norvicare
Thorne, B.J. (1985). *The quality of tenderness.* Norwich: Norwich Centre Publications
Williams, H.A. (1972). *True resurrection.* London: Mitchell Beazley
Williams, H.A. (1976). *Tensions: necessary conflicts in life and love.* London: Mitchell Beazley

5

An Even More Offensive Theory

Daniel B. Wile

Several theoretical concepts that I and many other therapists have commonly used in our everyday therapeutic work, and that we may have felt really helped us, I now see as countertherapeutic and as placing therapists at a serious disadvantage. In fact I view these theories as *the problem*. It is clients' own commitments to these theories, or rather to the versions of these theories that exist in the general culture, that lie at the root of their difficulties. These realisations were hard for me to arrive at since they contradicted my early training and were offensive to my colleagues. And following the experience to be described, my theory became even more offensive to them.

PRIOR THEORY AND PRACTICE

Let me begin by laying out the theory I had prior to seeing the couple in question. I shall do so in the traditional way — by tracing the roots of my theory to Freud. My approach is based on what Freud first discovered: that warding off an *ordinary* wish can convert it into a symptom. Freud made this discovery as early as 1892–1894 in his treatment of Elizabeth von R, although elements of the theory are present even in the case of Anna O.

Freud (Breuer and Freud, 1955) attributed Elizabeth's symptoms — her leg pains — to moral condemnations against herself for what were actually *ordinary feelings*. Elizabeth was in love with her sister's husband. When this sister died, Elizabeth had the flashing thought 'Now he is free again and I can be his wife' (p. 156). Elizabeth was appalled by this thought. She felt it was wicked and unforgivable of her to be in love with her sister's husband. She repressed awareness of this passing thought and of her love for this man and developed hysterical leg pains.

Freud saw Elizabeth's love for her brother-in-law as understandable and non-pathological. Elizabeth and this man were attracted to one another from the beginning. It was perhaps only because of the contemporary system of arranged marriages that Elizabeth's sister rather than Elizabeth herself was the one to marry him. Some kind of thought to the effect of 'Now he is free again and I can be his wife' would seem inevitable given the situation. Freud tried to console her by telling her 'that we are not responsible for our feelings, and that her behavior, the fact that she had fallen ill in these circumstances, was sufficient evidence of her moral character' (p. 157).

Not only did Freud see Elizabeth's passing thought and love for her brother-in-law as entirely ordinary, but he went further and asked Elizabeth's mother about the possibility of a marriage between the two. The mother was opposed. However, this was not because the proposed husband was Elizabeth's sister's former husband. The mother's main concern was that *this man was unsuitable for Elizabeth* because of his poor physical and mental health. In other words, Elizabeth's mother did not find it shocking that Elizabeth was in love with her brother-in-law. Only Elizabeth did.

Here, at the very beginning of his work, Freud discovered a simple and elegant principle: *squelching ordinary feelings produces symptoms*. The source of psychopathology is clients' own rejection of their underlying wishes; that is, their own tendency to condemn these wishes as unacceptable, wicked, childish, or pathological. The problem is not that something is wrong with Elizabeth's wishes. The problem is that *she thinks that something is wrong with them*. The root of the difficulty is her belief about her wishes rather than the wishes in themselves.

A person's belief that his or her reactions are childish or pathological can lead to ones that are. A man who suppresses ordinary assertiveness, believing such behaviour to be unacceptably aggressive, may end up by engaging in sporadic tantrums that are aggressive (i.e. suppression leads to tantrums). A wife who makes practically no requests of her husband, believing that such behaviour would be unacceptably dependent, may end up by engaging in sporadic demands that are clingingly dependent. And a woman who thinks that it is unacceptable to be in love with her sister's husband and to have the passing thought that her sister's death might mean she can marry him herself may end up by developing leg pains.

In the years that followed, Freud's theorising took a different turn, and by the early 1900s he came in essence to agree with Elizabeth. He now believed that there *was* something wrong with patients' underlying wishes. In fact, Freud now saw patients' wishes in even more negative terms than did these individuals themselves. Whereas individuals saw their wishes as childish, Freud saw them as even more regressed, that is, as infantile. Repression (warding off underlying wishes), which, in his treatment of Elizabeth, Freud saw as the pathogenic agent, he now viewed as not entirely bad. The *unrepressed* wish, were it to be acted on, would result in a perversion. If Freud were to have seen Elizabeth twenty years later, he might have traced her love of her sister's husband to incestous love for her father, homosexual love for her sister, oedipal competition with her mother, sibling rivalry with her sister, or a wish for a penis.

Freud has thus left us with *two* theories to explain how symptomatic behaviour obtains its infantile, primitive, or pathological character. The first theory — the one emerging from the case of Elizabeth — is that the processes of regression and suppression tranform what began as an ordinary wish into something primitive or pathological. The second — the one Freud came to emphasise — is that no transformation is involved. Rather, the original wish is in fundamental nature infantile and primitive. Thus, at the core of every neurosis is a perversion.

Freud's treatment of Elizabeth von R constitutes a rudimentary version of 'ego analysis',[1] the psychotherapeutic approach to which I subscribe. In later years, Freud (1959, 1961) turned back to some extent towards ego analysis, although it remained for Fenichel, in his 1941 book on psychoanalytic technique, to begin a systematic development of the approach. Apfelbaum (Apfelbaum, 1977, 1982, 1983; Apfelbaum and Gill, in preparation) has continued this development, and is the most forceful modern proponent of ego analysis. Wile (1981, 1984, 1985a, b) has also written extensively on the subject.

Why did Freud develop the second theory if, as I am arguing, the first — the theory he employed in the case of Elizabeth — provides a fully sufficient explanation? And why did he emphasise the second if, as I wish to argue, the first is more convincing? The apparent answer is that the first theory did not seem fully sufficient and was not more convincing *to him*. Freud appeared to prefer a theory that, based as it were on drives, approximated the mass-energy theories of the physics of his generation and thus appeared more scientific.

And why should it even matter which theory is more correct or which of the two theories a therapist employs? It matters because the two lead to incompatible therapeutic approaches, as Greenberg and Mitchell (1983) show in their discussion of psychoanalytic theory. It matters because therapists are in a very different position if their task is to break the news to people about their infantile and perverted wishes than if their task is to show how the wishes and feelings for which these individuals are already criticising themselves are actually ordinary.

And it matters because, from the standpoint of each theory, the other is iatrogenic. Telling people that their underlying wishes are infantile would be seen from the standpoint of Freud's first theory as feeding into the self-accusation that generates the problem. And telling people that their underlying wishes are ordinary would be seen from the standpoint of Freud's second theory as feeding into the defences and resistances that maintain the problem.

The case of Janet and Bruce taught me the extent to which therapists are caught between Freud's two theories. Most therapists subscribe to Freud's second theory. They attribute the problem to clients' defences and underlying immature or primitive impulses. In practice, however, these therapists often informally shift to Freud's first theory. Sensing that the problem is the way in which clients invalidate their own feelings, these therapists attempt to protect clients from self-accusations. This shift to Freud's first theory is not very firm, however. At a particular moment, therapists may see clients' *self-accusations* for being too dependent, self-centred or hostile as the major problem. The very next moment, however, particularly if therapists feel under pressure (e.g. they feel responsible to do something or are concerned because they are not understanding), they may see clients' *dependency, narcissism or sadism* as the major problem. In this manner, therapists shift back and forth between Freud's two theories.

The case of Janet and Bruce taught me the extent to which I am caught between Freud's two theories. Although dedicated to Freud's first theory, that is, to the recognition that the problem is the often hidden ways in which people are already accusing themselves, under the pressure of the moment, I started accusing them myself. The case of Janet and Bruce thus led me, not to a new theory, but to a further appreciation of the difficulty of applying the one I already had. The case also led me to an appreciation of the inevitability of what can be called *everyday momentary overload,* which people respond to by functioning in narrowed-down stereotyped ways.

DESCRIPTION OF THE KEY CASE

Janet and Bruce, a couple in their mid thirties, came to the fifth couples therapy session upset. The following is how I would have *liked* the session to have gone:

Janet We're back to square one. I thought we were making progress coming here. But what happened today makes me think we haven't got anywhere.
Bruce Maybe we just weren't meant to be a couple.
Janet I don't even know how it started. I was just talking on the phone with my friend, Sue. And Bruce started making angry faces at me. And when I got off the phone, he had this tantrum about my tying up the line.
Bruce Well you *were* tying up the line. You were on the phone for 45 minutes, for crying out loud.
Janet It wasn't that long. And anyway, Sue was upset. She just broke up with her boyfriend.
Bruce Sue's always upset. And she's always breaking up with her boyfriend. We ought to install a hot-line so she can be sure to get through when she's upset, which is every ten minutes.
Janet I hate it when you're sarcastic like this. And anyway, I don't even think it was about Sue. You came *home* angry. You were angry at your boss and so you came home and kicked the dog. And I'm the dog.
Bruce I didn't come home angry. What got me angry was what happened when I *got* home. Or rather what didn't happen. You acted as if I wasn't even there.
Janet Well, what do you expect? We hadn't exactly been getting along like Romeo and Juliet. I put on that special dress this morning — the one you think looks real sexy. And I did my hair the special way you like. And you didn't say anything about it. Talk about not being there, all you cared about was the eggs I put in front of you. I'm just the cook.
Bruce You're the cook and you're the complainer. I called you at work and the first thing you did was blame me for forgetting to put gas in the car. You don't like anything I do these days.
Janet I didn't blame you about the car. You're mixing it up.
Bruce I'm not mixing it up. I know when I'm being blamed. And I'm not mixing up the way you looked at me last night.
Janet What way I looked at you?
Bruce With pure disgust. I've never seen a look of such

utter disgust.

The session to this point may seem an inconclusive exchange of charge and countercharge. But something useful has occurred. Janet and Bruce came into the session not knowing what their problem was about or how it started. And in the course of this interchange, they threaded their way back to its source — the 'look of pure disgust'.

This look occurred while Janet and Bruce were in bed. And, as we were to find out shortly, it was key to all the charges and countercharges that they had just been making. They had been having sex and, right in the middle, Bruce lost his erection and was unable to get it back.

Bruce We eventually gave up and just lay there. Then I looked over at Janet and she was staring off into space with this look of utter disgust. (To Janet): You were disgusted with me for failing you sexually.

Janet was amazed at what Bruce was now telling her:

Janet I wasn't disgusted at you for failing me. I was worried that I failed *you*. That you didn't find me attractive. That I didn't turn you on.

Suddenly everything was clear. Bruce and Janet had come away from that incident with contrasting unexpressed worries.

Since Bruce was disgusted with himself, he could easily imagine that Janet was also. And the thought that she might be disgusted with him angered him. He took her long conversation with Sue as meaning that she was turning away from him in disgust and towards her friends. He had the passing thought that Janet and Sue were laughing at him for his sexual failure. Overtly he defended himself against Janet's complaints. Privately, however, he took them to heart. He saw his failure to comment on her dress as further indication that he did not have the proper responses that a husband should have. And he worried that he *might* be treating her as a cook rather than a lover. He shuddered at the double meaning implicit in Janet's complaint that he failed to put gas in her car.

Janet had her own unexpressed worries. She took Bruce's impotence with her as a sign that she was impotent with him in that she was unable to turn him on. She slept poorly and, the next morning, made a concerted effort to try to turn him on. She dolled herself up. And when he did not even seem to notice, she was mortified. At first she blamed herself; she felt she just wasn't pretty enough.

But when he criticised her for putting too much salt on the eggs, she suddenly felt justified to blame him: 'You want a cook; not a wife'.

The problem as they saw it now, was not Janet and Bruce's failure at sex. The problem was their failure to discuss their 'failure' in sex. If they were to have had such a discussion — the discussion they were having now — they might have been able to straighten things out. If Bruce had known that Janet's look of 'utter disgust' was actually worry about her own attractiveness, he would have been much less upset and might have tried to reassure her. And if Janet had known that Bruce was blaming himself for not being masculine enough rather than blaming her for not being feminine enough, she would have been much less upset and might have tried to reassure him.

And if they were to have had such a discussion about Bruce's episode of impotence — the discussion they were having now — they might have been able to figure out what had led up to it. They had been arguing that evening about where to spend their vacation. Janet initiated sex as an attempt to patch things up. She was still tense from the argument, however. And in the middle of sex, Bruce sensed Janet's tension and lost his erection. What Bruce had seen as his failure to meet his sexual responsibilities as a husband, and what Janet had seen as her failure to meet her sexual responsibilities as a wife, they now saw as Bruce's understandable reaction to Janet's tension. And they saw Janet's tension as her understandable reaction to their argument.

Such a discovery is likely to make the therapy session a useful one. The source of the immediate problem would have been uncovered and a less alienated and more hopeful spirit reinstituted. The problem is that the hour did not quite go this way. It *could* have gone this way. Two years before another couple came to a session reporting a very similar incident and the hour with them *had* gone this way. The reason the session with Janet and Bruce did not go this way is that they were themselves psychotherapists. And why this should matter is what this chapter is about.

In saying that the hour did not quite go the way I reported, I do not mean that Janet and Bruce did not say what I described them as saying. Everything reported here was said. The problem is that a lot of additional things were said. And these added comments changed the whole picture.

Interestingly, the difference between the discussion with the couple I saw two years before and the discussion with Janet and Bruce is similar to the difference between Freud's first and second theories. In the case of the couple I saw two years before, we traced the problem to ordinary feelings (Freud's first theory). The husband was worried about failing as a man and the wife was worried about failing as a woman. These are worries that any man or woman in such a situation might have. In the case of Janet and Bruce, the partners traced the problem to pathological impulses and reactions (Freud's second theory). Janet and Bruce attributed the difficulty to rescue fantasies, defensiveness, unresolved anger towards parents, a basic hatred of men, fear of intimacy, a power struggle, and an unconscious wish to punish.

Rescue fantasies

As already described, Bruce accused Janet of tying up the line in her conversation with Sue. But he added another comment that I have not mentioned. He accused Janet of having 'rescue fantasies'.

Bruce You were on the phone for 45 minutes, for crying out loud.
Janet It wasn't that long. And anyway, Sue was upset. She just broke up with her boyfriend.
Bruce Sue's always upset. And she's always breaking up with her boyfriend. *Your problem is that you're so insecure that the only way you can feel important is by finding people who are helpless and then rescuing them.*

Janet became upset and confused. Her face reddened and she fought off tears. She did not know what to say. How do you defend yourself when you are accused of having rescue fantasies.

Defensiveness

Bruce said that her becoming upset in response to what he said was an act. It was a defence.

Bruce (to Janet) *You're acting upset so you don't have to look at the truth of what I'm saying. You don't want to take responsibility for your feelings.*

Janet became further upset. And then she became angry. She accused Bruce of being insensitive and of not understanding how she felt.

You're really angry at your mother

As already described, Janet said that Bruce's anger at her was really anger at his boss. But Janet added another comment that I have not yet mentioned.

Janet (to Bruce) *And unconsciously you're really angry at your mother. And I'm tired of having to pay for what happened with your mother. Nothing's going to change until you go back into individual therapy and deal with your feelings about her.*

Now it was Bruce who was upset. He said that he did not need individual therapy, that his feelings about his mother have nothing to do with it, that, anyway, he's not angry at his mother, and that, anyway, Janet has problems with her own mother. Janet said that she doesn't have problems with her mother, to which Bruce responded by reminding her of the argument she had with her mother earlier that week. Janet said that it was just a misunderstanding not an argument. And anyway they had worked it out. And even if it were an argument, it was a lot better than what happens between him and his mother. He hasn't talked to her in two years.

Basic hatred of men

As already stated, Bruce criticised Janet for the way she looked at him following his episode of sexual impotence. But he added another comment.

Bruce (to Janet) You looked at me last night with pure disgust. I've never seen a look of such utter disgust. *I don't think you really like men. You enjoy putting them down. You're afraid of them. I think you have a basic hatred of men.*

This statement is a show-stopper. It's hard to hear such charges against oneself without wondering whether they might be true. Janet anxiously scans her past relationships with men, looking to see whether Bruce is right about her and that she does have a basic hatred of men. And she can't decide for sure. Bruce has not specifically used the words, but she feels accused of that most heinous of all crimes: *being a castrating woman.*

Fear of intimacy

Janet has a show-stopper of her own. She interprets Bruce's episode of sexual impotence as fear of intimacy.

Janet (to Bruce) *You're afraid of commitment. Your fear of your mother makes you unable to have a real relationship with a woman. You got too close to me. And being impotent is a way of pulling back to a safe distance.*

Now it's Bruce's turn to worry about himself. He scans his past romantic relationships looking for evidence that he might be afraid of intimacy, and he thinks he finds it. Of course he does. People can always find such evidence in the past. He remembers a couple of instances in which he cut off relationships before they got too intense.

Power struggle

Bruce does not tell Janet that he thinks she's right about his fear of intimacy. But he does admit to something else. He tells her that he thinks that they are having a power struggle. There is a hint of a softening tone in this comment. In attributing their problems to a power struggle, Bruce is blaming both of them and not just her. Janet is well aware that a struggle of some sort is occurring between them. And she is relieved that Bruce is willing to share the blame. She agrees with him that they are having a power struggle.

Setting me up

The conciliatory tone is short-lived. Janet and Bruce immediately run into trouble when they try to say what the power struggle is about.

Janet *You manipulated me. You set me up. You were trying to frustrate me. You agreed to having sex and then you lost your erection. You were trying to punish me.*
Bruce *I wasn't trying to punish you.*
Janet *You just weren't aware of it. You were trying to punish me unconsciously.*

'You statements'

Since Bruce is unable effectively to deny having wishes that his accuser, Janet, has already designated as unconscious, he changes the subject. He criticises Janet for failing to make 'I statements'.

Bruce *Listen to what you just said. You said 'you manipulated me' and 'you were trying to punish me'. Those are 'you statements'. We'll never get anywhere as long as you're always making 'you statements'.*

Janet *We'll never get anywhere as long as you're always using words like 'always' and 'never'. And, besides, you just made a 'you statement' yourself. And, besides, I don't always make 'you statements'. I was careful to make an 'I statement' when I told you this morning that 'I don't like the way you always accuse me'.*

Bruce *That's not an 'I statement'. That's a 'you statement' in disguise.*

In the session with the couple I saw two years before, the discovery of the critical misunderstanding produced a lessening of tension and a move towards reconciliation. In the case of Janet and Bruce, however, such a shift never occurred. Their initial discouragement and distress persisted through the hour.

Why did this happen? My immediate idea was that Janet and Bruce's professional knowledge had got in the way. The potentially conflict-resolving discovery — that Bruce blamed himself for failing as a man and Janet blamed herself for failing as a woman — came too late. By that time, Bruce had already accused Janet of being defensive, engaging in rescue fantasies, having a basic hatred of men, and making 'you statements'. And Janet had already accused Bruce of fear of intimacy, having unresolved anger towards his mother, needing personal therapy, and setting her up. Too many swords had passed through too many bodies to allow them to realise that there might have been no need for the war in the first place.

Ironically, being psychotherapists and having a working familiarity with these concepts placed Janet and Bruce at a disadvantage. The session might have gone better if these partners had no knowledge of these concepts; that is, if they had been electricians or physicians, or, as in the case of the couple I saw two years previously, a sales manager and a music teacher.

If stating such ideas to one's partner produces such negative effects, maybe stating them to one's clients is not such a good idea either. The comments that Janet and Bruce made to one another seem typical of the kinds of reasoning that psychotherapists often employ and the kinds of interpretation they frequently make. Is there a possibility that such reasoning and interpretation are countertherapeutic?

But why should terms and concepts associated with the specialised knowledge of psychotherapy be countertherapeutic? One might think, instead, that they would be helpful. These are some of the concepts, after all, that many psychotherapists depend on to produce a therapeutic effect.

Perhaps the explanation can be found in the well-known fact that even very good ideas can be turned into weapons. The distinction between 'I statements' and 'you statements' is an example of a very good idea. However, this useful distinction can easily be transformed into an accusation. This is what Bruce did when he criticised Janet for making 'you statements'. And then Janet turned Bruce's weapon back on him. She pointed out that his comment, 'You just made a "you statement"' is itself a 'you statement'.

The transformation of good ideas into weapons is not the whole explanation, however. Some ideas are more inflammatory than others. Certain ideas are so intrinsically accusatory that it is difficult to keep them from becoming weapons. This is the case with many of the standard ideas that therapists have. People can get pretty upset when they are told that they have a basic hatred of men or an unconscious wish to punish their partners.

Clients are less able than are therapists' partners to protect themselves from these accusatory ideas. Clients are generally more compliant than partners, more likely to give the therapist the benefit of the doubt, and more likely to accept the therapist's authority. Furthermore, therapists state these ideas to clients in a more neutral, more tactful, and less provocative manner than they do to their partners. They are not angry at their clients. Consequently, clients do not have the same opportunity to dismiss these interpretations as exaggerated statements made in anger.

Psychotherapists, and everyone else, underestimate the difficult of making truly neutral and non-accusatory statements. When is an interpretation an accusation and when is it useful information? An interpretation is an accusation *whether or not* it contains useful information when the implication is made that the person is doing, feeling, or thinking something that he or she should not be doing, feeling, or thinking.

The interpretation 'you are resisting' is clearly an accusation, since no one thinks that resisting is something a person should be doing, and few sophisticated therapists make it anymore. There are many other similarly accusatory interpretations, however, that therapists do commonly make. Therapists regularly describe clients as angry, dependent, controlling, competitive, jealous, self-centred, manipulative, afraid of intimacy, still angry at their fathers, and so on. These therapists make these interpretations believing that they are simply describing obvious facts. What these therapists fail to realise is that there is no way in which people in our culture can hear these things being said about them without immediately thinking they are doing something wrong. And if the therapist's comments reinforce the self-accusations that, as in Freud's early case of Elizabeth von R, constitute the source of the problem, then these comments have a clearly countertherapeutic effect.

The only way therapists can interpret someone as being angry or dependent without it being an accusation is if they immediately talk about how it makes sense that they would be feeling angry or dependent, that they may need to feel freer to have such feelings, and the problem may be that they are unable to enjoy these feelings. This is a key principle of ego analysis.

EMERGENT NEW DEVELOPMENTS

Now comes what might be the most dramatic event in this entire episode with Janet and Bruce. My whole approach is based on recognising the existence and danger of accusatory thinking. As alert as I was to this danger, I fell victim to it myself, and this really convinced me about the difficulty of avoiding it. I told Janet and Bruce that their comments to one another were accusations. Just as Bruce's criticism of Janet that she made 'you statements' was itself a 'you statement', my comments to both that they were accusing one another was itself an accusation. My implication was that they should not be doing this.

But what alternative was there? Janet and Bruce's criticisms of one another were producing an increasingly unworkable interaction. As the therapist — the person in the situation entrusted to guide the process — I felt responsible to do something. And as a therapist who believes in the value of giving clients an overview of what they are doing, the something-to-be-done was to show Janet and Bruce what they were doing; namely, accusing one another.

But such a statement is only a half-interpretation. The full interpretation is to show that, yes, Janet and Bruce are accusing one another, but that they are doing so because they are having difficulty saying what they need to say. People who accuse often appear to be *failing* to inhibit themselves and to be *lacking* self-restraint. This makes it easy to miss the fact that *accusations are inhibited assertions*. The individuals in question are unable to express their feelings because they are unaware of what their feelings are or because they think that they should not be having them. The rapid pace of events compounds the effect: people have insufficient time to deal with feelings that would be difficult to comprehend even with unlimited time. Individuals who are unable to give adequate expression to their feelings commonly resort to accusations. And that is what happened to Bruce, Janet and myself.

Bruce accused Janet of engaging in rescue fantasies because there was something he needed to say that he was having difficulty getting across. His accusation was the best approximation he could make at the time. What he needed to tell her, and to discover more fully for himself, was, among other things:

(1) that he felt humiliated about the incident of impotence;
(2) that he was worried that Janet was as disgusted with him for it as he was with himself;
(3) that he could easily think, when she talked for a longer time than usual with Sue, that Janet was withdrawing from him and becoming more involved with Sue;
(4) that he felt a little jealous of her involvement with Sue;
(5) that he could even imagine that Janet and Sue might be laughing about him;
(6) that he felt so hurt and angry that he felt like accusing Janet of engaging in rescue fantasies;
(7) and that, as a matter of fact, if she was wanting to rescue someone, he would enjoy her rescuing him.

What Bruce did say — accusing Janet of engaging in rescue fantasies — was a distorted fragment of what he really wanted to tell her.

And so were Janet's accusations that Bruce was afraid of intimacy, still hung up about his mother, and unconsciously seeking to punish her. What Janet needed to tell Bruce, and, also, to discover more fully for herself, was, among other things:

(1) that her immediate reaction to his impotence was that she had failed him;
(2) that her main feeling about the matter was that she wasn't sexy

or attractive enough and that she was lucky that he had agreed to marry her;
(3) but that there were times, however, particularly when they were arguing, when she would suddenly feel that everything was all Bruce's fault;
(4) that she feels this right now;
(5) that when she is feeling this way she can believe that he is afraid of intimacy, that his problem is with his mother, and that *he's* lucky that she had agreed to marry him;
(6) that she can quickly move back and forth this way between completely blaming herself and completely blaming him;
(7) that she is thus confused about what she thinks the truth really is;
(8) and that at times when she is blaming him she can even think that he might be trying to frustrate her on purpose.

It makes a big difference, of course, whether Janet says all these things, the effect of which would be *non*-inflammatory, or whether she simply accuses Bruce of being afraid of intimacy, being tied up with his mother, and trying to frustrate her, the effect of which would be *inflammatory*. Janet and Bruce were likely to have felt relieved if I had helped them formulate these fuller statements. Since they are trying to convey something, but are doing so inadequately, they would enjoy seeing how it could be conveyed adequately.

To turn to my own part in this, it makes a big difference whether I accuse Janet and Bruce of accusing one another, which is a distorted fragment of the full story, or whether I attempt a fuller depiction. Such fuller depiction would include discussing:

(1) how each seems frustrated because he or she can't get the other to agree to things that seem clearly true to him or her;
(2) that each feels that the other's accusations are at least partly unjustified;
(3) that this way of relating is what they feel has caused them most of their problems and is what they have come to therapy to change so that we're dealing now with some pretty critical issues;
(4) and that I feel responsible to help them do something about it;
(5) that statements about 'fear of intimacy', 'hatred of men', 'unconscious wish to frustrate', 'still hung up with your mother', and 'rescue fantasies' seem to sting or demoralise the other;
(6) and that we may need to look at these ideas one by one and see

how much one or both partners believe them and what they mean by them;
(7) that we need to consider the possibility that these statements are rough first approximations, that is, that they are global statements being made because the person saying them has not yet had the chance to figure out exactly what he or she feels;
(8) or that these are powerful statements being made to get the other's attention;
(9) that, in any event, clearly there are things that both need to get across to the other, maybe even things they have not quite figured out yet, that they are really frustrated about because they are not getting them across;
(10) and that the way to do so is to take a detailed look at the situations that generated these accusations.

Accusing is what Janet, Bruce, and I were left to do because we were unable to say, and may not even have fully realised, what we needed to say and to realise. This is the heart of everyone's difficulties. The key factor is hidden helplessness or impotence. No one notices, but the person goes on overload. If it's the client, he or she feels something like: 'Things are hopeless. I'll never get her (him) to understand. And besides, maybe she's (he's) right: it's all my fault and I'm a terrible person.' If it's the therapist, he or she feels something like: 'I'm supposed to be the therapist around here and know what I'm doing but I haven't the vaguest idea what's going on'. Or, in my case, 'These people are destroying one another using the kind of psychological jargon I've always hated. I've got to do something but I haven't a clue how even to start.'

The problem is not such feelings of helplessness in themselves. The problem is *discomfort* with and *rejection* of these feelings. People think that they should not have them. They fail to recognise that *everyday momentary overload* is part of the human condition. If they were to recognise this fact, they might be able to view the matter philosophically and matter-of-factly: to expect overload experiences, to take them into account, and to plan for them. Since they do not recognise this fact, they have no choice but to act. They try to counteract their sense of powerlessness and helplessness by making powerful statements.

The statements that Janet and Bruce made were too powerful and, at the same time, insufficiently powerful. They were too powerful in their squelching and demoralising effect. They were insufficiently powerful because they inadequately stated what the partners needed to say.

In their effort to make powerful statements, people automatically employ culturally sanctioned accusations. These are accusations that everyone in a particular culture or subculture accepts as serious faults. Examples in our cultures are: 'You're a nag,' 'You're dependent', and 'You're selfish'. Culturally sanctioned complaints are irrefutable. No one even thinks of replying 'What's so bad about being a nag?' (or being dependent, or selfish). We all just accept the fact that being these things is bad. People resort to irrefutable culturally sanctioned complaints when they feel overwhelmed, when they have difficulty getting their points across, or when they have difficulty believing their own arguments.

Such culturally sanctioned complaints so taint the persons accused that these individuals find it almost impossible to prove their innocence, even (or particularly) to themselves. Everyone just immediately thinks that he or she is guilty. A woman labelled a 'castrator' has a hard time proving and, at times, believing that she is not. And a man labelled a 'wimp' or 'sissy' has a similar difficult time proving and, at times, believing that he is not. Once Janet is accused of engaging in 'rescue fantasies', her actions are immediately given new meaning. What before had been viewed as a positive trait — as concern about and loyalty to her friends — is suddenly redefined as an obsession and a character defect.

Janet and Bruce invoked professional versions of culturally sanctioned complaints in their efforts to find some grounds from which to make a stand. Bruce did not feel comfortable in saying that he felt hurt and jealous. So he made a professionally sanctioned complaint. He accused Janet of engaging in 'rescue fantasies'. Janet felt uncomfortable about blaming Bruce for the problem. So she appealed to professionally sanctioned complaints that might reduce her uncertainty and increase her sense of justification. She accused Bruce of being 'afraid of intimacy' and of having 'unfinished business with his mother'.

We now have answers to what are perhaps the two main questions regarding Janet and Bruce's behaviour: (1) why they stated distorted fragments rather than complete accounts of what they are feeling; and (2) why they made unanswerable accusations; that is, why they weakened what they had to say by reducing it to a distorted fragment and why they then so strengthened it that they overwhelmed the other. Interestingly, the answer to both questions is the same. Janet and Bruce stated truncated distortions of their full feelings because they felt unjustified in having them, which is also why they engaged in unanswerable accusations.

I had trouble justifying my feelings also. The psychotherapeutic concepts that Janet and Bruce employed in their accusations of one another (e.g. 'You're afraid of intimacy', 'You have a basic hatred of men', 'You're engaging in rescue fantasies') were among those that most disturbed me and about which I was continually arguing with my colleagues. I instinctively wanted to refute what they were saying. My problem, actually, was not that I had strong feelings about Janet and Bruce's use of these terms. My problem was that I did not allow myself to have strong feelings. Thinking that I should not be so affected (isn't there the rule, after all, that therapists should not have strong emotional reactions), I was unable to deal with the fact that I was. I went on everyday momentary overload.

If I had felt it was OK to have strong feelings, I would have been able to take my reaction into account and to go on from there. Since I did not feel it was OK, I tried to talk myself out of these feelings. I was thus in much the same position that Janet and Bruce were in. I had feelings that I felt were unjustified. And I did what Janet and Bruce were doing. I appealed to a culturally sanctioned idea (i.e. 'blaming doesn't help') to justify these feelings. I accused Janet and Bruce of blaming one another. My implication was that they should stop doing it.

What made my reaction particularly interesting is that I did not even believe what I said. The pressure of the situation led me to forget momentarily what I believe about accusations, which is that people accuse one another when they have important points that they are unable to get across. Accusations are not things that should be squelched. I see them instead as clues to critical messages that it is important to decipher. What ideally I would have wanted to do, accordingly, is to have *started* by acknowledging that Janet and Bruce were accusing one another and then quickly go on to show how it makes sense that they might be doing so and, in fact, that I might be doing so if I were in their positions.

This realisation led to the following speculation. If, under pressure (i.e. having feelings I thought I should not be having), I reverted to a familiar cultural or professional idea that I no longer believe, perhaps others do this also. And there is evidence that they might. Colleagues who make the kinds of intervention that seem to me objectionable (i.e. subtly accusatory interventions) often state that they themselves are not completely happy with these interventions. They make them, they say, only because they feel overwhelmed, confused, anxious, helpless, overly responsible, or under pressure. (1) They feel that they do not understand what is going on and that they *should* understand. (2) They feel provoked by the client and think they should not feel so provoked. Or (3) they feel responsible to do something more active to help the client and do not know what else to do. At such times it is easy to fall into employing these accusatory psychodynamic constructs.

Clients have made similar comments. One client, who was himself a therapist, criticised his depressed wife for 'choosing to feel bad' and for 'wanting to suffer'. He later said that he made these statements in frustration and that he did not completely believe they were true. What had happened, we discovered, is that he felt that it was his responsibility to cheer up his wife. Saying that she must want to suffer was his way of dealing with his inability to cheer her up. The irony, of course, is that his wife did not want him to try to cheer her up. She felt burdened by such efforts since she felt it was then her responsibility to be cheered up. Instead, she wanted him to listen to how she felt, which, if he were to do so, might have cheered her up.

The culturally sanctioned ideas to which people appeal to justify feelings may be ones that they do not even fully believe. In times of uncertainty or when feeling pressured, people fall back on more solid ground, even if it is the solid ground of an earlier and rejected way of thinking. The classic example is agnostics who, on their deathbeds, revert to the belief in God that they had in their childhoods. The lesson I learned from this couple's therapy episode, accordingly, is *how difficult it can be for any of us to justify certain feelings and how we typically call upon irrefutable, culturally sanctioned accusations (ones that we may not even entirely believe) in our attempts to do so.*

IMPLICATIONS FOR OTHER THERAPISTS

The solution to this problem begins with an awareness of the extent to which accusatory ideas pervade our thinking. Society teaches us to think in accusatory terms. In fact, *many of the standard accusatory psychotherapeutic ideas are formalised cultural accusations.* They are professionalised forms of familiar cultural criticisms and put-downs. 'Projection' would seem to be a purely professional idea. However, the common saying 'the pot calling the kettle black' says very much the same thing. Almost every technical term has a rough popular equivalent. Describing people as narcissistic, symbiotic, passive-aggressive, or afraid of intimacy is often and in an important sense just another way of saying that they are self-centred, clinging, indirect, or afraid of commitment. Describing them as anal retentive, pre-oedipal, castrating, sadistic, bipolar, schizoid, obsessional, counterphobic, inauthentic or psychotic is in some sense just a fancier way of calling them miserly, babyish, bitchy, nasty, moody, withdrawn, indecisive, macho, phony or crazy.

Some popular accusatory terms are taken into the professional lexicon unchanged. Examples include dependent, perfectionist and manipulative. Some terms that began as professionalised cultural accusations have made their way back into the popular language. Examples include neurotic, paranoid, psychopathic and schizophrenic.

Therapists who seek to avoid accusatory thinking need to appreciate how psychotherapeutic theory not only accepts many of the accusatory ideas of our culture, but also *extends* them. Therapists use the familiar reproach 'You're doing it to youself' and take it one step further. They see people as 'doing it to themselves' *on purpose*, as enjoying being self-destructive, as obtaining masochistic pleasure.

Another common cultural idea that psychotherapists have accepted and then elaborated is the notion that adults who behave in offensive ways are immature; that is, they just never grew up. Psychotherapists seize upon this idea and take it one step further. They try to determine the exact infantile or childhood stage that the individual never grew up from (or has regressed to); that is, the exact early childhood stage at which the individual is thought to be functioning. A major, perhaps *the* major, dispute in contemporary psychoanalysis is whether the dominant fixation or regression point for most people is the mother-infant symbiotic stage or the mother-father-child oedipal stage.

A common error made by people in our culture (or perhaps in any culture) is to mistake effect for intent. A wife who feels guilty or angry sees her husand as *wanting* to make her feel guilty or angry. Psychotherapists have raised this error to a major psychodynamic principle. 'One clue to the "intention" of the symptom', Simon (1975, p. 194) writes, 'is the effect the symptom has on others.' 'What you [the therapist] are experiencing of course', Langs (1976, p. 25) writes, 'is in some way related to what the patient wants you to experience.' Emboldened by this general principle, some therapists are even able to suggest that the reason they fall asleep in their sessions with clients is because these clients want them to fall asleep.

Professional training has the effect of increasing the conviction of therapists in the validity of familiar cultural accusations. The partners I saw two years before — the sales manager and the musician — may have had some of the same thoughts as Bruce and Janet. The wife may have thought that her husband was afraid of commitment or still very angry at his mother. The husband may have thought that his wife was afraid of men or defensive. The two partners did not mention these things, however. They could not get themselves sufficiently to believe them.

Professional training causes people fully to believe such things. In this training, certain types of explanation are simply assumed to be true. Peterfreund (1983, pp. 19–50) provides dramatic examples of how even well known and well respected psychoanalysts arrive at their conclusions very early in the analysis, how they do so with hardly any evidence, how they make no effort to obtain substantiating evidence, and how they cling to their formulations despite overwhelming contradictory evidence. Each school of therapy has its own set of stock interpretations and formulations. The following are examples of those employed by certain psychodynamically oriented therapists.

(1) The oedipal conflict is so intrinsic to psychoanalytic theory that it is easy to overlook the fact that it operates as a stock formulation. Clients are *automatically* assumed to be suffering from oedipal wishes and castration fears if they are men, and from oedipal wishes, penis envy, and, usually also, pregenital rage against their mothers if they are women. Most of Peterfreund's examples are of analysts who conclude very quickly that their clients have oedipal problems and who stick to these views despite overwhelming contradictory evidence.

(2) If clients reject their therapists' interpretations, this automatically means, according to some therapists, that these clients are resistant and/or are unconsciously trying to defeat their parents. And if clients do not make the expected therapeutic changes, some therapists automatically conclude that these individuals are afraid to take risks, are trying to defeat the therapist, are getting too much from their symptoms to want to give them up, or are simply refusing to grow up and accept the responsibilities of adulthood. In making such stock formulations, these therapists often overlook the possibilities that (i) their interpretations

might be inaccurate and that clients might be right to reject them, and (ii) their clients' failure to change might be the result of limitations of the therapeutic method, deficiencies in their own skills as therapists, or the simple fact that changes are often difficult to make.

(3) If a client is depressed, some therapists immediately believe, in addition to whatever other factors might be involved, that the individual is angry and that his or her anger is turned inwards. This is a stock formulation when, as is often the case, it is maintained without evidence. The lack of any indications of anger is thought to mean simply that the anger is unconscious; that is, that it is truly turned inwards. (Such a formulation is unfalsifiable; there is no way to disprove it.) Here is an example of how a requirement of Freud's second theory, the need to trace the problems to basic drives, can lead to stock formulations. Alternative explanations for depression, such as self-hating ideas or severe loss, failure, or disappointment, are seen as insufficient because they are not basic drives. Aggression is viewed as the major explanatory principle, despite lack of clinical evidence, because it *is* a basic drive.

(4) I know at least some therapists who immediately assume, if clients come to sessions saying that they want to terminate therapy or to come less often, that this really means that they want to come *more* often. And if clients discontinue therapy after one session, this means, according to some therapists, that these individuals are afraid of intimacy, are unwilling to do the work required for therapy, or have taken flights into health. Therapists who employ these stock interpretations fail to consider the possibility that some clients might be wise to terminate. Therapy, or at least the particular types of therapy being employed, might be unhelpful to these individuals, at least at the present times in their lives.

(5) If the effect of clients' behaviour is to make their therapists sleepy, bored, or angry, this is seen by some therapists as what these clients unconsciously want them to feel. Therapists who make such stock formulations forget how difficult it is even *consciously* to affect others in a desired way. Consider how hard it is to get dinner guests who overstay their welcome to leave. And consider the difficulty many people have in getting people whom they most like to like them.

(6) Clients who become angrier at their bosses, spouses or therapists than it is thought they should be are seen by some

therapists as really angry at their fathers or mothers. Therapists who make such stock formulations may forget how easy it is for people to become very angry at others *whether or not* they have unresolved anger at their parents. They forget how holding back anger, which everyone does at least some of the time, produces tantrum-like outbursts that give the appearance of excessive and unwarranted anger.

(7) If clients are passive aggressive, this means to some therapists that these individuals are really very angry. These therapists do not consider the alternative, which is that these individuals may feel it is not OK to be angry (their agression, after all, is 'passive', i.e. inhibited or indirect) and that their problem is that they are *worried* that they are really very angry.

Bruce and Janet differed from the couple I saw two years before in being themselves therapists, and thus in having had training experiences in which principles such as the ones just stated can be taken as unquestioned truths. And with training experiences such as these, that is, with the full authority of the psychotherapeutic establishment behind them, Bruce and Janet made interpretations about one another that the partners I saw two years before might think of in passing but not have the nerve to begin to consider making.

This incident between these partners and myself challenges a traditional view of clients and their problems and, in fact, of human life and human nature. In this traditional view, which emerges from Freud's second theory, human beings are seen as being essentially primitive, regressive, and destructive. People are seen as having an underlying hate, greediness and selfishness, and as being unwilling to take risks, grow up, accept responsibility for their feelings, be honest with themselves, stop playing games, and stop blaming others for their problems.

The alternative view, which emerges from Freud's first theory and his treatment of Elizabeth von R, is demonstrated in the case presented here: the problem is that people are too ready to believe that they have primitive and unacceptable elements in their personalities. The readiness to believe this view of themselves leads people to disqualify and invalidate their feelings. And such self-invalidation is the source of their problems.

In the traditional view, psychopathology is traced to primitive strivings and characteristics. In the alternative view, life is seen as a struggle to justify feelings that the person erroneously views as primitive and unjustifiable. Therapists are likely to approach clients in a very different way if they see these individuals as struggling to justify feelings. And therapists are likely to approach themselves in a very different way if they see themselves as engaged in the same struggle.

The major implications that this episode involving Janet, Bruce and myself has for other therapists, accordingly, are the suggestions that (1) the effort to justify feelings is a central principle of human motivation — a major thing that people, both clients and therapists, are trying to do; (2) in pursuing this purpose, people revert to standard cultural ideas (and, in the case of psychotherapists, to standard professional concepts) that they might not even fully believe; (3) many of these standard professional concepts are simply recastings or elaborations of traditional cultural prejudices and ideas; (4) these standard cultural and professional ideas are hidden accusations and, thus, appealing to them involves shifting from a neutral to a moralistic, accusatory stance; (5) founded as they are on standard cultural prejudices, our whole set of traditional psychotherapeutic ideas and concepts need to be re-evaluated; and (6) a major part of the therapeutic task is for therapists to be aware of how, under pressure of feelings they see as unjustified, they and their clients keep falling back on these old accusatory theories.

NOTE

1. 'Ego analysis' developed in reaction to 'id analysis'. Two major principles of ego analysis are as follows:

(1) Whereas id analysis attributes symptomatic behaviour to clients' underlying pathology (infantile impulses, pathological defences, and developmental defects), ego analysis traces such behaviour to ordinary adult feelings and impulses that people are unable to recognise and express because they feel unentitled to them.
(2) Whereas id analysis views clients as gratified and resistant (wanting to maintain their pathological patterns because they are getting something from them), ego analysis views clients as deprived and stuck (wanting to give up their counterproductive patterns but not knowing how). Ego analysis must be distinguished from Hartmann's and Rapaport's 'ego psychology'. Ego psychology extends id-analytic thinking, whereas ego analysis challenges it.

REFERENCES

Apfelbaum, B. (1977). A contribution to the development of the behavioral-analytic model. *Journal of Sex and Marital Therapy, 3,* 128–38

Apfelbaum, B. (1982). The clinical necessity for Kohut's self theory. *Voices, 18,* 43–9

Apfelbaum, B. (1983, August). Introduction to the symposium, 'Ego analysis and ego psychology', presented at the American Psychological Association Convention, Anaheim, California

Apfelbaum, B. and Gill, M.M. (In preparation). Technical implications of the structural approach: a critique of Kanzer's 'good analytic hour'

Breuer, J. and Freud, S. (1955). *Studies on hysteria. Standard Edition,* vol. 2, London: Hogarth Press. (Originally published in 1895.)

Fenichel, O. (1941). *Problems of psychoanalytic technique.* New York: Psychoanalytic Quarterly

Freud, S. (1959). *Inhibitions, symptoms and anxiety. Standard Editiion,* vol. 20. London: Hogarth Press. (Originally published in 1926)

Freud, S. (1961). *The ego and the id. Standard Edition,* vol. 19. London: Hogarth Press. (Originally published in 1923)

Greenberg, J.R. and Mitchell, S.A. (1983). *Object relations in psychoanalytic theory.* Cambridge, MA: Harvard University Press

Langs, R. (1976). *The bipersonal field.* New York: Jason Aronson

Peterfreund, E. (1983). *The process of psychoanalytic therapy: models and strategies.* Hillsdale, NJ: Analytic Press

Simon, B. (1975). Psychoanalytic approach: the case of June. In C.A. Loew, H. Grayson and G.H. Loew (Eds), *Three psychotherapies.* New York: Brunner/Mazel

Wile, D.B. (1981). *Couples therapy: a nontraditional approach.* New York: Wiley

Wile, D.B. (1984). Kohut, Kernberg, and accusatory interpretations. *Psychotherapy: Theory, Research, Practice, and Training, 21,* 353–64

Wile, D.B. (1985a). Phases of relationship development. In D.C. Goldberg (Ed.), *Contemporary marriage: special issues in couples therapy.* Homewood, IL: Dorsey Press

Wile, D.B. (1985b). Psychotherapy by precedent: unexamined legacies from pre-1920 psychoanalysis. *Psychotherapy: Theory, Research, Practice, and Training, 22,* 793–802

6

Siding with the Client

John Rowan

This was a memorable case, which had a number of features that made it out of the ordinary, but I have tried in this account to keep to the main lines of the one incident and its aftermath.

PRIOR THEORY AND PRACTICE

The theoretical orientation to which I mainly hold is called primal integration. This is a form of therapy brought over to Britain by Bill Swartley, although it was also pioneered here by Frank Lake. It lays the major stress upon early trauma as the basic cause of neurosis, and enables people to regress back in time to the point where the trouble began, and then to relive it. For this reason some people call it regression-integration therapy.

It puts great emphasis on the whole person, and aims at getting the body, feelings, intellect and spirit into some appropriate harmony. This is why there is so much talk about the integration aspect. It is not enough to relive primal events, and to change one's personality accordingly; there is then the long task of exploring all the implications of the change one is making.

Primal integration is one of the heaviest forms of therapy, in the sense of going very deeply into unconscious material. Accordingly it is not recommended as a first approach to therapy: rather it is for those who have done some form of therapy already, and who now feel ready to go down into the very roots of their neurosis. Because it deals with old and strong emotions — often in situations which the person felt were too much to take — there may be a good deal of pain involved.

However, there is primal joy and primal love as well as primal pain, and there is also a spiritual aspect to the whole thing, often missed or even denied by some other approaches in this area. It seems that the deeper one goes into primal material, the more likely one is to have spiritual experiences too (Adzema, 1985). These can help a great deal in the process of integration, where we are calling on all the resources we can to build the person up again from scratch without the harmful assumptions of one's previous approach to life.

Primal integration sets very little in the way of limits for where the person can go to in the process of therapy. Some people may never get further back than childhood; some go back into infancy; some go back to the birth process; some go back into fetal life, or even further back than that. Each person is encouraged, with no help from hypnosis or drugs, to go into whatever most concerns them, in a direct and straightforward way. There are no special rules such as isolation periods or abstinence.

Both group work (usually with two leaders of opposite sexes) and individual work are carried out. The group work is good for bringing out and working through traumas, and the individual work is particularly good for working up to that, and for working through the implications of what happens in the group and enabling integration to take place. An interview is usually required before people are invited to join a group.

In this present chapter, it is only individual therapy which is the focus. In the individual session it is possible to take things up over and over again from different angles, so that they can be really worked through fully. Sessions may last for one hour, an hour and a half, two hours or three hours, depending on the client's needs.

Primal integration is an active form of therapy, using techniques and methods in all areas of the four functions established by Jung: sensing, feeling, thinking and intuiting. In the sensing area we use methods derived from Rank, Reich, Lowen and Lang, plus some of our own; in the feeling area we use methods from Moreno, Perls, Rogers, Jackins and others; in the thinking area we use theory from Freud, Klein, Bion, Berne, Ellis, Kelly and others; and in the intuiting area we use methods and insights from Jung, Desoille, Assagioli, Wilber and others. But we are not eclectic: primal integration is a synthetic or syncretic discipline which brings these elements into a systematic framework, which is described in full in Rowan and Dryden (in press).

In other words, each of the interventions we can make in psychotherapy starts from one of these functions. Obviously each real person operates on all these functions simultaneously, and we would never want to reduce a person to a set of functions, but the model seems useful in at least showing what not to ignore, what not to leave out, as I have argued in more detail elsewhere (Rowan, 1986).

All this is based on the fundamental belief that the inner core of the client is ultimately healthy, and that it is only the defences that are unhealthy. This is the basic humanistic belief in the real self, which I have discussed fully elsewhere (Rowan, 1983), and which is common to most people working in a humanistic way.

This makes primal integration therapists like me very confident in going into the very deepest and darkest place in the soul of the client. We have been into those places in our own training, and we do not believe that we are ever going to come to something which is not a person, and not to be met face to face. We do not have much respect for the idea that some people have a fragile ego, and must be treated very gently in case it shatters. For us the standard ego is the problem to be dealt with, not an entity to be preserved.

On the other hand, we do not believe that the client's defences must be attacked and undermined at the fastest speed possible. We place the responsibility for the process of therapy squarely in the hands of the client. It is the client doing it, not the therapist doing it, and the therapist must respect the pace and the readiness of the client to deal with each piece of material as it comes to the fore. This goes very much along with the belief in the real self which we have already mentioned.

My own view, expressed in my books, lectures and conversations, was that every time I do something for the client, I stop the client doing it. If I really respected and wanted to foster another person's autonomy, I had to do it all along the line. I believed in support and confrontation as the two wings of therapy, but felt that support meant only such things as empathy and resonance — in other words, encouraging people to get in touch with their own resources, their own inner world. A section in one of my books had the heading 'The therapist is not a rescuer', and this seemed to me the ultimate wisdom in therapy. 'Every time I take responsibility for the client, I stop the client taking responsibility. Every time I try to help, I get in the client's way.' I was quite dogmatic about this, because it seemed so basic. I still think it is very important.

The same view is held in another theory which I also found useful in therapy. This is the theory of Alvin Mahrer (1978), which says that people have potentials that they have disowned, and that often appear to them hateful or frightening. When one of these disowned potentials starts to rise to the surface, as a result of some cue, the person feels anxiety. This anxiety can be resolved in one of three ways: by changing the subject, or the scene — just escaping to a better place on the same level; by sinking into the 'zone of unfeeling' where we block off all our feelings and cease to take responsibility for them; or by adopting the deeper potential, giving in to it and becoming it. This last, which is the only solution leading to increased health and development, feels very scary, and it may take a therapist or other helper to enable the person to accept and go along with this action.

The implications of this theory are similar to those of the primal approach already mentioned. To put it crudely and baldly, both theories are saying that no matter how bad the person's monster, it is only by becoming that monster and taking its energy that the problem can be overcome. At the moment the client genuinely accepts and does this, that which was previously defined as monstrous changes into its good form — the form where it yields up its hoard of positive energy for the person to use. In both primal integration and Mahrer's theory, this is seen as a cathartic experience where old decisions can be remade and old wounds healed.

This approach, of finding where the client hurts most and going into that area more and more deeply and thoroughly, is very central to my way of working. Coupled with the emphasis on autonomy, mentioned earlier, this puts quite a heavy weight of responsibility on to the client, to open up and to take the apparently considerable risks. I remember times in my own therapy when the pain of discovery was so great that I cried out: 'If this is reality, I don't want reality, it's too much.' The client has to be encouraged to go on at such points, because the wounds of therapy can only be healed by deeper therapy.

The way that I espouse really tries to get to the bottom of a neurosis, and to deal with it completely. It is not content to patch the person up so that they can function more or less adequately. It is always trying to achieve real transformation of personality or character.

In my own therapy I have had a number of experiences of this kind of cathartic breakthrough, and these have been significant turning points in my life. I have seen a number of other people go through the process, and have taken part in a research study (Marina, 1982) which showed objectively that real personality change did take place. So at the point in time when this case came to its crisis, I was confident in using primal integration as my method of treatment for clients with serious problems who needed to make substantial changes.

One other point is worth mentioning here. As well as having a basic method, I have always felt it to be highly desirable for a therapist to be imaginative. By this I mean that each client is unique, and in order to do justice to this uniqueness it may be necessary for a therapist to improvise. This means saying something new, doing something fresh, suggesting something original. But there is another side to this too, which is seeing that it is possible to draw on the client's imagination. By believing in the creative imagination of the client, the therapist has an enormous resource to draw on, as Shorr (1983) and others have shown in detail.

An imaginative therapist can keep track of the client not only at the conscious level of words and phrases; not only at the emotional level of unspoken feelings; not only at the unconscious level of internal impulses and conflicts; not only at the body level of posture and gesture; but also at the symbolic level of imagery and intuition. This means being able to listen and intervene at this level, as I have explained more fully elsewhere (Rowan, 1986). But it also means being able to ask clients to use this level more in getting in touch with their own inner experience. This opens up a vast range of new resources which can be used in the process of therapy. A good discussion of this question can be found in Ferrucci (1982).

DESCRIPTION OF THE KEY CASE

This was a woman in her early thirties, recently married, about average height, dark, somewhat overweight. Her main problem seemed to be depression, though eating problems were also important at times. The depression had been severe enough to make her attempt suicide by cutting her wrists more than once, but she had never been hospitalised. She had been to a number of therapists before, and was taking a course to become a therapist herself. I shall call her Sarah.

Her history was probably the worst I had ever come across. It started before her conception, which took place when her mother was 40 years old. Her mother had just run away with Sarah's father, after an unhappy marriage of 15 years. Her husband was strongly opposed to children, and had made her have an abortion in the early days of the marriage. She had then talked him into having children, but after years of failure had been told she was infertile.

Sarah's father was a man of wide interests and varied talents, and 25 years older. He looked after Sarah's mother, who was in poor health with nervous complaints and poor nutrition. During the pregnancy, she was going through the stress of trying to get a divorce (to which her husband would not agree) and was consuming much black coffee and chain-smoking cigarettes all day.

Having been told that she was infertile, Sarah's mother did not know she was pregnant. As she began to feel a lump in her womb, she assumed it must be a growth of some kind. When it grew, she thought it must be cancer. When it moved, she went into total panic, thinking that it was a mobile cancerous growth of a particularly virulent kind. It appears that this panic must have got through somehow to the fetus (it is now believed that this is physically possible through the passage of catecholamines through the placenta and the umbilical cord (Verny, 1982)). In reconstruction, it seems that the chemical shock of these reactions coming into the fetus every time it moved actually conditioned it to move as little as possible, so that instead of a normally vigorous motion of the fetus in the womb there were just a few rather restricted movements — ironically just the sort of movements to confirm the mother in her beliefs.

William Emerson, a therapist who has specialised in this area of work, says that a trauma of negative recognition in the first trimester of pregnancy can produce later feelings of 'I don't have a right to exist'. Frank Lake (1980), another pioneer in this area, says that negative feelings coming through the unbilical cord can bring feelings of paralysis and paranoia: 'The whole world is against me, and there is no escape.'

Ten days before the birth, Sarah's mother had 'stomach pains' so bad that a doctor had to be called. He told her that she was pregnant. This sent her into a new panic, because she felt she was too old to have a baby, and knew that she had not been eating properly for the past few months.

The birth was prolonged and difficult, and the baby experienced anoxia (shortage of oxygen) and extreme paralysing terror as the walls of the uterus closed in and there seemed to be no way out. The mother's hair and nails dropped out after the birth, and she had no milk. The baby had two fingernails not properly developed, and the mother thought she might be mentally deformed or retarded.

Sarah's mother had been brought up very strictly and religiously. She felt extremely guilty at having brought an illegimate child into the world. As the baby grew, she saw it as fat and ugly and badly behaved. She didn't like it.

Now of course it is not possible to check whether any of this is factually true, and in fact the mother and father are both dead, so we cannot ask them. Sarah was an only child, and that is some evidence of the mother at any rate not being over-fond of having children.

This early bad start also affected Sarah's schooldays, which were miserable and traumatic, with many vividly remembered incidents of being put down and made to feel unworthy. She remembered an incident where a girl she had thought was her friend had turned against her. This reinforced her view that the whole world was hostile.

To Sarah her Jewish mother was an oppressor, and her mother's mother even worse, if anything. She hated and feared both of them. Incident after incident came up of her mother punishing her, belittling her, making her feel unwanted and unsupported. On the other hand, she loved and idolised her Gentile father. He was the one perfect thing in her life, and she resolved to live her life in such a way as to be worthy of him. When Sarah was seven years old, he had a stroke, and she was afraid of losing her one support and strength.

When Sarah was nine, her father died from a second stroke. It happened in a very particular way. He was talking to her at home, and she lied to him, by telling him that a woman had told her off and hit her on the way home from school for making too much noise. He got upset about this incident, and suddenly his speech became jumbled up. Sarah became hysterical and continued to be extremely disturbed until she fell asleep. Her mother, for whatever reasons, did not comfort her or pay attention to her, which she desperately wanted. The following morning her mother walked into her room, said 'Your father's dead', and walked out again.

Sarah was struck by terror and guilt and went to school to get some sympathy, but got none there. Her memory is that she was made to sit in a room alone all day. Her family was sitting around the corpse in the bedroom, she thought like vultures. She felt them all looking at her accusingly. Her grandmother made her stay in the room with the dead body of her father. His feet were sticking out at the end of the bed; she reached out to them but could not touch them. She felt as guilty as it was possible to feel.

Her mother blamed her for her father's death, and treated her even worse from that point on, convinced that she was not only fat, ugly and badly behaved, but also evil and destructive.

Her mother gradually became arthritic, and had to use sticks to walk. Sarah felt that her family blamed her for her mother becoming a cripple. But according to Sarah, her mother would accept help from anyone except her. All through her adolescence, then, which is often a difficult time in any case, Sarah was getting the continual insults which made her life a misery.

At the age of 17, Sarah did actually lose weight and become the normal attractive girl her mother had continually asked her to be. But her mother then switched to attacking her sexuality. The only answer seemed to be to find the suitably nice Jewish boy that her mother wanted for her.

Just as she was going out with such a boy, her mother got cancer. When Sarah was 22 her mother died. At the funeral, she realised how much she hated her mother's family, and they hated her. One of the family at the funeral turned on her and accused her of hastening her mother's death. She ran away and hid, and then locked herself in her house for several weeks. She hid in a wardrobe every time any family member knocked on the door. Eventually she collapsed from nervous exhaustion.

This is the basic background, and it can be seen that for Sarah her childhood was a very black-and-white matter, populated by clear heroes and definite villians. She herself was a victim throughout.

But she was not just a victim. She also had from her father a very ambitious project: to be different from the rest of her family, to be brilliant, to be scholarly, to be a winner. In this respect she was very much like Kohut's (1971) characters, full of grandiose imaginings which only produce collapse and disappointment because of their excessive character.

The combination of these two phases — the depressive and the narcissistic — is illustrated in one of the worst and vivid memories of her childhood. She had been given the part of a fairy in the school play at the age of seven or so, and had gone home in great excitement to tell her mother. And her mother's response had been 'A fairy?! More like an elephant, if you ask me!' This had produced a flood of tears and an upsurge of bad feelings which could be clearly remembered many years later. The swing from 'on the peak' to 'in the pit' was instantaneous. This pattern was something which repeated itself all too easily.

Once in the pit of depression it was impossible to get out of it by any act of will, direct or indirect. Time had to pass and health to return. So this was the situation at the start of therapy.

In the early days of the therapy, which began in September 1981, we spent most of the time on Sarah's mother, just following her feelings back into her childhood again and again. We found that her mother kept on turning up in the most extraordinary disguises, in dreams and in fantasies: for example, we spent some time wrestling with a 'death skeleton' which was extremely frightening and threatening, and this turned out in the end to be her mother again. One of the most fearful versions for Sarah was the Black Witch. The Black Witch came up in dreams and fantasies, and actually laid a spell on the child (Sarah) to strike her dumb. This was a very accurate statement of what happened when Sarah's mother came on the scene: Sarah was dumbstruck.

Each time she was attacked by her mother, she went into the pit of hopelessness. This was a sort of grey, cold place, with the word '*not*' the most consistent feature: *not* OK, *not* breathing, *not* feeling, *no* resources of any kind, and *no* right to exist.

Some specific difficulties emerged about working in this way. One was that her mother, when she arrived on the scene in the therapy session, was too terrifying to face. Try as I could in one way after another, I failed to get Sarah to answer back to her mother's accusations of being evil, destructive, cancerous and so on. She simply agreed with them and could not reply. She was struck dumb, as it were. She gave in and sank into the pit. On a couple of occasions when she did seem to have a little more spirit, and seemed to be making some sort of reply, I encouraged her to answer back more loudly, repeating the same sentence in a stronger voice, to bring the feelings more to the surface, and to admit that she was angry with her mother for treating her so badly. But on those occasions she backed down, saying that she couldn't shout at her mother, because her mother always shouted. If she herself shouted, she would be like her mother, the one thing she wanted most not to be! This is of course a classic piece of self-sabotage, which I now see through much more easily and quickly. But session after session went by, with no real change in the situation. We had reached an impasse.

It was no help to invoke Mahrer's theory and to point out that her mother was her own deeper potential, and that the thing to do was to embrace this potential and own it. Sarah knew Mahrer's theory, having learned it on her course, and she could even use it herself and explain it to people, but she could not make the necessary move. Panic prevented her.

The other difficuly was with the pit. My past experience had been that the way to deal with pits is to take people to the bottom of them. If they can really get to the bottom — the very deepest, darkest, murkiest spot in the whole pit — that is the place where something can change. The first time I tried this, Sarah went deeper and deeper but never reached the bottom, and at the end of the session felt very much worse than when she came in. Nothing daunted, some time later we set up a two-hour session, and spent the entire two hours trying to get to the bottom of the pit. Again we failed, and Sarah felt so bad afterwards that she went home and cut her wrists. This was the first time this had happened in my experience, and I didn't like it. I felt baffled and disappointed, and sorry for Sarah.

It is important to see why this incident did not make either of us want to stop the therapy, or seek medical advice. From her point of view, she had made her point, expressed her feelings, gone as far as she dared. Her husband had taken care of her, and made sure that she was all right. She did not blame me, because of her previous experience and self-knowledge. She knew that she had gone into the two hours as a definite decision on her part, for which she took responsibility.

From my point of view, I knew that she had cut her wrists before, so it was not such a terrible shock as it might otherwise have been. It was not right outside the range of the possible. It was serious, but I believe everything in therapy is serious and to be taken seriously. It was painful, but some things in the process of therapy are painful: they just are. It was an occasion for concern but not for panic.

I have found it difficult to explain to people just why this seriously distressing incident was so unimportant in the process of therapy. They keep on wanting to go back and discuss this incident, instead of the more central issues in the case history. But it was not in fact very revealing, or very horrifying to either of us.

What really happens, perhaps, is that this incident touches off in the reader a whole lot of anxieties about death, and that the extended discussion is more about the reader's own anxiety than about the significance of the incident to Sarah or to me.

It is important to say, too, that at no time in the two hours did I push Sarah to go any further than she was ready to. As with all my attempts at therapy, it was more a giving of permission to go into the relevant areas than any effort to get the person to go where I wanted them to go. In this case, I believed that at the bottom of the pit lay her strength. But what Sarah showed me was that she had immense strength in refusing to own her strength. She had immense resources for refusing to have any resources. It seemed that this paradox had to be tackled somehow if we were to get anywhere. By the time I got to this point we had been working together for over a year.

I remember at one time Sarah had a series of dreams which seemed to be about subpersonalities, and we explored the resources of each one of them. None of her subpersonalities seemed to hve any real strength except the Black Witch. All the others were either weak to start with, like Charlie Chaplin, or showed weaknesses as soon as we tried to call upon them for aid, like King Arthur. So this was the impasse. It seemed that we could not go any further along this line.

The event that triggered a change was a lecture which I went to on the work of John Rosen. The lecturer said that one of the problems Rosen had tackled successfully was a client who had an extremely heavy and punitive superego. It was as if the superego sat on top of the ego and squashed it, with such weight and force that the ego had no chance at all to respond or resist or retaliate in any way. What Rosen did was to line up with the client and throw his own weight against the superego as well. This released more energy in the client, by giving explicit permission to answer back, as it were, and also by giving a model of how to do it.

Although in my own theory there is no superego, and no ego either, in the strict Freudian sense, I could see that the superego functioned just like a subpersonality. So I could understand what was being said in my own terms, and see the relevance of that to Sarah's case. Sarah also had a heavy and punitive subpersonality sitting on top of her and squashing her, as it were.

But could I use this method? On the one hand it did fit in with my ideas about being imaginative and trying new things, but on the other hand it went right against my ideas about the client being autonomous and self-responsible. So it was as if one voice was saying 'Try it!', while another voice was saying 'Don't you dare!' I loved the idea of trying something which had some promise of breaking the terrible impasse we had got into; but I hated the idea of taking away from the client her own responsibility and power: it was *she* who had to fight back; it was she who had to find her own resources and her own answers, not me to find them for her, or use my own as a substitute, or know better than she what she was ready for.

In the event, my curiosity won out over my conscience. At the next opportunity, I lined up with Sarah against her mother. In my way of working, where Sarah is sitting on one cushion and her mother (in whatever guise) on the other, this was in fact very easy to set up. I simply put another cushion next to Sarah's and sat on it myself, saying things to support Sarah's own statements.

However, this did not work. Sarah's mother (what I would call the bad mother subpersonality) was still too strong for both of us together. Again we had to retire, baffled and frustrated. But something seemed to have shifted slightly, though I wasn't quite sure what it was. There was a definite movement, such that I felt that here was a promising approach, if only some way could be found of taking it further.

In talking about this incident with Sarah later, she said that nobody had ever stood up for her like that before. So she was rather taken aback, and couldn't quite believe it was happening. It was nice, but somehow she didn't think it applied to her! This helps to explain why it didn't work immediately.

The next time the opportunity arose, we were both more ready to grab it and use it constructively. What happened was that we were working on a dream about a giant spider. Sarah had done a painting of the dream which I have in front of me as I write (see Figure 6.1). It shows a fetus in the middle of the page, pinkish on a blue background, with a huge purple umbilical cord going out to the left, through the red border of the womb, to a yellow moon hung in a night sky with yellow and silver stars. Below the sky, on the left of the picture, is a blue-green sea with smooth waves.

On the right of the picture, filling the whole space, is a huge black hairy spider, with red eyes and what look like two horns with knobs on the ends. The legs are too big to be contained on the page, and disappear over the edge of the paper to the right, and behind the womb to the left. The background on the right-hand side is red, except at the top, where it becomes red and yellow flames against a violet background. So it looks like a sort of devil-spider. One of the legs curves right over the top of the spider's head, and looks almost like an alternative umbilical cord.

As I often do, I suggested, after going through the dream and finding that the spider represented the mother, that we put the spider on to a cushion and talk to it. Sarah agreed to this, and we set it up, but I could see that she was experiencing some fear. I remembered the previous incident where I had taken her side, and it suddenly occurred to me how we might make it work better this time.

This time I said 'Now there is a magic glass screen just here (I indicated a line) between you and the spider. You can talk to the spider, but the spider can't get through the screen. The spider can still hear and see and talk through the screen, but is completely blocked by the screen. You can get at the spider if you want to, but the spider can't get at you. And the screen will stay there until I take it down again.'

Now I lined up with Sarah as before, and supported her against the spider, shouting back at the spider that she had no right to attack Sarah, that Sarah had seen through her game, that she wasn't going

Figure 6.1: Sarah's painting.

to stand for it anymore, and so on. This time, as we went back and forth between Sarah and the giant spider, the spider diminished in size and paled in colour. It became smaller and smaller and weaker and weaker, until Sarah felt capable of facing it and dealing with it by herself.

For the first time, we had the feeling of victory against the mother. For the first time, the mother respected Sarah. We had broken through, and the positive feeling was tremendous. In talking with Sarah afterwards, she said that the magic screen was like a protection that made her feel safe. It allowed her to feel that she was allowed to communicate. Before this, she had felt no right to communicate at all, particularly so far as her mother was concerned (the dumb-child motif mentioned earlier).

But of course there were other things going on too. It may be felt that I was perhaps functioning on one level as a bigger magician than the Black Witch, and beating her on a magical level. At an unconscious level, perhaps I was her father come back to rescue her. Perhaps the glass screen was simply a schizoid defence, a temporary neurosis. Sarah's own view, expressed later, was that I was showing her how to talk back to her mother: she had no model or script for it, so did not know how to do it until she saw me do it. Once she had picked up the model, she was able to use it, and this seemed to break the dumbness spell put on the child by the Black Witch.

But as a therapist with the theory outlined in the first section above, I was in turmoil. To line up with the client seemed to go against everything I believed. It was taking responsibility away from the client and giving it to the therapist. It was making the client dependent on the therapist. It was not respecting the inner strength of the real self. It should be the client doing it, not the therapist doing it. I could not reconcile what I had done with the theory I held.

I recognised afterwards that this was just the same sort of confusion as existed in a Marxist who came to one of my creativity groups, got the answer to his problem, and then complained of being mystified. He didn't know how he had got his answer. He had arrived at a solution, but not by the correct route, and that felt mystifying. Much in the same way, I had got a result, but not by the correct route, and I felt as if I would either have to change my theory or my practice.

The magic glass screen I did not feel so bad about. This fitted in quite well with the approach to fantasy of people like Will Schutz and Jay Stattman, who had taught me these techniques. Both of these men were quite prepared to give the client a bulldozer to clear an obstacle, or a magic cake to give to the dragon, if the occasion seemed to demand it. I had done this sort of thing in group work many times, though never in the same context as we were doing it now.

However, my supervisor supported me in lining up with the client, saying that it seemed quite legitimate to him in the particular circumstances at hand here. He reminded me of my old slogan, 'You alone can do it, but you don't have to do it alone'. He made me recall times in groups when I had done just this kind of thing. Once, for example, when a woman was facing her father and feeling that she could never win, I had encouraged another woman to stand side by side with her and support her. The father had immediately felt much weaker, and now the woman had a chance to say what she had never dared to say before, and to be heard by him. Another time, I had encouraged a woman to pick up the cushion representing her bad parent and take it round the group so that each member could take a punch at it as it went past. The bad parent had then felt so chastened that it could be talked to and worked with in a really constructive way.

It seems that these bad parents (or bad part-objects sometimes) can have such an inflated sense of their own power and importance that they intimidate the client unduly. In order to do any useful work, the difference in perceived power must be reduced. This can be done by giving the client an ally or allies. These allies don't even have to be very strong or impressive: the mere alteration of one victim into two or more resisters is enough to make the bad parent feel quite different. The difference is that the client must be treated with greater respect, and listened to more. This makes dialogue and negotiation much more possible. In the examples given, it was not I myself who was the ally, but these were sufficiently close to be helpful in enabling me to understand the principle involved.

So what I have moved to now is a belief that what we are talking about here is not therapy, but a preliminary act of clearing the ground so that any therapy can take place at all.

This makes a distinction between doing therapy and doing other things that help the therapy and in that sense are therapeutic. There are many examples of this: some people may have a very poor sense of boundaries and limits in their lives, and finishing the session on time may be therapeutic for such a person, although it is not therapy; one may ask a client to lie down to make fantasy or regression easier, and lying down my be therapeutic in this sense, but it is not therapy; I may ask clients to take off their glasses before going into an active phase of the session, but taking off glasses is not therapy.

Similarly here, siding with the client may take some of the pressure off temporarily, long enough to enable the client to muster more resources, but it is not therapy. The therapy is when the client does it on her own and for herself.

There seem to be many instances where the therapist does this sort of activity, clearing the way, or laying foundations, or offering choices which may not have been seen before by the client. They are all part of the therapeutic process, but they are all things the therapist does, rather than things the client does. And it is the things the client does which are the real therapy. This has always seemed to me a very important distinction, and now more so than ever with the new example in this case history.

In the present instance, I sided with the client once or twice more. After that it was not necessary. Sarah became able to talk back to her mother on her own, and later the whole relationship started to change.

With the weight of her mother now lifted or lightened, Sarah's dreams started to take a different turn, and about two years after the start of therapy she had a whole series of dreams about dangerous weeds and gardens being spoilt and so on. This turned out to be all about her experience as a fetus, being defined as cancer and actually seeing herself as bad and cancerous. So this enabled us to do some deep work on her very early experience; this was very important work for her whole therapy, which had been quite impossible for her to tackle until we had got her mother out of the way to some extent. (If anyone reading this still has doubts about fetal experience being remembered, Verny (1982) provides the evidence.)

So now I consider this episode to have been extremely important as a turning point in the whole process of therapy for Sarah. Without it, I feel as if we would still be stuck with her mother, totally blocking off any other areas we might need to be working on. Her mother did in fact remain an issue for some time after this, but we have found it much more possible to deal with her, and in a recent session Sarah even found herself feeling sorry for her mother.

EMERGENT NEW DEVELOPMENTS

This led me into a new period in my own practice, when I took less seriously the precepts of good therapy that I had absorbed and uttered over the years. I found myself taking more risks and using more of myself than I had ever done before, I even found myself giving advice every now and then, which before had been the sin of sins. It was as if I had given myself permission to break the bounds.

But I hardly used the idea of siding with the client again, because none of my other clients had the same problem. I still regard it as a rather dangerous procedure, only to be used when it is really needed. One time when I did use it, in the first and last session with a client who seemed very poorly motivated (his wife had brought him in), it had no appreciable effect. It may be that it works best when a good therapeutic relationship has been built up.

It may also be that it would work best with a client who has little experience of answering back to authority figures. This is because of the modelling effect. In other words, it can be a very direct lesson in what to say and how to say it for someone who is lacking in these particular skills. Seeing someone else do it (a model) not only gives permission, but also shows you how.

What did happen more and more was that I started, in my lecturing and writing, to draw attention to a key paradox in all therapy: that what the therapist does is not therapy. Or to put it another way, most of what is done in a therapy session is not therapy.

Therapy is a process of giving up our assumptions. So in therapy the best, final, ultimate approach is to encourage and enable the client to question all his or her assumptions without exception. As Levin (1981) says:

> *All* conceptual constructions of the experiential process are *defence mechanisms*, to the extent that they solidify into patterns of response that obscure a clear perception of one's situation and block an appropriate, effective and spontaneous involvement (p. 248).

The ideal therapist is someone who can approach the client in a mood expressed by the phrase 'emptily perfect and perfectly empty'. There is then no distortion of the client's experience, no twisting of it to suit some theory. This enables the client to move in the same direction: that is, towards more openness, less restrictiveness. Levin says:

> The therapist thus prepares a spacious clearing, a comfortable openness, for the other . . . to open out into . . . We might call this quality 'spaciousness': the gracious hospitable spaciousness we need to grow, to live, to open up (pp. 254–6).

There is no statement here of any stages or levels of development, nor of any person or system by which change takes place. The emptiness in the therapist allows the client to move towards her or his own emptiness. But this, as Suzuki (1970) says:

> does not deny the world of multiplicities; mountains are there, the cherries are in full bloom, the moon shines most brightly in the autumnal night; but at the same time they are more than particularities, they appeal to us with a deeper meaning, they are understood in relation to what they are not. (Quoted in Wilber, 1979.)

These things do not make us unhappy unless we see them as denying us, frustrating us or unattainable by us. The constant thing in all unhappiness and distress is that it is 'I' who am unhappy or distressed, and all therapy is based on the premiss that is the 'I' which needs to change, to be worked on. But from our new point of view we can now see this differently. As Wei Wu Wei put it:

> Why are you unhappy?
> Because 99.9 percent
> Of everything you think and
> Of everything you do
> Is for yourself —
> And there isn't one. (Quoted in Wilber, 1979.)

This is the equivalent in therapy terms of the statement I made once about Harold Walsby's ultimate ideology, the ideology that enables us to describe and account for all ideologies (Lamm, 1984). I said that 'the ultimate ideology must be understood and accepted by nobody', simply because there is absolutely nothing to understand or accept. I went on to point out:

> In fact, the metadynamic level (the ultimate ideology) can have no expression at all, except the negative one of showing that all basic assumptions are self-contradictory, each in its own distinct way . . . We have seen through all other basic sets of assumptions, and we have nothing to put in their place (Rowan, unpublished manuscript).

Similarly in therapy, as we reject false self after false self in the search for the true self, we discover that there is no end to this process. When we realise that, there is nowhere for unhappiness or suffering to belong to or connect with. To put it another way, you behold your original face on all sides. Ken Wilber (1979) puts it like this:

> The more I look for the absolute self, the more I realise that I can't find it as an object. And the simple reason I can't find it as a particular object is because it's *every* object! I can't feel it because it *is* everything felt (p. 58).

This is the sort of empty paradoxical talk to which one is reduced when one tries to talk about what cannot really be talked about. But we have said enough to make it clear that from such a point of view the idea of measuring therapy, or of specifying the outcomes of psychotherapy, is absurd.

This is all very well, and very true. I could actually live up to it at times. But when I tried to do this and only this in therapy, I found that I usually could not do it. Always there seemed to be something needed first, some more immediate aim which had to be carried out before we could get on to the real emptiness. This now seems to me the essential paradox of psychotherapy: we can hardly ever do what is the best thing to do because there is always something better to do first.

If we just do the real therapy, the ultimate therapy, we restrict ourselves to the clients who are ready for that, and clients are hardly ever ready for it. This is not in any way to blame the clients: it is merely to recognise that the process of development is long and slow. When I am the client, I am no better than many of my own clients.

It seems that both therapists and clients are equally adept at avoiding the real issue, and perhaps this is necessary. Maybe the periphery is just as important as the centre. Maybe to concentrate on the centre all the time is too pure, too obsessive, too rigid, too arrogant; but at least it seems worth knowing: the difference between the centre and the periphery, the ultimate and the proximate.

Perhaps in the final analysis there are many levels of therapy, and we need to work on all of them at different times with different clients. If so, the sooner we know more about how many levels there are and how to work on each of them, the sooner we shall get out of empty arguments as to which level is the best. Wilber (1984) has some marvellous ideas about this.

These are wide-ranging thoughts to come out of one therapy

session, but it does seem as if it was this case that really opened my eyes to this deeply disconcerting vision.

IMPLICATIONS FOR OTHER THERAPISTS

The danger of purism

It seems to me that if I had been purist about my theory I would have said in effect something like: 'I don't believe in the superego, and these analysts are always trying to take over the client's experience, so I won't touch this approach with a bargepole.' I think it's very good to have a definite theory and stick to it, but if you stick too hard to it, you can become so rigid that marvellous opportunities like this one are let slip.

The key thing here is that I made the move before working it out in theoretical terms. It seems to me that this is the right way round. The practitioner always has to follow intuition and the sense of what is fitting, in the session itself. This is the eternal paradox, which I have written about also in a research context (Reason and Rowan, 1981), that the better our plan and our preparation, the better it is to let go of it in the actual moment of encounter. If we are too purist, in the sense of being determined to hang on to our theory at all times, we cannot do justice to this paradox.

The dangers of eclecticism

I would not like the idea of using any old technique in any old order with any old client. I think there is a very real danger of taking over the therapy, and taking over the client's experience, and making the client more dependent. A sort of slap-happy eclectic mishmash seems to me all too common among therapists, and I value a clear line and a clear demarcation of responsibility such that the client does the therapy and the therapist facilitates that process. I would not like siding with the client to become a regular thing or even a common thing. The client might like it too much, and the therapist might like it too much — both at the expense of any real therapy. But used in a genuinely preparatory way, as a way of opening up the possibility of working with the bad parent (bad breast, bad womb) material, this approach can fall into its appropriate role and be a valuable adjunct. It can then sink into the background and be superseded by the ordinary process of therapy proper.

The importance of serendipity and flexibility

If I had not gone to the lecture, I might never have heard the idea of John Rosen: it is not a common idea, and I have never read it anywhere. That is serendipity — or perhaps synchronicity: the lucky happening of something just at the moment when you need it most. Unless I had been keeping my eyes and ears open, I would have missed this, even then.

But equally, I had to have the flexibility actually to use it. It seems equally possible to be rigid and to dismiss the possibility of using something: 'It may be all right for him, but it would be artificial for me.' Unless we are flexible enough actually to try new things — things we didn't learn in our training — therapy will never change or develop. And we will never change or develop as therapists. We have to be able to try things which seem at first artificial or strained or formal or odd, because new things seldom seem smooth the first time we do them. It is only later that they may come to seem second nature.

The importance of imagination

Without imagination, I could never have invented the magic glass screen. (I don't mean I invented it in the sense of nobody ever having done it before; I am sure Moreno or somebody else thought of it years ago.) This kind of symbolic move is extremely useful in therapy, and I often use symbol and fantasy to help the client to move on. This can be done in many ways. A very good source of ideas on this whole area is Shorr (1983), and I would strongly recommend this book to anyone who likes working with imagery.

Translating a problem into symbolic form is an important way of making it concrete and easier to handle. That is why drawing and painting are such useful adjuncts to therapy. I often ask clients to draw or paint their problem or their conflict, and usually this makes it easier to proceed. Drawing a scene from a dream can be extremely useful. Drawing monsters is good, too.

If a dream is not available, it seems equally good to make up a dream or to use a guided fantasy. Ferrucci (1982) has many good suggestions along these lines. I have also used Winnicott's 'squiggle' technique, where he simply takes a piece of paper, does a squiggle on it with any pen that happens to be handy, and hands it across to the client with the words, 'Turn that into a picture.' The material elicited in these ways can be used just as one would use dream or art material.

I have also used Tarot cards, not in their 'official' interpretations, but simply as stimuli, so that the client can pick out cards that seem particularly appealing or offputting or otherwise meaningful, and talk about them, or talk as them. I used to use the old Rider pack for this, but more recently the Motherpeace pack (Noble, 1983) seems much more stimulating and up to date and defensible.

But the main thing is simply to allow the imagination free rein, so that the therapist is continuously using and cultivating the imagination for what it can offer. This is one of the main ways in which the therapy can stay alive and fresh at every moment.

The importance of having a good theory

It seems obvious that if your theory does not permit you to be flexible or imaginative, it is going to stop you from making important leaps and breakthroughs. It was only because my theory incorporated the idea of subpersonalities that I could work so easily with the idea of 'a heavy superego'. All subpersonalities are very much like the Freudian idea of the superego, and so it is a small step to transfer the idea and to talk instead about 'a heavy subpersonality'. We can then work with it as we work with any other subpersonality.

Without a good theory, it is hard to work with new ideas in any coherent way. The tendency is to break down into a sort of mindless eclecticism which uses anything and everything, or to rest with a rigid theory in which everything that is not commanded is forbidden. A good theory enables useful ideas to be incorporated without either of these two things happening.

I now feel, at the end of it all, that Bergantino (1981) was right when he said:

> The appropriate response may be as tricky as it is genuine. Being tricky and authentic can be two sides of the same coin. Being an authentic trickster will not destroy the patient's confidence if the therapist's heart is in the right place (p. 53).

The importance of creating new theory

The points I have made about the paradox of therapy emerged from the experience of therapy. Presumably all or most of the theory in therapy emerges from one's own therapy and the therapy of one's clients. It is from difficult cases like this one that new theory can emerge most readily. So from the point of view of developing theory further, the worst clients are the best. Here is another paradox of therapy.

REFERENCES

Adzema, M.V. (1985). A primal perspective on spirituality. *Journal of Humanistic Psychology*, 25 (3), 83–116
Bergantino, L. (1981). *Psychotherapy, insight and style.* Boston: Allyn & Bacon
Ferrucci, P. (1982). *What we may be: the visions and techniques of psychosynthesis.* Wellingborough: Turnstone Press
Kohut, H. (1971). *The analysis of the self.* New York: International Universities Press
Lake, F. (1980). *Constricted confusion: exploration of a pre- and peri-natal paradigm.* Oxford: Clinical Theology Association
Lamm, Z. (1984). Ideologies in a hierarchical order: a neglected theory. *Science and Public Policy*, February, 40–6
Levin, D.M. (1981). Approaches to psychotherapy: Freud, Jung and Tibetan Buddhism. In R.S. Valle and R. von Eckartsberg (Eds), *The metaphors of consciousness.* New York: Plenum Press
Mahrer, A.L. (1978). *Experiencing. a humanistic theory of psychology and psychiatry.* New York: Brunner/Mazel
Marina, N. (1982). Restructuring of cognitive-affective structure: a central point of change after psychotherapy. Brunel University: unpublished doctoral dissertation
Noble, V. (1983). *Motherpeace: a way to the Goddess through myth, art and Tarot.* San Francisco: Harper & Row
Reason, P. and Rowan, J. (Eds) (1981). *Human inquiry: a sourcebook of new paradigm research.* Chichester: John Wiley
Rowan, J. (1983). *The reality game: a guide to humanistic counselling and therapy.* London: Routledge & Kegan Paul
Rowan, J. (1986). Holistic listening. *Journal of Humanistic Psychology*, 26 (1), 83–102
Rowan, J. and Dryden, W. (Eds) (in press). *Innovative therapy in Britain.* London: Harper & Row
Shorr, J.E. (1983). *Psychotherapy through imagery* (2nd edn). New York: Thieme-Stratton
Suzuki, R. (1970). *Zen mind, beginner's mind.* New York: Weatherhill
Verny, T. (1982). *The secret life of the unborn child.* London: Sphere

Wilber, K. (1979). *No boundary: Eastern and Western approaches to personal growth.* Boulder: Shambhala

Wilber, K. (1984). The developmental spectrum and psychopathology: Part I, Stages and types of pathology. Part II, Treatment modalities. *Journal of Transpersonal Psychology, 16* (1), 75–118, and *16* (2), 137–66

7

Better the Devil You Know

Trevor Butt and Don Bannister

PRIOR THEORY AND PRACTICE

Although this chapter is penned jointly by two authors, we should explain at the outset that the prior theory and practice referred to is that of Trevor Butt. The chapter is an account of his growing dissatisfaction with the behaviour therapy approach that crystallised around a number of clients referred for social skills training. Two cases which best exemplify this rethinking are outlined, along with the emergence of a construct theory approach that developed in discussing the cases with Don Bannister.

There is no general agreement about what constitutes behaviour therapy. It ranges from the application of techniques based on classical and operant conditioning to the use of 'cognitive behaviour modification' which has left psychoanalytic renegades like Albert Ellis finding that he has been talking behaviour therapeutic prose if not all his life, at least for the last 30 years (Ellis, 1975). Erwin (1978), in an attempt to arrive at a statement of what behaviour therapy is, distinguishes between doctrinal definitions, which talk in terms of the application of particular theories and learning principles, and epistemological definitions, which characterise therapy in terms of a scientific approach to clinical problems. The problem is that whereas doctrinal definitions are too narrow, with many theorists excommunicating others not of the true faith, epistemological definitions are too broad, threatening to incorporate the therapies of Kelly, Rogers, or anyone else who adopts a broadly scientific posture in therapy.

We would argue that, in common with any other human venture, the development of behaviour therapy can only be properly understood when considered in its historical context. Like the 'problem behaviour' of the clients to be discussed, it must be appreciated not only for what it is, but also for what it is not. From contact with 'great men' like Gwynne Jones, we get the flavour of the radical alternative that behaviour therapy must have represented in the early 1960s. In contrast to psychoanalysis, it took clients' complaints at face value and certainly seriously. It rejected speculative theorising, where there was always the danger that the therapist knew best, and did not assume unproven links between behavioural problems and other disturbances. However, it was prepared to tackle complicated networks of complaints (e.g. Meyer, Sharpe and Chesser, 1976) when, as a result of an experimental approach to a case, this became a viable therapeutic proposition.

As well as being at the contrast pole to psychoanalysis, behaviour therapy stood in contrast to the medical model. Problems were seen either as behavioural excesses that arose through unlucky learning strategies, or behavioural deficits born of a lack of learning of appropriate skills (either through a lack of opportunity or perhaps the encountering of consequences that had led to avoidance). A behavioural analysis (Kanfer and Saslow, 1969) approached each individual open-mindedly, attempting a formulation of the problem in concrete terms having agreed aims and objectives openly with the client. Clients, in our experience, readily take to such an approach, are not insulted by it, and are recruited as agents in the resulting therapeutic programmes. Progress is monitored and reformulations are attempted, if there is little therapeutic movement.

Perhaps the most important modification in the behaviour of behaviour therapists has been their change towards a reliance on cognitive explanations of psychopathology, coupled with attempts to change beliefs directly (Mahoney, 1974; Bandura, 1976; Meichenbaum, 1977); Increasingly, clients are encouraged to elaborate their attitudes and beliefs, particularly about themselves. In the spirit of rational-emotive therapy (Ellis, 1975), it is emphasised that unpleasant feelings such as anxiety do not come out of the blue, but are a result of some personal belief or stance towards the world. Bandura (1977) pointed to a paradox in the later research findings of behaviour therapists: although there was general agreement that action-based techniques were most potent in bringing about therapeutic change, there was also a general disenchantment with conditioning theories as explanations. He proposed that the final common pathway to overcoming anxiety lay in the modification of what he termed 'efficacy beliefs'. Snake phobics knew that snakes were harmless, but had no confidence in their ability to carry out the simple task of picking one up. It is this lack of confidence that is challenged in any successful therapy, when the client is persuaded that he can and should do it.

If this proposition fits the bill for snake phobics, it seems even more appropriate for people phobics. Most shy people who are referred for social skills training think they know what effective/ social behaviour looks like, but they just feel they cannot carry it out. Given the alternatives that seem to face many clinical psychologists, social skills training appeals as an optimistic enterprise. A social skills training perspective views 'shy' and 'inadequate' behaviour as a behavioural deficit which can be remedied with the appropriate training. Complaints of lack of social confidence are seen as reflecting lack of perceptual and motor skills and consequential social failure. Better social performance is taught, hopefully resulting in the client's experience of increasing competence and confidence. All this is in line with Bandura's claim that performance is the most powerful source of efficacy beliefs.

There are many varieties of training procedure. The one used and described here is not atypical.

(1) Individual sessions in which the client's complaints are elaborated and operationalised in terms of target behaviours. The client is oriented towards a social skills approach and encouraged to see his or her life story in these terms. It is emphasised that change is not easy and depends on the client's commitment to attempting sometimes difficult behavioural homework between sessions.
(2) Group sessions — in a closed group lasting 10 to 12 weeks. Clients are encouraged to rehearse and discuss difficult tasks in the relatively safe setting of the group, where they can receive guidance, support and encouragement before exporting their skills to the outside world.

So, in social skills training, client and therapist are jointly engaged on the same venture, in pursuit of agreed goals. The issue in therapy is not what is wanted, but how it is to be achieved, and the therapist's job is to help the client remedy his or her lack of ability in achieving these objectives.

DESCRIPTION OF THE KEY CASES

The case of Jane

Jane was 23 when first referred for social skills training. She complained of being 'scared of people', and during the first session spoke very quietly, occasionally peeking out from a veil of long hair. She reported that she felt anxious during the most simple and ritualistic encounters (e.g. buying cigarettes) but felt most anxious with acquaintances. It did not matter if they were men or women, old or young, attractive or not, though it did make matters worse if they were extroverted and intelligent. She complained that people expected her to act in 'a silly, girlish way' and she found herself doing so, especially in her work as a secretary.

Jane had married young and divorced soon after, and was now living with a man she described as 'safe, reliable and boring'. He was apparently devoted to her, but she was really using him for temporary stability. She wanted to strike out on her own and find a new man, but had not the confidence to do so.

There appeared to be no sudden onset for her presenting problems, just a gradual realisation that her relationships were unsatisfactory. Her anxiety had led her to prune all social encounters to minimum contact. When she was forced into company, she would avoid eye contact, speak only when spoken to and generally discourage interaction.

It seemed that social skills training might well have something to offer her, and this approach was described to her, emphasising the importance of her willingness to attempt social tasks of increasing difficulty. It was explained that sessions could be used to report progress and prepare for future targets, both through discussion and the use of behaviour rehearsal. As soon as possible she could join a group that would provide more realistic possibilities for practice, feedback and encouragement, vital components of the skills training procedure.

Jane was enthusiastic about this scheme, and the first three sessions were spent drawing up hierarchies, examining the records she had started to keep, and planning and executing the first steps of treatment.

The general optimistic and business-like atmosphere evaporated during the fourth session, however, in which Jane was quiet and preoccupied. When the therapist enquired into this, she said that she had become infatuated with him and had been entertaining elaborate sexual fantasies about him. The therapist's initial reaction of surprise and embarrassment was followed by his assertion that this should not be allowed to interfere with the task in hand. Lacking guidelines from the behavioural framework we are left with common sense, which suggests that this issue should not be ignored. Generally it should be dealt with as a sort of therapeutic aside; it might be seen as indicating problems she was likely to have with men, but the therapist's main job was to continue to act as advisor and teacher while she pursued her goals between sessions.

Jane, though, was determined to focus all attention on the therapeutic relationship. Why couldn't we meet outside? Wasn't she attractive? (she was). Attempts to question her about her progress with the tasks that had been designed were countered with questions about the therapist. What had he done? Was he married? Faced with this impasse, he turned to the issue of whether such dramatic changes in her behaviour were characteristic of her elsewhere. She responded that she often appeared to have soured her relationships. For example, her boss was now frequently angry and sarcastic with her, and she did not know what she had done to earn this. Replicating such situations in role play suggested that she was either too dominating or submissive in her relationships at work. Jane found this a useful interpretation and said she saw human relationships very much as a battlefield; the world was divided into the strong and dominant on one hand and the weak and submissive on the other. The question always was, how to get yourself on the winning side.

Already a simple skills training perspective seemed too simple to guide Jane's therapy. The therapist was not happy about helping her to become more dominant; helping her change from being a doormat to a foot. Anyway this did not seem like a skill she needed to learn. She seemed to go from one to the other. It was more that 'dominant or submissive' was the wrong question to ask of relationships, and she needed to be helped to explore alternative perspectives and questions.

The therapeutic strategy adopted was to continue doggedly, trying to focus on events outside, while she persisted in focusing on the therapist. When, after three months, the time came for her to join a group, she felt rejected. However, during the course of the group's 12-week life, she became more relaxed and happy. She became friendly with several group members and said that she felt more confident. She left her job, went on a short college course and left her man to live in a bedsit. By the end of the group she was going out with a man whom she found interesting and exciting, and she made a number of friends and acquaintances. She was seen twice more for individual sessions and she declared that she felt no more need of therapeutic contact.

Fifteen months later, Jane asked to be seen again. This time she complained of no anxiety, just an overall feeling of unhappiness. Having married the exciting man, she now found him dull and boring. She was depressed by her inability to respond to his love, loyalty and genuineness. His affection merely served to highlight her own shortcomings. Her complaints are best displayed in her own words:

> Why do I always destroy something that's going well?
> I'm a masochist — self-destructive.
> I'm turning my husband into another Peter (previous man friend). The more depressed I get, the more boring he gets and this just makes me worse!
> I feel as though I'm cut off from life, just observing but not involved.
> I don't like the facade of happy wife I'm supposed to put up.
> Nothing can be done for me — I'm doomed to be unhappy.

A recurring theme was that she ought to be happy but wasn't. She saw herself as sabotaging her happiness and this is illustrated in the following episode:

Jane	*Husband*
Acts cold and off-hand.	Tries to find out what's wrong.
Shuns his interest.	Persists; suggests going out.
Wants to be alone. Persuades him to go out alone.	Does so reluctantly.
Drinks heavily; cries with rage and feels guilty.	Returns late.
Attacks him verbally/physically.	Is still tolerant.
Sleeps alone and cries herself to sleep.	

Therapy now addressed this 'neurotic paradox'. Why did Jane 'find herself' acting in ways that were not in her own best interests? She acknowledged that her current predicament reflected a recurring aspect of her lifestyle. All intimate relationships with men followed a similar pattern. She would become infatuated with a man, 'seduce' him, and once he had committed himself to the relationship she would sabotage it, denying herself the love she wanted. Feelings of self-pity, worthlessness and guilt marked the end of the cycle. Jane speculated that perhaps she was scared of being loved and was unsuited to a conventional monogamous lifestyle. Such 'insights' were hollow and infertile though, since they did not enable her to act or see herself differently. She had a clear image of what a wife 'ought to be' (always supportive, uncomplaining, compliant, docile, responsible and happy in her role). She saw herself as the exact opposite (miserable, moody, uninterested in sex or housework, tired and useless). The self-pity that was associated with the rejection of the 'good wife' role entailed a form of self-acceptance ('well I'm not cut out to be a bloody wife, and sod it why should I be?'). Nevertheless, Jane hoped that she could be helped to stop sabotaging her marriage. She had long since got over her brief infatuation with the therapist, and it would be no obstacle to concentrating on the goal. Yet the therapist's theoretical model faced difficulties in accommodating to this sort of request: 'Help me stop doing what I voluntarily do'.

Therapy focused on episodes such as the one outlined above, trying to identify the angry thoughts and self-statements that accompanied and arguably fuelled rejections of her husband with a view to getting her to challenge them and generate positive thoughts. In role play new strategies of relating to her husband were rehearsed.

The problem was that to Jane this always seemed like acting, hiding her real feelings, being a 'good little wife'. She was being asked to take on a role that just did not fit. The fact that the therapist did not see avoiding arguments as being submissive mattered not; the alternative courses of action as *she* saw them, along with their implications, were quite different for her.

Formulations of the problem in terms of emitting the wrong behaviour or cognitions, or a lack of interpersonal skills, now seemed quite sterile. It seemed that Jane was in a dilemma; faced with a choice of bad alternatives she was severely restrained in the possible types of marriage open to her. Rather than helping her to find silly answers to silly questions, therapy should be concentrating on helping her find better questions.

The therapist therefore set about trying to explore new ways in which she might develop a satisfactory relationship with her husband. There were various things Jane liked about herself. Some trait labels she attached to herself were 'curious about people', 'powerful', 'open-minded', 'bright' and 'amusing'. Perhaps if better ways of relating what she saw as evidence of these strengths could be found, she would feel less artificial, more prepared for change. Therapy centred on elaborating on how these aspects of her might be brought into play. How would a curious and open-minded person react in this situation?, and so forth.

Although Jane launched into the exercise with enthusiasm, after a few weeks she began to cancel sessions, due apparently to a series of minor mishaps (cold, car broke down, too much work). When she next came it was to announce that things were going from bad to worse with her husband. She had become infatuated with a man at work, adopted 'girlish and mindless' postures with him, and was purposely making her husband jealous. She felt compelled to follow up this new passion even though she was sure it would follow the same course as all the rest. As it happened, she became disillusioned with this affair very quickly and it led to her resigning her job and becoming unemployed. Very soon after this, she reported that her husband had a new job up north and she would be going with him. She would be pleased to leave the area.

There were four sessions left, and these were spent attempting to summarise important themes that had recurred throughout therapy. Jane became very sullen, never taking the initiative and only speaking when directly questioned. When she was asked about the change in her behaviour she professed surprise, saying nothing was wrong. The very last session was unnervingly like the first, some two years previously. Jane sat silently behind a veil of hair, rarely peeking out. When, at the end of the session she walked out without a 'goodbye', one was left with the feeling that therapy had made no difference at all to her life.

To the therapist, this case highlighted two problems:

(1) The conflict about taking complaints at their face value. Focusing on the social anxiety presented turned out to be inadequate, and seeing it as a skills deficit inappropriate. How can the therapist best appreciate the complex of issues and their relation that are relevant to the complaint?

(2) The failure of the behavioural framework to explain the neurotic paradox. How can we conceptualise a very intelligent client's repeating patterns of behaviour that she knows to be self-destructive? In this facet of the old free will versus determinism issue the therapist is faced with the conflict of how to recognise the client's agency while avoiding the blame that by custom

accompanies responsibility. Indeed, if the client is voluntarily committed to a course of action, what right have we to 'help' him or her to do differently?

Contact with Jane ended suddenly and unexpected but left the therapist in considerable confusion. It was during this period that he began to explore the approach of personal construct theory to psychotherapy, through contact with Don Bannister. The impact of this becomes increasingly evident in the case of Kevin.

The case of Kevin

Kevin lived in fear of men's violence. He pictured it erupting in a variety of situations, but especially at work. His world was peopled by aggressive, insensitive and uncaring men who were eager to spot and expose weaknesses in others. His fear led him to adopt a submissive posture lest he provoke others to verbal and even physical violence.

He lived in a bedsit and reported that he had a small circle of good friends with whom he felt safe but in whom he rarely confided. He had been through a course of social skills training, had been a sensitive and helpful member of the group, and found the main benefit had been the comfort he had got from the group cohesiveness. Although he had attempted all his assertive tasks unreservedly, he never felt at home in the role, feeling somehow it did not fit. Soon after the end of the group he found an American self-help book on assertiveness. This emphasised the importance of the attitudes and beliefs behind assertive action. Kevin was optimistic that this could help him achieve the 'suit of armour to protect his soft centre' that he wanted and was enthusiastic about embarking on a new course in social skills training based on this book.

The therapist, however, had become sceptical about the value of more of the same, and wanted to investigate more fully the implications of change. The evidence was building up from a number of clients, but particularly from Kevin, that people cannot don an ill-fitting role, however much they might appear to want it. It was jointly decided that further therapy should be preceded by an examination of what he would become, and what he would make of himself should be acquire the social armour he wanted. Radley (1973) has proposed that in self-change the person must be able to see clearly what he or she will become before acting and finally actually becoming a new role.

Kevin, of course, did not want to change in all respects. He saw himself as understanding others' point of view, tolerant and accepting, likeable and popular. These attributes contrasted with the typical quality of hostile individuals. They were inconsiderate, thick-skinned and aggressively domineering. An investigation of how Kevin saw himself in a whole range of social situations showed that he saw these good qualities as constant. At any time, he saw himself as being consistently understanding, tolerant and likeable. In Kellyan terms, these are preferred poles on core constructs. If he saw himself at the contrast poles, i.e. acting in an inconsiderate, hostile and obnoxious way, the very basis of the identity through which he related to others would be threatened.

On the other hand, he saw himself as too anxious, self-conscious, passive, defensive, quiet and immature, and longed to have the contrasting qualities of the relaxed, spontaneous and assertive extravert. His 'target behaviours' were tailored to bring this change about:

Talk loudly and confidently.
Remain quiet when I feel the need, in conversation.
Talk more about myself.
Talk back in arguments.
Act in a calm, relaxed way.

When asked to imagine himself attempting these targets, Kevin saw each one as clear evidence of the construct poles to which he wanted to change. They were consistent with becoming more relaxed, spontaneous, assertive and extraverted. But what about the implications for the core-role constructs? When talking loudly and confidently, for example, could be retain the image of himself as a tolerant and understanding man? In order to examine these implications, a grid was devised in which the target behaviours were taken as elements to be construed in terms of the core-role constructs.

When imagining performing each action, Kevin was asked to take each as evidence of either a preferred or non-preferred pole position on a four-point scale (see Figure 7.1).

Since Kevin's ideal self was a + + on each construct, we can see that he anticipates movement away from this in achieving any of these targets. However, some present far more threat than others, so the core role is completely lost in being assertive. Even being quiet presents more of a problem to him than would be supposed by

Figure 7.1: Target behaviours grid.

(Preferred Pole)	being calm and relaxed	talking confidently	being quiet in conversation	talking about myself	being assertive/aggressive	talking back in argument	(Non-Preferred Pole)
Understanding	+	+	−	+	=	−	Inconsiderate
Tolerant, pleasant	++	+	−	+	=	−	Hostile
Likeable	+	+	−	+	=	−	Obnoxious

++ extreme evidence of preferred pole.
+   evidence of preferred pole.
−   evidence of non-preferred pole.
=   extreme evidence of non-preferred pole.
o   out of range of convenience — does not apply.

an observer/therapist from the vantage point of a different construct system.

It was put to Kevin, then, that change as he saw it was a package deal with definite benefits but also considerable costs. It seemed like a desperate 'if you can't beat 'em, join 'em' strategy, where he would sacrifice cherished qualities in favour of those that he despised in others. However, what was at issue for him was social survival; if he were to swim and not sink, he felt he had no choice but to train himself in the assertive skills that a harsh world demanded.

It appeared to the therapist that like Jane with her dominant-submissive construct, Kevin, with a similar construction but different verbal labels, was approaching social life with the wrong question. Still, with the remnants of the behaviour therapists' view that the customer is always right, a new social skills training venture was launched.

Kevin approached the exercise with a surge of hope, energy and experimentation. He kept records of how he actually felt in terms of complaint and core-role constructs each time he attempted a target behaviour. In the first five weeks he successfully attempted many different tasks, that is, he was successful in that he saw himself as more extroverted, confident, gregarious, etc. through his activity. But this movement *was* accompanied by unwanted change on the core-role constructs. He saw himself as becoming simultaneously more inconsiderate, hostile and disliked. Perhaps this correlation explains why, in the subsequent four weeks, the targets were completed less successfully, but at least he became the nice considerate loser he knew.

In the period of despair that followed this 'relapse', therapy centred on gently raising the issue of whether he had been asking the best questions of himself and others. In an effort to replace the silly questions and their inevitable silly answers with better questions and constructs, the main therapeutic task focused on encouraging Kevin to become a constructive alternativist. That is, he should be helped to appreciate that the same events look very different from different perspectives; everyone has their story to tell.

The obvious place to start looking at this is in therapy; the client can say how things are from his viewpoint, and the therapist can agree or disagree with this. They can swop impressions of each other and back them up with evidence, in the spirit of Mair's (1970) conversational model. It was put to Kevin that the therapist's impression was that he was not always the passive victim he thought but a challenge to others. He had a definite vivid presence and his shyness might be mistaken for a mild arrogance. It is, of course, vital to the spirit of constructive alternativism that the therapist is not seen to be giving the true version of events; just another version.

The next step was to try to look at things from the point of view of the feared and hostile men. How did these Panzer Grenadiers see their social world, and their options? Kevin was asked to try to enter the role and write a sketch from this hostile, assertive point of view:

> I know what I want from life and haven't time for people who make excuses for their situation. They should help themselves. That's why I dislike certain people. Nervous people just annoy me. I don't enjoy their company and they're difficult to talk to. Why bother — they get over-sensitive to what I say anyway. I respect people who stand up for themselves even if it means they're unpopular. I don't care what other people think — it's my life after all.

Kevin was also asked to say from this point of view how he, Kevin, would have to change if he were to become more like this hostile man. Radley (1973) had found such exercises fertile in producing novel insights into other roles.

If Kevin were to become more like me, he would change in the folowing ways: would do what he wanted; wouldn't care what others thought of him; would be more confident, self-assured and assertive; would say what he thinks — wouldn't agree with people all the time.

An inspection of these statements shows the marked resemblance to Kevin's target behaviours, supporting the proposition that change in an assertive direction implied embracing this despised but envied identity.

Several sessions were spent questioning the evidence for the above outlook, and probing for alternative constructions. Might the behaviour of these feared men be defensive? Might they find Kevin difficult to deal with — interpret his shyness as dismissiveness or even arrogance?

At this stage Kevin was less disheartened and more interested in therapy, and it was decided that he might benefit from a fixed role enactment (see Epting, 1984). In this technique, the client is asked to act the part of a completely new character, who is outlined by the therapist. The role must be believable to the client and is not written to resemble his or her ideal self, but entails the challenge of adopting some novel perspectives on the world. The client is encouraged to become thoroughly immersed in the new role for a period of perhaps 2 or 3 weeks. This will involve going beyond the information given in the sketch, perhaps in terms of moving, talking, thinking and even eating as the new character would. The enactment is discussed in therapy sessions, and it is accepted that at the end of the exercise there is no expectation that the client will become the new character. However, it is hoped that he or she will have experimented with different ways of thinking and acting, and the results may have suggested new channels of movement. The fixed role sketch was written jointly by both authors. It was designed not to bring about the slot change that the training procedure had aimed at — going from submission to dominance — but as an encouraging experimentation with an orthogonal identity. This focused on a curious and inquisitive individual, who incorporated Kevin's qualities of being understanding and perceptive without being submissive.

Barry is an inquisitive young man who is fascinated by what makes people 'tick'. His absorbing interest takes the form of painstaking observation and questioning of others. With women, Barry is concerned to discover the ways they deal with their femininity. Many women impress him with the way they are neither hostile and aggressive, nor fawning and sycophantic. Through careful questioning, listening and observation, Barry draws up a plan of each woman's position from her perspective and likes to forecast how, from such a vantage point, she would react to difficult situations.

Barry will usually write down what people have said and what he has noticed about them, often in a very unstructured way before attempting tentative conclusions. The highly individualistic solutions people have to their problems he has found tend to defy classification. He has sometimes attempted to group them under five or six headings.

Barry is a thoughtful and reflective character, and although he is sometimes quiet in company, this is not due to shyness.

After two weeks of trying the fixed role, Kevin made the following observations:

It motivated me to absorb myself in other people and their problems and consequently not to be so self-conscious.

I see hostility in many actions/words which would not occur to others. I assume that all people behave the way that I do, so if someone acts in a way that I see negatively, that's because I would use that behaviour towards them with a negative intention.

Soon after this Kevin decided that he could do without therapy. In his work he was managing to coexist with difficult people without feeling that he would have to leave his job. This gave him confidence in coping with crises. Although he was in no sense the ideal self that he had envisaged at the start of therapy, and certainly had no suit of armour to cover his soft centre, he appeared to be engaged on a more profitable enterprise.

EMERGENT NEW DEVELOPMENTS

It is interesting to note how the client's difficulty in changing can be so similar to the therapist's, thereby reflecting Kelly's principle that an adequate explanation of human behaviour should be reflexive (i.e. apply to scientist as well as subject).

Once the therapist finds that the facts do not appear to fit his theory, and the theory cannot be elaborated to accommodate them, he is faced with another choice: make a deal with life and settle for eclectisism, or find a new theory (providing that he rejects the hostile attitude of insisting that the facts are 'wrong' and the clients are simply hysterical or malingering). The eclectic option is something of a slot-rattle — going backwards and forwards between theories and raiding them for their fruits. The new theory option is what Kelly called shift change, the search for a new construction. The shift to a new theory is not likely to be — and was not here — a sudden jump. A therapist without an articulated therapeutic language is unable to practise. New propositions are tried on for size gradually, and for a time exist side by side with old.

In response to the issues and conflicts raised by the cases of Jane and Kevin, the new developments that emerged in the therapist were of the radical shift-change variety. Similarly, we would argue that what Jane and Kevin needed was not the piecemeal acquisition of skills, but the development of new theories about themselves and others which would entail new ways of relating to others; new behavioural experiments.

A construct theory view of personal change argues that when people find themselves in a mess, it is not due to skills deficits, neither are they unconsciously motivated; they choose their course of action because the alternatives as they see them *leave no option*. The therapist's job is to open up new sets of alternatives, in order to get them moving again. He must understand that people are understandably loath to make any leap into the unknown, however attractive the fantasy may be to them. They must have some understanding of the implications of new roles. They can be encouraged to experiment, to try on new roles without commitment in the hope that they begin to glimpse new possibilities for themselves.

Clients come to the therapist in a crisis; their ways of dealing with it have not helped, the terms in which they see it offer no way out. From behaviour therapy's perspective with its impartial observations from without, the client's 'behaviour' or lack of it may seem puzzling. If what they ought to do looks obvious, then surely, as the behaviour therapist sees it, the answer lies in teaching them how to do it. The skills-training approach sees the skill as the alternative to the nothing they are doing now, it does not question what clients really want to do, taking at face value their request for change.

The construct theorist's stance is phenomenological, primarily interested in the client's version of reality. Kelly proposed that whereas the therapist sees a paradox, the client sees only a dilemma; a choice between bad alternatives:

> Over and over again, it appeared that clients were making their choices, not in terms of the alternatives we saw open to them, but in terms of the alternatives they saw open to them. It was their network of constructions that made up the daily mazes they ran, not the pure realities that appeared to us to surround them.

And

> ... the behaviour of the so-called neurotic client does not seem paradoxical to him until he tries to rationalise it in terms his therapist can understand. It is when he tries to use his therapist's construct system that the paradox appears. Within the client's own limited construction system he may be faced with a dilemma, but not with a paradox.
>
> (Kelly, 1979, pp. 84–5)

Of course, the client does not necessarily experience himself as choosing in the sense of consciously deliberating. Nevertheless, construct theory sees all action as meaningful, intentional and not irrational, or as the result of unconscious motivation. People are always 'doing' something (man is a form of motion), and often their action is best understood in terms of what they are *not* doing. Two people 'behaving' in the same way are not necessarily *doing* the same thing. One person may vote Labour because of a commitment to socialist ideals whereas another might do so because it seems like the only realistic alternative to Conservatism. An act of violence may be calculated and instrumental, or it may be a desperate measure resorted to only because it is preferable to the perceived alternative of defeatist compliance.

Understanding another's intention becomes more difficult in the light of the fact that an individual's choice never remains about one issue only; the organisation of the construct system into a set of ordinal relationships means that people are faced with a complicated network of choices: package deals that might carry a host of implications that are not immediately clear to the therapist, or the client him/herself.

The therapist, seeing only the single issue that he has helped the client to define, often fails to realise that, within the system of personal constructs that the client has erected, the decision for action is not necessarily based on this issue alone, but on a complex of issues. (Kelly, 1955, pp. 67-8)

Nevertheless, clients present with complaints they want to tackle and with lives they find deeply unsatisfactory. Why should they not be prepared to swop the problem package for one that appears to promise a better deal?

It is here that we see the weakness of the analogy of social action as a skill. Learning to type or to ride a bike is unlikely to have far-reaching consequences in terms of self-image for most of us. For some, the prospect of becoming a bike-rider may be laden with dark implications, but generally we are likely to accommodate it without too much disturbance. Becoming the sort of person who confronts others as Kevin wanted to, or becoming an 'ideal wife' as Jane feared, is likely to be a very different kettle of fish. Although in many ways appealing, we are likely to see it as radically changing our relationships. The individual is faced here with a moral choice: a fundamental decision about how to conduct himself with others (cf. Smail, 1977). Not the least of his problems is whether other people would recognise him as the same person, indeed whether he would recognise himself.

Kelly's choice corollary states that a person will choose that alternative through which he anticipates the greater possibility for the extension and definition of his system. Like the therapist, who cannot afford to be left theoryless, the client is going to have difficulty even envisaging a new core role that has no threads connecting it with the old. Both Jane and Kevin discovered serious implicative dilemmas in their sought-after change. For Jane change involved becoming a 'good little wife', and for Kevin it would entail becoming a hostile belligerent. The return, in both cases, to a familiar, well-trodden path of misery is only a paradox if one is taking an observer's perspective and operating a simple, hedonistic theory of people.

This view, that people are motivated by simple and uncomplicated pleasures, had its focus of convenience in the animal psychology on which behaviour therapy was initially based, but it barely explains the behaviour of the domestic cat, surely the best contender for this model of humankind (Bannister, 1981). Personal construct psychology rejects the idea that we are essentially passive, waiting for some drive or other to kick us into action. Instead, it proposes that it is anticipation (beating the world to the punch) and not pleasure-seeking or pain avoidance that is at the centre of the human enterprise. People tend to do what they know how to do — to recognise themselves in action, even if this does entail problems.

For Kelly, then, the human enterprise centres on anticipation, particularly social anticipation. In this antithesis of reaction the person is seen as one who initiates action, guided and informed by their assumptions about the nature of the (social) world. The psychology of personal constructs does not resolve psychological processes along a cognition-behavioural dimension, but instead sees intention and meaning as residing in action. A person's theories and propositions are woven into what he or she does. No theories: no meaningful action. People who find themselves acting in ways that are just 'not them' experience threat or guilt, and it is not surprising that they hop back into the old and familiar frying pan.

The therapist's job, then, is to encourage the client to develop new and more productive theories and questions. The client is likely to want quick answers to questions within his own framework, but in the view of construct theory this is likely to lead to untenable superficial (though possibly behaviourally dramatic) slot change. His ideal self will be couched in terms of his problem theory.

Kelly (1970) once remarked that there was nothing wrong with behaviour therapy except the way in which it was written up. The move from being a behaviour therapist to a construct theorist does not entail dramatic behavioural change in the sense that one abandons one set of techniques in favour of another. There remains the emphasis on action and experiment, but within the new theoretical framework (see Bannister, 1975). The therapist must help the client achieve the stance of a constructive alternativist. His or her problems, far from issuing from irrational thought, are seen as highly rational and meaningful from his viewpoint, and it is this viewpoint that is the focus of therapy. The client may tell you how things are (e.g. I'm a failure: people aren't to be trusted). The therapist can tell him or her how he or she sees things, can raise questions about how others do, and can encourage inquiry and experiment.

Although construct theory therapy is essentially an educational exercise, it is not concerned with training. The therapist does not have a prescription for what social behaviour should look like: no ideal that he measures clients up against. Therapy is educational in that it encourages the asking of new questions. Alternative construction should be allowed to coexist with the old. The client is not encouraged to choose the 'right' pathway, but to examine each for what it can offer. Fixed roles are designed explicitly to do this. They should be written so as to encourage experimentation with at least one major aspect of a new role. However, it is helpful if themes from the client's core role are present and he or she has the freedom to fit the new role with some flexibility.

It has already been noted that the construct theory approach was developing in the context of Kevin's therapy. This case illustrates some of the spirit and the techniques that are characteristic of the Kellyan approach.

IMPLICATIONS FOR OTHER THERAPISTS

What does a therapist do when he or she encounters clients who appear to cling to their problems, who 'find themselves' acting in ways which they know will lead to trouble; clients who do not seem to be able to learn skills despite the best efforts of both themselves and the therapist? Behaviour therapists have described this behaviour as a 'neurotic paradox' (Maher, 1966), but can only furnish descriptions, and not proper explanations of it. The therapist is left to draw on his or her experience and common sense for remedies, concluding that 'there's nowt so queer as folk'; he or she is left talking two languages — the science of behaviour, and the art of therapy.

Dissatisfaction with the behavioural perspective in general and with social skills training in particular is evident in even the work of Trower (1984), once a foremost proponent of the paradigm and now in search of a 'radical agency approach'.

We would argue that a therapist cannot begin to help people change until he or she realises that, in some sense, clients are responsible for their plight, are the authors of their own stories. The problem that both simple common sense and behavioural views share is that being responsible and needing help to change is seen as something of a contradiction. This is perhaps why neurotic patients who fail to respond to treatment are so often labelled as hysterical or manipulative. Initially they are given the benefit of the doubt as victims, and subsequently they are seen as having only themselves to blame.

An elaborated version of responsibility recognises that people choose their courses of action, but choices are appreciated as having implications, some far-reaching and threatening. Smail (1977), working primarily within a Sartrian framework, provides an excellent elaboration of this theme. Tschudi (1977) provides a model of choice and change which draws on both construct theory and decision-making theory.

Certainly the therapist must not assume that new bits of behaviour can be grafted on to old. Assessment should focus on making explicit the network of choices the client is facing. The optimum point of entry into the system is unlikely to be at the most subordinate level of drilling the client in new scripts and behaviour. Within the system subordinate change must be accounted for at the superordinate core-role level. The question to be addressed is not simply how can the client show assertiveness, but does he or she really want to? Exploration of change, e.g. using fixed roles, must work at both levels simultaneously.

It follows that although we must take the client's initial complaint seriously, we must not confuse this with taking it at face value. The therapist would be wise to assume that even a client with an apparently simple spider phobia is expressing a fear about a number of things, including spiders. None of us, including the client, can articulate easily everything that fear, anger or grief is about. Neither are we in a position to know exactly what we want, though from a Kellyan viewpoint this knowledge is not ultimately inaccessible.

The end point in therapy cannot therefore be described in terms of the presenting complaint, and certainly not in behavioural terms. Since therapy is about getting the client moving again, generating new and better questions and choices, it will be difficult to forecast what the issues will be as time moves on and new constructions develop. For this reason, as Bannister (1980) points out, there can be no simple measure of effectiveness in psychotherapy.

Perhaps the most quoted comment of Kelly's is his advice that 'if you don't know what's wrong with the patient, ask him, he may tell you'. This should not be taken to mean that we should take what we are told uncritically; rather that we will only glimpse the meaning of problems from an appreciation of perspectives. The client may not be able to tell us exactly 'what is wrong', but at least he can tell us where to start looking.

REFERENCES

Bandura, A. (1976). Behavior therapy and the models of man. In A. Wandersman, P. Poppen and D. Ricks (Eds), *Humanism and behaviorism: dialogue and growth*. Oxford: Pergamon

Bandura, A. (1977). Self efficacy: towards a unifying theory of behavior change. *Psychological Review, 84* (2), 191-215

Bannister, D. (1975). Personal construct theory psychotherapy. In D. Bannister (Ed.), *Issues and approaches in the psychological therapies.* London: Wiley

Bannister, D. (1980). The nonsense of effectiveness, *New Forum, 7,* 13

Bannister, D. (1981). The fallacy of animal experimentation in psychology. In D. Sperlinger (Ed.), *Animals in research.* London: Wiley

Ellis, A. (1975). Rational-emotive psychotherapy. In D. Bannister (Ed.), *Issues and approaches in the psychological therapies.* London: Wiley

Epting, F. (1984). *Personal construct counseling and psychotherapy.* London: Wiley

Erwin, E. (1978). *Behavior therapy: scientific, philosophical and moral foundations,* Cambridge: Cambridge University Press

Kanfer, F. and Saslow, G. (1969). Behavioral diagnosis. In C.M. Franks (Ed.), *Behavior therapy: appraisal and status.* New York: McGraw-Hill

Kelly, G.A. (1955). *The psychology of personal constructs.* New York: Norton

Kelly, G.A. (1970). Behavior is an experiment. In D. Bannister (Ed.), *Perspectives in personal construct theory.* London: Academic Press

Kelly, G.A. (1979). Man's construction of his alternatives. In B. Maher (Ed.), *Clinical psychology and personality.* New York: Kreiger

Maher, B. (1966). *Principles of psychopathology,* New York: McGraw-Hill

Mahoney, M.J. (1974). *Cognition and behavior modification,* Cambridge, MA: Ballinger

Mair, J.M.M. (1970). Psychologists are human too. In D. Bannister (Ed.), *Perspectives in personal construct theory.* London: Academic Press

Meichenbaum, D. (1977). *Cognitive behavior modification,* New York: Plenum

Meyer, V., Sharpe, R. and Chesser, E. (1976). Behavioural analysis and treatment of a complex case. In H.J. Eysenck (Ed.), *Case studies in behaviour therapy.* London: Routledge & Kegal Paul

Radley, A.R. (1973). A study of self-elaboration through role change. Unpublished PhD thesis, University of London

Smail, D. (1977). *Psychotherapy: a personal approach,* London: Dent

Trower, P. (Ed.) (1984). *Radical approaches to social skills training.* London: Croom Helm

Tschudi, F. (1977). Loaded and honest questions. In D. Bannister (Ed.), *New perspectives in personal construct theory.* London: Academic Press

8

On the Origin and Development of Rational-Emotive Therapy

Albert Ellis

PRIOR THEORY AND PRACTICE — 1

From 1947, when I began to undergo didactic psychoanalysis, until 1953, when I became quite disillusioned with practising it, I believed that people largely learn to be disturbed by the teachings and actions of their parents or parent surrogates and that only by understanding what happened to them in their childhood and by rewarding their attitudes and feelings in their relationship with an accepting therapist could they achieve a deep and long-lasting change in their neurosis. Becoming increasingly sceptical of psychoanalytic theory and practice, however, I began experimenting from 1953 onwards with other methods, and published two monographs on my discoveries: 'New approaches to psychotherapy techniques' (Ellis, 1955a) and 'Psychotherapy techniques for use with psychotics' (Ellis, 1955b).

The more I began to add cognitive, behavioural and other methods to my psychoanalytic procedures, the more I began to see that the theory of early childhood indoctrination and conditioning gave a very poor explanation of how people originally become disturbed — or, in RET terms, mainly disturbed themselves — and what they could effectively do to reduce their self-adopting and self-created neurosis. However, I was in conflict at this time because although I was using a number of non-psychoanalytic methods, I still largely believed that people learned to upset themselves and that they mainly did so by adopting the views that were presented to them and the behaviours that were modelled for them by their parents, by their peers, by their teachers, and by other significant people who were part of their early childhood.

Although by this time I had abandoned classical psychoanalysis, I was still doing psychodynamic psychotherapy and was showing my clients, mainly on a once-a-week basis, how their activities and relationships were highly motivated by their unconscious thoughts and feelings, and how, if they understood what their unconscious motivations were, they could change some of their dysfunctional behaviours and practise new ways of dealing with themselves, with others, and with the world around them. My interpretations were hardly Freudian, and owed more to several neo-Freudians and neo-Adlerians, especially to Karen Horney, Erich Fromm, and Harry Stack Sullivan. But along with the psychodynamic underpinnings of my therapy, I also began to include a good deal of philosophic advice, activity homework assignments (such as urging my phobic clients to take risks and to do what they were irrationally afraid of doing), and some pioneer skill training techniques — particularly with my shy and inhibited heterosexual and homosexual clients, to whom I gave specific instructions regarding how to approach desirable partners and how to communicate more effectively with these partners (Ellis, 1956).

At this time, I had already published several articles and books on sex and marital therapy, and was consequently seeing many clients with sex, marriage and family problems. With them, I used a more active-directive approach than I used with my regular psychotherapy clients, and I developed a cognitive-behavioural form of sex therapy which started to influence other therapists, including (a little later) Masters and Johnson (Ellis, 1953a, b, 1954a, b, c, 1955c). My sex and family therapy was, once again, far from being Freudian, but it was fairly heavily psychodynamic as well as cognitive-behavioural.

DESCRIPTION OF KEY CASE — 1

My practice of psychotherapy began to be much more cognitive and much less psychodynamic as a result of the following key case. I had, at this period of my psychotherapeutic practice, a 37-year-old female client whom I had been seeing for two years and who had made considerable progress, but who remained on a kind of therapeutic plateau after making this progress. When she first came to therapy she had been fighting continually with her husband, getting along poorly at her rather menial office job, and paranoidly believing that the whole world was against her. It quickly became clear in the course of the first few weeks of therapy that her parents (both of whom were rather paranoid themselves) had literally taught her to be suspicious of others and to demand a good living from the world, whether or not she worked for this living. They had also convinced her that unless she catered to their whims and did almost everything they approved, she was ungrateful and incompetent.

With this kind of upbringing, it was hardly surprising that my client thought that her husband never really did anything for her, and that, at the same time, she herself was essentially worthless and undeserving of having any good in life. She was shown, in the course of psychoanalytic-eclectic therapy, that she had been thoroughly indoctrinated with feelings of her own inadequacy by her parents (and by the general culture in which she lived). She was specifically helped to see that she was demanding from her husband the kind of unequivocal acceptance that she had not got from her father; and that, after railing at him for not loving her enough, she usually became terribly guilty, just as she had become years before when she hated and resisted her parents when she thought they were expecting too much from her.

Not only was this client shown the original sources of her hostility towards her husband and her continual self-deprecation, but she was also encouraged actively to decondition herself in these respects. Thus, she was given the 'homework' assignments of (a) trying to understand her husband's point of view and to act towards him as if he was not her father, but an independent person in his own right, and of (b) attempting to do her best in her work at the office, and risking the possibility that she might still fail and might have to face the fact that she was not the best worker in the world and that some of the complaints about her work were justified.

The client, in a reasonably earnest manner, did try to employ her newly found insights and to do her psychotherapeutic 'homework'; and, during the first six months of therapy she did significantly improve, so that she fought much less with her husband and got her first merit rise for doing better on her job. Still, however, she retained the underlying beliefs that she really was a worthless individual, and that almost everyone with whom she came into contact recognised this fact and soon began to take undue advantage of her. No amount of analysing her present difficulties nor of tracing them back to their correlates in her past seemed to free her of this set of basic beliefs.

Feeling, somehow, that the case was not hopeless and that there was some method of showing this client that her self-depreciatory and paranoid beliefs were ill-founded, I persisted in trying for a therapeutic breakthrough. And suddenly, as I myself began to see things rather differently, this long-sought breakthrough occurred.

The following dialogue with the client gives an idea of what happened. It is slightly abridged, grammatically clarified, and cleared of all identifying data.

'So you still think', I said to the client (for perhaps the hundredth time), 'that you're no damned good and that no one could possibly fully accept you and be on your side?'

'Yes, I have to be honest and admit that I do. I know it's silly, as you keep showing me that it is, to believe this. But I still believe it; and nothing seems to shake my belief.'

'Not even the fact that you've been doing so much better, for over a year now, with your husband, your associates at the office, and some of your friends?'

'No, not even that. I know I'm doing better, of course, and I'm sure it's because of what's gone on here in these sessions. And I'm pleased and grateful to you. But I still feel basically the same way — that there's something really rotten about me, something I can't do anything about, and that the others are able to see. And I don't know what to do about this feeling.'

'But this "feeling", as you call it, is only your beliefs — do you see that?'

'How can my feeling just be a belief? I really — uh — feel it. That's all I can describe it as, a feeling.'

'Yes, but you feel it because you believe it. If you believed, for example, really believed you were a fine person, in spite of all the mistakes you have made and may still make in life, and in spite of anyone else thinking that you were not so fine; if you really believed this, would you then feel fundamentally rotten?'

'Uh. Hmm. No, I guess you're right; I guess I then wouldn't feel that way.'

'All right. So your feeling that you are rotten or no good is really a belief, a very solid even if not too well articulated belief, that you are just no good, even though you are now doing well and your husband and your business associates have been showing, more than ever before, that they like you well enough.'

'Well, let's suppose you are right, and it is a belief behind, and — uh — causing my feelings. How can I rid myself of this belief?'

'How can you sustain it?'

'Oh, very well, I'm sure. For I do sustain it. I have for years, according to you.'

'Yes, but what's the evidence for sustaining it? How can you

151

prove that you're really rotten, no good?'

'Do I have to prove it to myself? Can't I just accept it without proving it?'

'Exactly! That's exactly what you're doing, and have doubtlessly been doing for years — accepting this belief, this perfectly groundless belief in your own "rottenness", without any proof whatever, without any evidence behind it.'

'But how can I keep accepting it if, as you say, there is no proof behind it?'

'You can keep accepting it because —'. At this point I was somewhat stumped myself, but felt that if I persisted in talking it out with this client, and avoiding the old psychoanalytic clichés, which had so far produced no real answer to this often-raised question, I might possibly stumble on some answer for my own, as well as my client's, satisfaction. So I stubbornly went on: '— because, well, you're human.'

'Human? What has that got to do with it?'

'Well —' I still had no real answer, but somehow felt that one was lurking right around the corner of our collaborative thinking. 'That's just the way humans are, I guess. They do doggedly hold to groundless beliefs when they haven't got an iota of evidence with which to back up these beliefs. Millions of people, for example, believe wholeheartedly and dogmatically in the existence of God when, as Hume, Kant and many other first-rate philosophers have shown, they can't possibly ever prove (or, for that matter, disprove) His or Her existence. But that hardly stops them from fervently believing.'

'You think, then, that I believe in the "truth" of my own rottenness, just about in the same way that these people believe in the "truth" of God, without any evidence whatever to back our beliefs?'

'Don't you? And aren't they — the theory of God and of your own rottenness — really the same kind of definitional concepts?'

'Definitional?'

'Yes. You start with an axiom or hypothesis, such as: "Unless I do perfectly well in life, I am worthless", or, in your case, more specifically: "In order to be good, I must be a fine, self-sacrificing daughter, wife and mother." Then you look at the facts, and quickly see that you are not doing perfectly well in life — that you are not the finest, most self-sacrificing daughter, wife and mother who ever lived. Then you conclude: "Therefore, I am no good — in fact, I am rotten and worthless".'

'Well, doesn't that conclusion follow from the facts?'

'No, not at all! It follows almost entirely from your definitional premises. And, in a sense, there are few facts in your syllogism, since all your "evidence" is highly biased by these premises.'

'But isn't it a fact that I am not a fine, self-sacrificing daughter, wife and mother?'

'No, not necessarily. For actually, you may well be as good a daughter to your parents as most women are; in fact, you may be considerably better than most in this respect. But your premiss says that in order to be good, you must be practically perfect. And, in the light of this premiss, even the fact of how good a daughter you are will inevitably be distorted, and you will be almost bound to conclude that you are a "poor" daughter when, in actual fact, you may be a better than average one.'

'So there are few real facts at all in my syllogism?'

'Yes, damned few! But even if your "facts" were accurate — even, for example, if you were not even an average daughter or wife — your syllogism would still be tautological: since it merely "proves" what you originally postulated in your premiss; namely, that if you are not perfect, you are worthless. Consequently, your so-called worthlessness or rottenness is definitional and not factual.'

'Are all disturbances, such as mine, the same way?'

'Yes, come to think of it —' and, suddenly, I did come to think of it myself, as I was talking with this client '— all human disturbances seem to be of the same definitional nature. We assume that it is horrible if something is bad — if, especially, we are imperfect or if others are not acting in the angelic way that we think they *should* act. Then, after making this assumption, we literally look for the "facts" to prove our premiss. And invariably, of course, we find these "facts" — find that we are or someone else is behaving very badly. Then we "logically" conclude that we were right in the first place, and that the "bad" behaviour we found conclusively "proves" our original assumption. But the only real or at least unbiased "facts" in this "logical" chain construct are our own starting premisses — the beliefs we tell ourselves to begin with.'

'Would you say, then', my client asked, 'that I literally tell myself certain unvalidated sentences, and that my disturbance stems directly from these, my own, sentences?'

'Yes', I replied with sudden enthusiasm. 'You give me an idea, there. I had not quite thought of it that way before, although I guess I really had, without putting it in just those terms, since I said to you just a moment ago that it is the sentences we tell ourselves to begin with that start the ball of definitional premises, semi-definitional "facts", and false conclusions rolling. But, anyway, whether it's your idea or mine, it seems to be true: that humans who feel disturbed really are telling themselves a chain of false sentences — since that is the way that humans seem almost invariably to think, in words, phrases, and sentences. And it is these sentences that really *constitute* their neuroses.'

'Can you be more precise? What are my own exact sentences, for instance?'

'Well, let's see. I'm sure we can quickly work them out. You start by listening, of course, to the sentences of others, mainly of your parents. And their sentences are, as we have gone over many times here, "Look, dear, unless you love us dearly, in an utterly self-sacrificing way, you're no good, and people will find out that you're no good, and they won't love you, and that would be terrible, terrible, terrible!"'

'And I listen to these sentences of my parents, told to me over and over again, and make them mine — is that it?'

'Yes, you make them yours. And not only their precise, overt sentences, of course, but their gestures, voice intonations, critical looks, and so on. These also have significant meaning for you: since you turn them, in your own head, into phrases and sentences. Thus, when your mother says, "Don't do that, dear!" in any angry or demanding tone of voice, you translate it into, "Don't do that, dear — or I won't love you if you do, and everyone else will think you're no good and won't love you, and that would be terrible!"'

'So when my parents tell me I'm no good, by word or by gesture, I quickly say to myself: "They're right. If I don't love them dearly and don't sacrifice myself to them, I'm no good, and everyone will see I'm no good, and nobody will accept me, and that will be awful!"'

'Right. And it is these phrases or sentences of yours that create your feeling of awfulness — create your guilt and your neurosis. You, of course, don't have to only put your beliefs into phrases and sentences, because you can use images, symbols, and other cognitions, too. But like almost all humans who learn a language, you normally state your beliefs or philosophies to yourself as well as to others, verbally.'

'But how? What exactly is there about my own sentences that creates my awful feeling? What is the false part of these sentences?'

'The last part, usually. For the first part, very often, may be true. The first part of your beliefs, remember, is something along the lines of: "'If I don't completely love my parents and sacrifice myself for them, many people or some people, including my parents, will probably think that I'm a bad daughter — that I'm no good.' And this part of your ideas may very well be true.'

'Many people, including my parents, may really think that I'm no good for acting this way — is that what you mean?'

'Yes. They actually may. So your observation that if you are not a perfect daughter, various people, especially your parents, won't approve of you, and may consider you worthless, is probably a partly sound and valid observation. But that isn't what does you the damage. It's the rest of your self-statements that do the damage.'

'You mean the part where I say "Because many people may not approve of me for being an imperfect daughter, I am no good?"'

'Exactly. If many people, even all people, think that you're not a perfect daughter, and that you *should* be a perfect daughter, that may well be their true belief or feeling — but what has it really got to do with what you have to believe? How does being an imperfect daughter make you, except in their eyes, *worthless*? Why, even if it is true that you are such an imperfect child to your parents, is it *terrible* that you are imperfect? And why is it *awful* if many people will not approve of you if you are a poor daughter?'

'I don't have to believe I'm *awful* just because they believe it? I can accept myself as being imperfect, even if it is true that I am, without thinking that this is *awful*?'

'Yes. Unless your definition of "awful" and "worthless" becomes the same as their definition. And that, of course, is exactly what's happening when you feel upset about your parents' and others' view of you. You are then making their definition of you your definition. You are taking their assumed beliefs and making them your own. And it is this highly creative, self-defining act on your part which manufactures your disturbance.'

'I have the theoretical choice, then, of taking their definition of me as worthless, because I am an imperfect daughter, and accepting it or rejecting it. And if I accept it, I make their definition mine, and I upset myself.'

'Yes, you illogically upset yourself.'

'But why illogically, necessarily? Can't they be right about my being an imperfect daughter making me worthless?'

'No — only, again, by definition. Because, obviously, not every set of parents who have an imperfect daughter considers her worthless. Some parents feel that their daughter is quite worthwhile, even when she does not completely sacrifice herself for them. Your parents obviously don't think so and define your worth in terms of how much you do for them. They are, of course, entitled to define you in such a way. But their concept of you is definitional; and it is only tautologically valid.'

'You mean there is no absolute way of proving, if they consider me worthless for not being sufficiently self-sacrificing, that I actually am worthless?'

'Right. Even if everyone in the world agreed with them that your being insufficiently self-sacrificing equalled your being worthless, that would still be everyone's definition; and you still would not have to accept it. But of course, as we have just noted, it is highly improbable that everyone in the world would agree with them — which proves all the more how subjective their definition of your worth is.'

'And even if they and everyone else agreed that I was worthless for being imperfectly interested in their welfare, that would still not mean that I would have to accept this definition?'

'No, certainly not. For even if they were right about your being worthless to *them* when you were not utterly self-sacrificing — and it is of course their prerogative to value you little when you are not doing what they would want you to do — there is no connection whatever, unless you think there is one, between your value to them and your value to yourself. You can be perfectly good, to and for *yourself*, even though they think you perfectly bad to and for *them*.'

'That sounds all very well and fine. But let's get back to my specific sentences and see how it works out there.'

'Yes, you're quite right. Because it's those specific sentences that you'd better change to make yourself undisturbed. As we said before, your main sentences to yourself are: "Because they think I am worthless for not being utterly self-sacrificing to them, they are right. It would be terrible if they continue to think this of me and don't thoroughly approve of me. So I'd better be more self-sacrificing — or else hate myself if I am not".'

'And I have to change those sentences to —?'

'Well, quite obviously you don't *have to* but *had better* change them to: "Maybe they are right about their thinking I am worthless to *them* if I am not a much more self-sacrificing daughter, but what has that really got to do with my estimation of *myself*? Would it really be *terrible* if they continue to think this way about me? Do I *need* their approval that much? Should I *have to* keep hating myself if I am not more self-sacrificing?"'

'And by changing these sentences, my own versions of and belief in their sentences, I can definitely change my feelings of guilt and worthlessness and get better?'

'Why don't you try it and see?'

This client did keep looking at her own sentences and did try to change them. And within several weeks she improved far more significantly than she had done in the previous two years I had been seeing her. 'I really seem to have got it now!', she reported two months later. 'Whenever I find myself getting guilty or upset, I immediately tell myself that I am saying some silly sentences to myself to cause this upset; and almost immediately, usually within a few minutes of my starting to look for it, I find this sentence. And, just as you have been showing me, my belief invariably takes the form of "Isn't it *terrible* that —" or "Wouldn't it be *awful* if —". And when I closely look at and question these sentences, and ask myself "How is it *really* terrible that —?" or "Why would it *actually* be awful if —?", I always find that it isn't terrible or wouldn't be awful, and I get over being upset very quickly. In fact, as you predicted a few weeks ago, as I keep questioning and challenging my own beliefs, I find that they stop coming up again and again, as they used to do before. Only occasionally, now, do I start to tell myself that something would be terrible or awful if it occurred, or something else is horrible because it has occurred. And on those relatively few occasions, as I just said, I can quickly go after the "terribleness" or the "awfulness" that I am dreaming up, and factually or logically re-evaluate it. I can hardly believe it, but I seem to be getting to the point, after so many years of worrying over practically everything and thinking I was a slob no matter what I did, of now finding that *nothing* is so terrible or awful, and I seem to be recognising this in advance rather than after I have seriously upset myself. Boy, what a change that is in my life! I am really getting to be, with these new attitudes, a quite different sort of person.

True to her words, this woman's behaviour mirrored her new attitudes. She acted much better with her husband and child, and enjoyed her family relationship in a manner that she had never thought she would be able to do. She quit her old job and got a considerably better paying and more satisfying one. She not only stopped being concerned about her parents' opinion of her, but started to help them to get over some of their own negative ideas towards themselves, each other, and the rest of the world. And, best of all, she really stopped caring, except for limited practical purposes, what other people thought of her, lost her paranoid ideas about their being against her, and began to accept herself even when she made errors that others brought to her attention in a disapproving manner.

EMERGENT NEW DEVELOPMENTS — 1

As these remarkable changes occurred in this client, and I began to get somewhat similar (though not always as excellent) results with several other clients, the principles of rational-emotive therapy began to take clearer form; and, by the beginning of 1955, I had formulated the basic theory and practice of RET.

I finally, at least to my own satisfaction, solved the great mystery of why so many millions of humans not only originally become emotionally disturbed, but why they persistently, in the face of so much self-handicapping, remain so. The very facility with language which enables them to be essentially human — to talk to others and to talk to themselves — also enables them to abuse this facility by talking utter nonsense to themselves: to define things as terrible when, at worst, these things are inconvenient and annoying.

In particular, their talking and their self-talking abilities encourage people to forget that their real needs, or necessities for human survival, are physical or sensory — that is, consist of the need for sufficient food, fluids, shelter, health, and freedom from physical pain. And their self-talk helps them to translate their psychological desires — such as the desires for love, approval, success and leisure — into definitional needs. Then, once they define their desires or preferences as necessities, or accept the false definitions of their parents or others in this connection, their self-talking abilities beautifully enable them to continue to define their 'needs' in this nonsensical manner, even though they have no supporting evidence to back their definitions.

I discovered clinically, when I realised how important talk and self-talk was, that disturbed individuals often take their preference to be loved or approved by others (which is hardly insane, since there usually are concrete advantages to others' approving them) and arbitrarily define and keep defining this preference as a dire need. Thereby, they become anxious, guilty, depressed, or otherwise self-hating; since there is absolutely no way, in this highly realistic world in which we live, that they can thereafter guarantee that they will be devotedly loved or approved by others.

By the same token, disturbed people frequently take their preference for ruling others, or getting something for nothing, or living in a perfectly just world (which again are perfectly legitimate desires, if only one could possibly achieve them) and demand that others and the universe accede to their desires. Thereby, they make themselves become hostile, resentful, and grandiose. Without human talk and self-talk, some degree of anxiety and hostility might well exist; but not, I realised, the extreme and intense degrees of these feelings which constitute emotional disturbance.

Once I clearly began to see that neurotic behaviour is not merely externally conditioned or indoctrinated at an early age, but that it is also internally reindoctrinated or autosuggested by people to themselves over and over again, until it becomes an integral part of their presently held (and still continually self-reiterated) philosophy of life, my work with my clients took on a radically new slant.

Where I had previously tried to show them how they had originally became disturbed and what to do now to counter their early-acquired upsets, I saw that I had been exceptionally vague; and that, still misled by Freudian-oriented theories, I had been stressing psychodynamic rather than philosophic causation, and had been emphasising what to undo and not what to unsay and unthink. I had been neglecting (along with virtually all other therapists of the day) the precise declarative and exclamatory sentences which the clients once told themselves to create their disturbances and which, even more importantly, they were still specifically telling themselves to maintain these same anxieties, depressions and rages.

IMPLICATIONS FOR OTHER THERAPISTS — 1

I had relatively little conflict in giving up some of my last vestiges of heavily psychodynamically oriented thinking by the time I worked with this key case, since I had already been incorporating rational philosophies into my therapeutic procedures and had been finding them to be quite effective. Moreover, my main hobby, from the age of 16 onwards, was philosophy, and particularly the philosophy of happiness. I was therefore distinctly influenced by Epictetus, Marcus Aurelius, Baruch Spinoza, Friedrich Nietzsche, Arthur Schopenhauer, John Dewey, George Santayana, Bertrand Russell and other philosophers, and during my late adolescence I was particularly attracted to Immanual Kant's *Critique of pure reason* (Ellis, 1981). I therefore had a natural affinity to what Schopenhauer called 'The World as Will and Idea'.

When I began discovering, through my work with my clients, that cognition was central to virtually all neurotic disturbance, I rather enthusiastically accepted this concept and I had no real trouble incorporating it into RET.

Even while practising psychoanalysis and psychoanalytically oriented therapy, moreover, I had been highly critical of Freudian orthodoxy and had written several papers attempting to revise psychoanalytic theory and practice (Ellis, 1948, 1949, 1950). So I was theoretically prepared to change my therapeutic procedures long before I actually started to do so; and the knowledge that I learned from the key case I just described fell on quite receptive ears.

As a result of this key case and of my rethinking that followed it, I began, at the beginning of 1955, to call myself a rational therapist and to set up the new practice of RET. Since the term 'rational psychotherapy' was misunderstood by many people, who mistakenly started to identify me as an eighteenth-century rationalist, I later changed the name to rational-emotive therapy. Actually, however, as Raymond Corsini keeps pointing out to me, RET, right from the start, has been rational-emotive-behavioural therapy and therefore could well be known as REBT.

Some of the points that other therapists, of whatever school, might take from my originating RET in the manner described above include these:

(1) Some of the most important theories and practices of psychotherapy can be learned from working with and listening carefully to our clients. They have their own ideas of how they became disturbed and how they might change; and these ideas can importantly supplement the knowledge that therapists take from their teachers, their books, and their supervisors.

(2) Dogmatic and orthodox allegiance to any form of therapy, no matter how good it is, can help stultify neophyte therapists and can hinder progress in the field of psychological treatment. Dogma and absolutism, according to RET, seem to be at the very core of most neurotic disturbances; and they are also fundamental to many forms of psychotherapy itself.

(3) Every session of psychotherapy, as Yates (1970) has aptly pointed out, had better be an experiment in its own right; and when it is seen in this manner, clients can be helped more individualistically; and therapists and the entire field of psychotherapy can maximally benefit. In this key case I saw the client as a unique

individual who had better be uniquely convinced that she was not worthless. So I tried using logical and empirical arguments that I had never thought of trying before. Ironically, I later saw that many of my arguments also could be used with other individuals who had severe feelings of inadequacy. But I first experimented by plunging off my usual therapeutic path and using new arguments with her. My client's consistent arguments that she could not *just* accept herself as human spurred me to figure out ways in which she *could* do so. Because she kept pointing out to me that she accepted her 'rottenness' without any proof, I was pushed to see that her disturbance was definitional and that she could accept herself unconditionally, because she was human and could therefore *choose* self-acceptance.

(4) Psychotherapy, as many authorities have indicated, had better be a collaborative process, and not merely stem from the authoritative stand of the therapist. As I have noted in the previous paragraph, my client was indeed argumentative and resistant, but I *viewed* her opposition as a plea for my working with her and overcoming it; and her negative thinking led to some of my own constructive thinking. In a sense, she *dared* me to undo some of her disturbance; and I rose to the challenge, used her arguments to incite and supplement my own, and collaborated with her to reach together a better solution than either of us, individually, would probably ever have reached. Therapists can learn by this kind of open interchange and collaborative 'arguing' that clients can not only benefit themselves by intensively collaborating with their therapists but can also sometimes help the growth and development of the art and science of psychotherapy itself.

(5) I learned from this case that a 'deeper' understanding of client problems and a more 'intensive' method of psychotherapy can follow from ideological and philosophical rather than historical analysis. I now believe that if therapists of various persuasions assume that virtually all their clients are, in some respects, philosophers and not merely experientialists and self-suggesters, they will add considerably to their understanding and helping these clients.

(6) I realised that there are two major levels of disputing irrational beliefs: (a) Checking them empirically and proving to clients that conditions are not as bad as they perceive; and (b) taking things at their worst, accepting 'wrong' facts and judgements as the clients perceive them and *still* not defining bad events as *awful* nor clients' bad *behaviour* as making them bad *people*. Thus, my client might not have been a poor daughter to her parents and I might well

have argued that she was not as bad or imperfect as she and they saw her. But I went further and showed her that even if, at the worst, she *was* 'bad' or 'imperfect' as a daughter, she would still not have to define herself as a 'worthless person'. This technique of showing clients, first, that they are not actually as bad as they unrealistically 'perceive', and that, secondly, if they really are that bad it still is not *awful* and that they are never *bad people* often distinguishes RET from other kinds of cognitive-behavioural therapy; and it is a philosophic argument that can be effectively used by almost all therapists.

PRIOR THEORY AND PRACTICE — 2

After creating RET in 1955, using it successfully with hundreds of clients and volunteers at my public and professional workshops, and teaching it to scores of professionals who also reported clinical and experimental successes, I added to its theories and practices and was pleased with its growth and development during the next 20 years. During this time, I taught virtually all my clients the famous ABCs of RET — namely, that environmental situations or Activating Events (A) do not normally cause people to feel and act in a disturbed manner at point C (their emotional and behavioural Consequences). Rather, their disturbances are largely created or 'caused' by B (their Belief System *about* A).

I especially showed them that they had rational Beliefs (rBs) that helped them create appropriate feelings (such as sadness, frustration and annoyance) when some important thing (failure and rejection) occurred at point A; and that they also had a set of irrational Beliefs (iBs) that helped them create inappropriate feelings (such as panic, depression and rage) when they were faced with blocks and discomforts at A. In my very first paper on RET, given at the American Psychological Association convention in Chicago in 1956, I outlined twelve basic irrational Beliefs that people frequently accepted or created to upset themselves (Ellis, 1957a, 1958); and I and other researchers constructed irrational belief tests to diagnose these iBs and to determine whether they really are correlated with emotional disturbance. I created a special personality data form incorporating 50 irrational Beliefs which has been clinically employed with thousands of clients at the Institute for Rational-Emotive Therapy in New York since I originated it in 1968 (Ellis, 1968).

For a good many years, then, RET became almost synonymous

with looking for several major irrational Beliefs that clients held, distinguishing these from the rational Beliefs that accompany them, and then active-directively showing the clients how to dispute and challenge their iBs. Hundreds of therapists throughout the world began to do RET in a somewhat similar manner, and many outcome studies on its use have now been done, the vast majority of which indicate that when it is employed with experimental and control groups, the experimental groups who learn to use RET make significantly greater improvements than the control groups who do not learn it (DiGiuseppe, Miller and Trexler, 1979; Ellis, 1979; McGovern and Silverman, 1984).

I was naturally pleased with RET's growth and development from 1955 to 1975. But two aspects that I had vaguely noted from the start and had included in *Reason and emotion in psychotherapy* (Ellis, 1962) became much more dramatically and effectively clear to me in the early 1970s.

First, I began to see that the twelve original irrational Beliefs that lead to disturbance that I had posited in my first paper on RET can be condensed into three major irrationalities or *must*urbatory self-statements:

(1) 'I *must* perform well and be approved by significant others, or I am an inadequate, worthless person'. This musturbatory thought often creates feelings of inadequacy, anxiety, and depression and avoidant behaviour.

(2) 'Other people *must* treat me considerately and fairly or they are no damned good!' This Jehovian command usually creates feelings of hostility and rage and aggressive behaviours.

(3) 'Conditions under which I live *must* be comfortable and undangerous or else my life is hardly worth living!' This dogmatic belief frequently leads to feelings of self-pity and depression and to procrastinaiton, withdrawal, and phobias (Ellis, 1973, 1977; Ellis and Harper, 1975; Ellis and Grieger, 1977; Ellis and Whiteley, 1979; Ellis and Becker, 1982; Dryden and Ellis, 1986).

Realising that these three basic grandiose demands were core irrational beliefs from which stemmed the original dozen irrationalities that I posited, I began to look more closely for my clients' discomfort disturbances (or low frustration tolerance) in addition to their ego disturbance (or self-downing). To my surprise, I found that they almost always had a considerable degree of *both* these major forms of needless upsetness.

DESCRIPTION OF KEY CASE — 2

A keynote case that helped me firmly crystallise my views on the three major *musts* that lead to serious emotional problems, and to give more importance than I had previously done to helping clients discover, understand and uproot their discomfort disturbance, was that of a recovered alcoholic of 35 who was working as a counsellor in a detoxification centre. He came to therapy because he was not doing as well as he thought he *should* do at work and in his intimate relationships, and consequently felt self-hating and depressed, and angry at those who slighted him.

We worked quite well on his self-downing problems for the first few months of therapy, and conquered some of them so well that he was able unashamedly to let everyone know that he had serious emotional problems and was in therapy once again even though he was a substance-abuse counsellor. He did several of the RET shame-attacking exercises — including wearing dirty and tattered clothes to work and yelling out the station stops in the New York subway — and managed to feel little shame while doing them. After a while, he became one of the most unashamed clients I had ever had and I felt very good about his progress!

Time and again, however, he kept saying that he felt 'anxious' about trivial things — such as waiting for a subway train or bus, getting to appointments on time, and being kept waiting by a friend. Some of this anxiety was related to his fear that people would not respect him, and was therefore ego-anxiety or self-downing — which he had clearly had all his life and still had, despite his RET gains. Much of his fear, however, and the depression that went with it seemed to stem from his abysmal low frustration tolerance (LFT). I began to realise that he was anxious (indeed, often panicked) because he might, first, be very uncomfortable about some frustrating event and, secondly, think that he *couldn't stand* this discomfort and *had to* be able to prevent it or stop it.

He *also* was afraid that he *couldn't handle* frustration or his extreme discomfort about it; that he might literally go crazy and have to be hospitalized; and that he then could never tolerate the restriction and frustration of hospitalisation. To some degree, he put himself down for not being able to handle frustration and for being so vulnerable to going crazy; but he largely made himself anxious about being balked, deprived, restricted and frustrated rather than about being inadequate and unloved. Even when he felt he needed others' approval, he only mildly berated himself for not getting it.

Mainly, he made himself angry at *them* for not giving him sufficient approval (as they *should*!) and for thereby depriving him of caring, consideration, and comfort.

One dialogue that I had with this client particularly helped me realise how comfort-oriented he was and how he demanded that people and things absolutely *must* cater to his 'needs'.

Client I felt like killing three noisy high-school kids who were on the bus with me coming here, and also was very angry at the bus driver for not making them stop their obnoxious noise.

Therapist What were you telling yourself about the boys?

Client They *should* know better than to annoy people like that on a public bus. Let them take a cab if they want to act like that!

Therapist Let's assume you are right and that they were acting very obnoxiously. Why *must* they act politely and nicely?

Client Because *I* wouldn't ever act that way. I would always be considerate of others, especially when we are all confined in a public bus.

Therapist I am sure you *would*. But why *must* they behave in a polite and considerate way that you and most others would?

Client Because they're bothering me and others so much.

Therapist That's why their *behaviour* is so annoying. But where is it written that they *have* to be less obnoxious?

Client Because I want them to be!

Therapist And you run the goddamned universe! Right? Whatever you *really* want *must* exist!

Client Yes, if it's right! And if I would act nicely to them.

Therapist You're telling yourself — and upsetting yourself — with two *non sequiturs* or conclusions that do not follow from your facts and premises. First, 'Because *I* would not act in that obnoxious way, *they* must not do so'. Secondly, 'Because they, the boys and the bus driver are indubitably wrong, they *must* not act in that wrong manner.' Now, do your conclusions, by which you needlessly upset yourself, really follow from your premises?

Client No, I can see that logically they don't. But I still *feel* that they do.

Therapist Because you still strongly *believe* that *you* absolutely *must* not be thwarted or annoyed by others, no matter what are *their* tendencies and behaviours.

Client Yes, I guess I do.

Therapist And where will your devout musturbatory beliefs get you?

Client Constantly angry and depressed. I see that. But I can't seem to change them.

Therapist You can't?

Client No, I've tried and only after a long time am I able to give up my anger and depression.

Therapist By doing *what*? How do you give it up?

Client Well, sometimes I figure out ways to avoid people like these boys or to get the bus driver to get them to stop.

Therapist Well, that's all right. That's being assertive and changing the A — the Activating Events — in the ABCs of RET. But suppose you can't figure out ways to change A. Then how do you get rid of your anger and depression?

Client I often don't. I just forget about these horribly annoying things after a while. Until the next one occurs. Then I get angry again.

Therapist *Get* or *make yourself* angry again?

Client Make myself, I guess. But it just seems that I *can't* control it.

Therapist *Can't*. No, not with your *philosophy*.

Client You mean that people *must* not act inconsiderately?

Therapist Yes, absolutely *must* not. With that philosophy, how could you possibly *not* upset yourself when people *do* act as they presumably must not?

Client I guess I have to keep upsetting myself — as I've done for many years.

Therapist Yes, until you change your *musts* to *preferences*. And how could you do that?

Client By working on them, I suppose.

Therapist Yes, and by giving up your assumption that you can't change them. Or that it's *too hard* to change them — which is an important second part of your low frustration tolerance. First, you tell yourself that others *must* not be the way they indubitably are and that it's *too* hard to tolerate their behaviour. Then you tell yourself that you *shouldn't* have to work so strongly and persistently at giving up your intolerance: once again, that it's *too hard* to do so.

Client But if I haven't succeeded so far, doesn't that *prove* it's too hard for me to change?

Therapist No — only that it is *quite* hard. But by telling yourself 'It's *too* hard' you make it even harder. That's the irony of low frustration tolerance. By saying that something is *too hard* to bear, you *increase* the hardness of bearing it and *add* to your frustration instead of minimising it.

Client Maybe you're right.

Therapist I probably am. But I still don't hear you saying — and determining to act on — 'Just because it's so hard to give up my low frustration tolerance, I'm going to work *much harder* to reduce it!'

Client Isn't it *too hard* for some people to change even when they know what's wrong with them and how to correct it?

Therapist Very unlikely. It's just about impossible for them to change *fast* or *completely*. It's interesting to see that you think that you can't change, when you clearly can. For don't forget that you trained yourself, consciously or unconsciously, not only to dislike pain and discomfort but to absolutely insist that it *must* not exist and to whine and swear when it does. If so, *you* can train yourself, however hard it may be, to change your *musts* and the whining that stems from them.

Client I can?

Therapist Of course you can! But let me ask: do you think that, by holding that you *can't* change and *have* to keep making yourself angry and depressed about the hassles of your life, you *therefore* are not downing yourself for not improving and giving up your anger and depression?

Client No. I honestly don't think so. The one thing I've learned from RET, which I didn't learn from my other years of therapy, is that I don't have to blame myself for my disturbances. So I think that I no longer do that. But I find it almost impossible to change and I often think I can't.

EMERGENT NEW DEVELOPMENTS — 2

Thinking about this case, and working hard to help the client overcome his low frustration tolerance, I realised that many clients may start with ego anxiety and ego depression. 'I *must* do better than I am doing and I am an inadequate person if I don't!' and they often get over that because they change their philosophy to, 'I'd *like* to do better than I am doing but it's not *necessary* and I can still accept myself if I don't'.

Although it is not easy for them to change their attitudes in this manner, it is also not too hard because they may not have to *work* at doing it and because they gain almost immediate satisfaction — lack of the pain of self-downing — when they do make this attitudinal change. Even clients with LFT may work at changing *ideas* more than they may work at changing actions and giving up immediate gratifications.

In terms of LFT, however, the problem of working to give it up is often much harder for several reasons:

(1) People with LFT have to, as it were, pull themselves up by their own bootstraps and to gain higher frustration tolerance while working against their low frustration tolerance. This is something like people with poor muscle coordination becoming adept at soccer. They can only do so by working harder than people with moderate or good muscle coordination would have to work. And since they have to work harder and longer than others, they are more likely to give up after a while and try some other activity (or inactivity) which requires less muscular training. Similarly, people with LFT normally have to work harder to discipline themselves than those without LFT and are therefore afflicted with catch-22!

(2) People with LFT not only have to change their ideas (which may require considerable cognitive effort) but also have to change their physical habits and energy levels to overcome the state of inertia that normally accompanies LFT. Thus, my client could without too much effort adopt a philosophy of self-acceptance; but since he was already habituated to angry outbursts (which get into one's viscera and lead to physical acts) and since he was already habituated to depressed feelings (which encourage one to be physically and muscularly inert) he would have to *push himself*, physically as well as mentally, to fight to overcome his LFT. And when one has LFT to begin with, *pushing* oneself physically and mentally is no easy thing to do!

(3) LFT, as in the case of the client, commonly leads to feelings of anger, which is a disruptive but none the less a *pleasurable* reaction, since when people are angry they feel superior to others at whom they are enraged. Depression, too, may have some pleasurable components, since it can include feelings of self-pity ('The horrible world is unfair to poor nice me!') and it encourages people to withdraw from life and its pain and hassles. Whereas self-downing, then, is almost completely painful, depression and, especially, anger have pleasurable components. People with LFT, who focus on the horror of pain and the need for immediate gratification, may well be willing to give up their self-denigration long before they surrender their anger and depression.

I saw that this was true in the case of my difficult client. Being bright and interested in getting rid of pain, he fairly easily gave up much — not all — of his self-denigration. But he still thought he *needed* respect and help from others, and though he recognised, after learning some RET, that his 'needs' made him angry and depressed, they also led to some gratification — and he would have to work hard, long and unpleasantly to give them up. Therefore, he only tried half-heartedly to do so; and like most people with LFT, he didn't want to work harder, convinced himself that he *couldn't* change, and *indulged* in his anger and depression.

This case — and several others somewhat like it — led me to see the great power of LFT or what I first called discomfort anxiety and then discomfort disturbance (Ellis, 1976, 1979, 1979–1980, 1985). I realised that the most difficult clients, those who resisted changing even though they previously wanted to do so, usually had *both* ego problems *and* LFT problems, and that the two importantly interacted with each other. Thus, my client originally *had to* perform well and *needed* others' approval and put himself down when he failed or got rejected, so he clearly had ego disturbance. But he also insisted on utter freedom from pain, discomfort and injustice, so he clearly had discomfort disturbance or LFT.

At first, his LFT made him resist working at therapy and made him dependent on a series of kindly therapists who *had* to help him instead of his working to help himself. When I refused to cater to him as they did and confronted him with his arrant self-downing and need for comfort, he began to work on the former and reduced much of his ego disturbance. But giving up his need for immediate gratification and his consequential LFT and anger was, for the reasons given above, much more difficult, and it took some time for him to reduce it.

When he finally did begin to catch his anger and depression soon after he produced these inappropriate feelings, he swiftly went to work to rid himself of them and to make himself feel only what RET calls appropriate negative feelings of frustration and disappointment when hassles occurred in his life. He then made a significant admission:

'I did what you were encouraging me to do for a long time and assumed that I *could* work on and eliminate my depressed and angry feelings. Three days ago I felt enraged and depressed when one of my women friends was to meet me for dinner and not only didn't show up but failed to call and cancel the appointment, as she had plenty of time to do. I got so angry that I was convinced that I *couldn't* work on my shoulds until some time had passed and could feel good enough to do so. As you would say, I decided to indulge in my anger for a while and to work on it later.'

'As I keep telling you that you *don't* have to do,' I said.

'Yes, I remembered, this time, what you have kept trying to show me, and I assumed that maybe I *could* work on my anger right away. So I did so.'

'What, exactly, did you do?'

'First, I told myself very strongly that Nancy *should* have acted inconsiderately to me because that's the way she frequently acted. That was part of her nature — along with the good parts that I really like about her.'

'Fine! Normally, you would have got around to telling yourself this much later — after you indulged in hours or even days of rage. But this time you forced yourself to make this self-statement much earlier.'

'Yes, I made it soon after I started to feel very angry at Nancy. And, as we have discussed, I *forcefully* told myself that Nancy *should* act as Nancy, and not act the way I demand that she act. That forceful self-statement helped a lot.'

'Right. That gave your RET a highly emotive quality — which is what we want you to have when you dispute your irrational Beliefs and state some rational ones. Good! And what action did you take to interrupt and remove your rage?'

'I called Nancy from the restaurant and unangrily asserted myself. I told her that I didn't at all like her not calling and telling me she was not coming and that the fact that she had, was really no good excuse.'

'So you really asserted yourself and didn't merely hold your displeasure in?'

'Yes, I took a chance that Nancy would not like my criticising her actions and risked her disapproval. But I also told her that I didn't think that she was a louse even though her behaviour was very lousy. And I said that I would never again agree to meet her outside a restaurant — where it happened to be cold and wet — but only inside wherever we planned to meet. And, because of my unangry tone of voice, she took what I said very well and, if anything, I think I helped strengthen instead of weaken our relationship.'

'Good! So you used thinking, emoting and action to work against your anger and your depression. And what happened?'

'To my surprise, I quickly felt only disappointed and sorry about Nancy's behaviour, but no longer angry and depressed. And to my even greater surprise, I enjoyed my meal alone, really enjoyed it, and had a very good evening by myself as well. Normally, I would have kept myself enraged for at least several hours, maybe for two or three days, and would not have been able to think of anything but Nancy's delinquency during that time, nor to enjoy myself at all. I now see that what you have been saying all along is true: I actually *indulge myself* in my feelings of anger and depression and I *convince myself* that I can't do otherwise. My low frustration tolerance really *is* bad. But I now see that I can reduce it — and am determined to do so!'

As a result of my work with and my thinking about this key case, I added significantly, I believe, to the theory and practice of RET by seeing the enormous importance of discomfort distress and low frustration tolerance in the creation — and especially the maintenance — of human disturbance. Other RET practitioners have tended to agree with me and follow my lead in this respect (Bard, 1980; Grieger and Boyd, 1980; Walen, DiGiuseppe and Wessler, 1980; Wessler and Wessler, 1980; Grieger and Grieger, 1982; Ellis and Bernard, 1983, 1985. Dryden, 1984). RET therapists still routinely look for ego disturbance in their clients and usually find it. But they also specifically look for discomfort disturbance, and find it, too. Humans usually upset themselves with two grandiose demands — for guaranteed competence and approval and the demand for immediate gratification and comfort. RET seeks out both these demands and shows clients how to reduce them significantly.

This is easy for me to say now, because I have actively sought for clients' low frustration tolerance as well as their self-downing for the last decade and have usually discovered that they do not merely have either/or but both/and. This is particularly true with what I call the DCs — the difficult customers. Most of them have arrant ego problems and berate themselves as humans for their main inadequate traits and performances. But they also 'know' how disturbed they are and — especially after they have had several RET sessions — they 'know' how they are disturbing themselves with profound *musts* and how they can change their irrational Beliefs. But they stubbornly refuse to work at giving up their irrationalities and at doing the homework assignments that would help them do so.

At the time I worked with this key case, however, I was much more concerned with the drama of clients' self-defamation and their overwhelming feelings of panic and depression that went along with this drama than I was concerned with their less dramatic LFT and the somewhat boring lack of change and progress that went with their resistance. So I myself had something of a conflict about letting go of their self-castigation and getting back to their inordinate demands on the universe. But once I realised that just about all human irrationalities that lead to emotional disturbance include clear-cut (explicit or implicit) musts, I was able to see that the demands leading to low frustration tolerance are just as grandiose and sacredising as those leading to self-immolation, and I lost my own resistance to seeing them as a most important aspect of neurosis and of borderline disorders.

IMPLICATIONS FOR OTHER THERAPISTS — 2

My impression, which is of course somewhat prejudiced, is that the two main points that I clarified in my own mind after working with my second key case are also of extreme importance in virtually all kinds of psychotherapy. Freud and the psychoanalysts are basically correct when they insist that disturbed people are much more motivated by their unconscious thoughts and feelings than they realise before coming to therapy. The Freudians are wrong, I believe, in insisting that unconscious ideation is frequently deeply hidden and has to be dredged up in the course of a long therapeutic process. I have noted for many years that our unconscious irrational Beliefs are almost always just below the level of consciousness, and exist in what Freud (1965) first called the preconscious (Ellis, 1962).

If I am correct about conscious and unconscious Beliefs including musts, shoulds, oughts, demands, and commands that lead to disturbance, then the discovery that these Beliefs can be categorised under three major headings is quite important, since it helps therapists to look for and very quickly find their clients' unconscious or explicit irrationalities. Thus, when one of my clients tells me that she became severely depressed when she did not study hard enough at school and consequently failed her exams, I immediately assume that she has one, two or three of the major irrational *musts*. I first assume that she is probably using an ego-oriented *must*, such as 'I absolutely *should* have studied for those exams, and am an incompetent idiot for not doing so!' I also assume that she may well have an LFT-oriented *must*, such as 'Those exams *ought not* have been that hard, and it's horribly unfair that they were!' I finally assume that she may also have a hostility-creating *must*, such as 'That damned professor *should have* given us a better exam, and he's a rotten person for not behaving as fairly as he *must!*'

Keeping in mind, the RET theory of unconditional *musts* that people easily and frequently lay on themsleves, I can quickly zero in on this client's basic irrational Beliefs, even if at first she is quite unconscious of them. For the theory of *mus*turbatory thinking leads me to infer what her inner commands probably are, and to ferret them out during the first few sessions of RET. Similarly, therapists from other schools can search for their clients' fundamental dogmatic demands and insistences, fairly easily find them, and help their clients consciously accept that they exist.

The RET theory of the importance of low frustration tolerance that I derived and expanded from this key case also can prove clinically helpful to many therapists. For they can look for *both* the self-downing elements (which probably exist in the great majority of their clients) *and* the fundamental allergicness to hard work and discomfort (which most clients also significantly seem to have), and can thereby help them surrender both these serious blocks to happy and effective living.

It seems odd that humans will severely berate themselves and consider themselves worthless slobs when they function poorly and are not approved by significant others, and that, at the same time, they will grandiosely demand that other people always act considerately towards them and that their environment be totally easy and enjoyable to live in. At first, these two demands seem rather contradictory: for the first one leads to self-abasement and the second to hubris and self-inflation. In RET, however, we now clearly recognise that self-downing is basically grandiose, because it stems from the godlike philosophy, '*I* must always do well and arrange for others invariably to approve of me — and I'm a *terrible person* when I don't do as well as I absolutely *must!*' But low frustration tolerance is also grandiose, because it stems from the godlike idea, 'Now that I am alive and kicking, people and the universe unconditionally *must* recognise my value and importance and give me exactly what I want whenever I want it!'

Virtually all therapists, I believe, if they clearly understand and use the RET insights about feelings of worthlessness and of grandiosity being different sides of the same *mus*turbatory coin, will be able to help themselves and their clients in a more efficient and effective way.

REFERENCES

Bard, J. (1980). *Rational-emotive therapy in practice.* Champaign, IL: Research Press

DiGiuseppe, R.A., Miller, N.J. and Trexler, L.D. (1979). A review of rational-emotive psychotherapy outcome studies. In A. Ellis and J.M. Whiteley (Eds), *Theoretical and empirical foundations of rational-emotive therapy.* Monterey, CA: Brooks/Cole

Dryden, W. (1984). *Rational-emotive therapy: fundamentals and innovations.* London: Croom Helm

Dryden, W. and Ellis, A. (1986). Rational-emotive therapy. In W. Dryden and W.L. Golden (Eds), *Cognitive-behavioural approaches to psychotherapy.* London: Harper & Row

Ellis, A. (1948). A study of trends in recent psychoanalytic publications. *American Imago, 5*(4), 3–13

Ellis, A. (1949). Towards the improvement of psychoanalytic research. *Psychoanalytic Review, 36,* 123–43

Ellis, A. (1950). An introduction to the principles of scientific psychoanalysis. *Genetic Psychology Monographs, 41,* 147–212

Ellis, A. (1953a). Is the vaginal orgasm a myth? In A.P. Pillay and A. Ellis (Eds), *Sex, society and the individual.* Bombay: International Journal of Sexology Press

Ellis, A. (1953b). Marriage counseling with couples indicating sexual incompatibility. *Marriage and Family Living, 15,* 53–9

Ellis, A. (1954a). *The American sexual tragedy.* New York: Twayne; rev. edn New York: Grove Press and Lyle Stuart, 1962

Ellis, A. (1954b). The psychology and physiology of sex. In A. Ellis (Ed.), *Sex life of the American woman and the Kinsey report.* New York: Greenberg

Ellis, A. (1954c). Psychosexual and marital proablems. In L.A. Pennington and I.A. Berg (Eds), *An Introduction to clinical psychology.* New York: Ronald

Ellis, A. (1955a). New approaches to psychotherapy techniques. *Journal of Clinical Psychology Monograph Supplement, 11,* 1–53

Ellis, A. (1955b). Psychotherapy techniques for use with psychotics. *American Journal of Psychotherapy, 9,* 452–76

Ellis, A. (1955c). Masturbation. *Journal of Social Therapy, 9,* 141–3

Ellis, A. (1956). The effectiveness of psychotherapy with individuals who have severe emotional problems. *Journal of Consulting Psychology, 20,* 191–5

Ellis, A. (1957a). *How to live with a neurotic.* New York: Crown. Revised paperback edn: North Hollywood, CA: Wilshire Books

Ellis, A. (1957b). Outcome of employing three techniques of psychotherapy. *Journal of Clinical Psychology, 13,* 344–50

Ellis, A. (1958). Rational psychotherapy. *Journal of General Psychology, 59,* 35–49. Reprinted New York: Institute for Rational-Emotive Therapy

Ellis, A. (1962). *Reason and emotion in psychotherapy.* Secaucus, NJ: Citadel Press

Ellis, A. (1968). *Personality data form.* New York: Institute for Rational-Emotive Therapy

Ellis, A. (1973). *Humanistic psychotherapy: the rational-emotive approach.* New York: McGraw-Hill
Ellis, A. (Speaker) (1976). *Conquering low frustration tolerance.* Cassette recording. New York: Institute for Rational-Emotive Therapy
Ellis, A. (1977). *Anger — how to live with and without it.* Secaucus, NJ: Citadel Press
Ellis, A. (1979). Rational-emotive therapy: research data that supports the clinical and personality hypotheses of RET and other modes of cognitive-behavior therapy. In A. Ellis and J.M. Whiteley (Eds), *Theoretical and empirical foundations for rational-emotive therapy.* Monterey, CA: Brooks/Cole
Ellis, A. (1979-1980). Discomfort anxiety: a new cognitive behavioral construct. *Rational Living, 14* (2), 3-8; *15* (1), 25-30
Ellis, A. (1981). The place of Immanuel Kant in cognitive therapy. *Rational Living, 16*(2), 13-16
Ellis, A. (1985). *Overcoming resistance: rational-emotive therapy with difficult clients.* New York: Springer
Ellis, A. and Becker, I. (1982). *A guide to personal happiness.* North Hollywood, CA: Wilshire Books
Ellis, A. and Bernard, M.E. (Eds) (1983). *Rational-emotive approaches to problems of childhood.* New York: Plenum
Ellis, A. and Bernard, M.E. (Eds) (1985). *Clinical applications of rational-emotive therapy.* New York: Plenum
Ellis, A. and Grieger, R. (Eds) (1977). *Handbook of rational-emotive therapy,* vol. 1. New York: Springer
Ellis, A. and Harper, R.A. (1975). *A new guide to rational living.* North Hollywood, CA: Wilshire Books
Ellis, A. and Whiteley, J.M. (Eds). (1979). *Theoretical and empirical foundations of rational-emotive therapy.* Monterey, CA: Brooks/Cole
Freud, S. (1965). *The standard edition of the complete psychological works of Sigmund Freud.* New York: Basic Books
Grieger, R. and Boyd, J. (1980). *Rational-emotive therapy: a skills-based approach.* New York: Van Nostrand Reinhold
Grieger, R. and Grieger, I.Z. (1982). *Cognition and emotional disturbance.* New York: Human Sciences Press
McGovern, T.E. and Silverman, M.S. (1984). A review of outcome studies of rational-emotive therapy from 1977 to 1982. *Journal of Rational-Emotive Therapy, 2*(1), 7-18
Walen, S.R., DiGiuseppe, R. and Wessler, R.L. (1980). *A practitioner's guide to rational-emotive therapy.* New York: Oxford
Wessler, R.A. and Wessler, R.L. (1980). *The principles and practice of rational-emotive therapy.* San Francisco: Jossey-Bass
Yates, A.J. (1970). *Theory and practice of behavior therapy.* New York: Wiley

9

Listening to Oneself: Cognitive Appraisal Therapy

Richard L. Wessler

PRIOR THEORY AND PRACTICE

The evolution of my thinking about psychological therapy into what I now term cognitive appraisal therapy began in the late 1950s with my earliest study of clinical psychology. My truly formative years as a therapist were spent at the Institute for Rational-Emotive Therapy in the 1970s, first as a post-doctoral fellow and later as a supervisor and director of training. Both the practice of Rational-Emotive Therapy (RET) and my efforts to train others led me first to expand the RET model, and eventually to move further and further away from it. This chapter outlines some of the experiences that shaped my thinking and practice. Although it discusses cases, there has not been any single key case in my experience; my thinking evolved gradually rather than changed cataclysmically. My dissatisfaction with RET grew; it did not occur suddenly.

My graduate degree was awarded by Washington University in St. Louis, where the PhD programme was basically experimental psychology plus an additional year of clinically relevant courses and a four-year traineeship with the Veterans Administration (VA) hospitals and outpatient clinics. Many of the clinical courses bore the apologetic title 'experimental', e.g. experimental psychopathology. Scepticism was encouraged and indeed modelled by the faculty. Probably a year-long course in the philosophy of science has had a more lasting impact on my thinking than any of the psychology courses.

A seminar in psychotherapy was introduced to the curriculum during my final year of courses. This was considered a very innovative and even daring move, for clinical psychoogy itself at that time emphasised diagnostic testing and intellectual evaluation.

It, like most of the clinical courses, was taught by part-time faculty who were full-time clinical psychologists. The seminar leadership rotated among several interested faculty, with the result that it had no particular theoretical orientation. It was vaguely psychoanalytic, but with a strong element of Rogerian non-directiveness as well. The seminar was supposed to integrate our practical externship experiences, but since the supervision I received from VA psychologists was more extensive and the seminar leadership so fragmented, I felt a sense neither of continuity nor of integration.

My dissertation was on the so-called experimenter expectancy effect, or the social psychology of the psychological experiment. The choice of topic reflected both my scepticism about psychology and my growing interest in other areas of the social and behavioural sciences. The fact that I could not obtain the 'robust' experimenter effects the research literature of the 1960s reported added to my disenchantment with psychology. I emerged from the PhD programme with a broad background in psychology and interests that diverged from those of my fellow graduate students. I had become more interested in the organisation and operation of hospitals than in the pathology of patients.

To pursue this interest, I accepted an assistant professorship at the other university in my home town, the Jesuit-controlled Saint Louis University in the department of sociology and anthropology, where I taught research methods, statistics, and organisation theory. After several years and believing that I knew enough about organisations to operate one myself, I moved to Parsons College in Iowa as an administrator and teacher of social psychology. My convictions about my administrative abilities were strengthened by a summer at Harvard University's Institute for Educational Management, but since my college had closed due to bankruptcy a week before I left for Harvard, I never had an opportunity to make my mark in this field.

By that time, I developed anew my interest in psychological therapy. For in the interim not only had America seen profound social changes in civil rights and war attitudes, but behaviour therapy had matured to offer a new technology of personal change. I had read Albert Ellis's (1962) *Reason and emotion in psychotherapy*, and recognised that his conception of therapy coincided with attitude theory. I was never much of a behaviourist (my graduate education did not require fidelity to any one system of psychology), but RET seemed to fit nicely into what I knew about social psychology.

Ellis pioneered the assumption (in therapy, not in social psychology) that cognition, affect and behaviour interact and are interdependent. Therefore, affect or feelings do not have an independent existence but are shaped and influenced by the content of one's thoughts, and can be brought under conscious control. I understood this to mean that the cognitive component of an attitude can influence the affective component, and the research literature on attitude formation and change generally supports this point. Further, attitudes towards oneself are crucial in understanding how one creates neurotic disturbance, especially feelings of anxiety and depression. The key to treating neurosis, then, is to change beliefs.

Ellis's ABC theory is a shorthand way of expressing these interrelations. (A = Activating event, B = Belief, C = Consequence.) An emotional and/or behavioural consequence is not directly due to the events, but to the beliefs one has about them and about oneself. In its broadest outline, this formulation is not unlike ones I knew from experimental psychology (Woodworth's paradigm that places organismic factors as mediators between stimuli and responses) and social psychology (Lewin's formula that behaviour is a function of both personal characteristics and perceived environmental events $[B = f(p,e)]$). Indeed, unless one strictly opposes thinking of mediating variables or believes that all action and affect stem from environmental cues or unconscious material, it is difficult to fault the general ABC model. However, Ellis's theory goes on to say considerably more than 'cognitive interpretations affect emotions and actions', and it is with these aspects of RET principles that I eventually fell into disagreement.

RET theory holds that there are two separate and distinct types of beliefs: rational and irrational. Irrational beliefs lead to 'inappropriate' and dysfunctional emoting and acting, and underlie neurosis. Rational beliefs also mediate emotions, but are 'appropriate' and do not lead to neurotic reactions. For example, irrational beliefs are said to lead to anxiety and depression, whereas rational beliefs lead to concern and sadness. This hypothesis is crucial to all else in RET, and there is no evidence to support it. I was willing to accept it as an untested assumption, provided the methods of treatment were effective.

I applied for a post-doctoral training fellowship at the RET Institute when the closing of Parsons College appeared certain, and in 1973, a month after leaving Harvard, moved to New York. Training at that time consisted of weekly two-hour sessions with Albert Ellis, followed by another two-hour session with one of the co-directors of training. Ellis's session was held in his office with himself in his recliner chair and twelve fellows seated in a square. The arrangement was exactly that of his nightly therapy groups. In fact, on alternate weeks he acted as our therapist as we were supposed to work on personal problems, especially as they affected our work as RET therapists. We fellows were not impressively open about our problems, and we seemed to care little about what was bothering anyone or how to help. We showed more interest in impressing Ellis with our ability to fire RET questions to the fellow with a problem; this had to be done in rapid succession, for another fellow awaited a chance to fill any split second of silence with his or her own question or interpretation. Ellis's contribution was to reveal the irrational beliefs we had missed and to urge the presenter to work hard at changing them.

On alternate weeks, Ellis supervised our work as his assistant in his nightly therapy groups. Our assignment was to take attendance, record homework assignments, and encourage silent members of the group to participate. We ourselves were instructed to speak at least as much as the most talkative group member, and to do so audibly and clearly. Immediately following 90 minutes with Ellis, group members attended an aftergroup session in which the fellow was in charge. There were little or no instructions as to how to conduct these sessions, except to imitate the therapeutic model Ellis furnished.

I had expected Ellis's group-therapy clients to know his well published ABC theory, which he demonstrated at his Friday night public workshops with volunteers from the audience. However, when I asked group members if they could express a problem in ABC format, they could not, and seemed rather surprised that ABC was anything other than the beginning of the alphabet. (I felt relieved, since I had worried upon entering the fellowship training program that I had not memorised Ellis's much-published list of irrational beliefs.) I soon realised why no one understood the ABCs of RET: Ellis seldom mentioned them in the group, and did not speak of irrational beliefs much, either; he more often labelled clients' thinking as 'nutty' or even 'autistic'.

Ellis's conduct of group therapy did not correspond to his own descriptions of his work. He claimed to use a variety of cognitive, emotive and behavioural methods. In fact, he almost never used any technique other than the cognitive disputing of irrational beliefs, and by his own admission not much of that: 'I do not devote the bulk of my therapeutic efforts to combating irrational beliefs' (Ellis, 1979, p. 98). The version of RET he demonstrated for professional and lay audiences routinely included rational-emotive imagery, behavioural homework assignments, and self-administration of rewards and punishments. Yet, as Becker and Rosenfeld (1976) showed in their analysis of Ellis's initial individual therapy sessions, he did not mention imagery or self-administration of rewards and punishments. His homework assignments consisted of a single statement, and he made no homework assignment in 25 per cent of the cases in the study. 'Ellis spent a large portion of the session utilizing didactic teaching of a general nature, which was supplemented by frequent concrete examples' (Becker and Rosenfeld, 1976, p. 875).

The confrontation of clients with their irrational beliefs and attempts to effect their surrender is called 'Disputing', thereby adding a D to the ABC model. (Disputing is supposed to lead to new 'Effects' or E.) Disputing takes the general form of asking 'where is the evidence or proof' that a belief is true. Three general types of so-called irrational beliefs are (1) an event is or would be 'awful'; (2) 'I can't stand it!' (i.e. anything that I find disagreeable); (3) any should- or must-statement, e.g. 'I must not make mistakes'. Thus, to help a person overcome anxiety or depression, Ellis recommends challenging his or her statements: 'Prove that it is awful!' 'Where is the evidence you cannot stand to be criticised for making mistakes?' 'Why must you not make mistakes?' Any reply would be neatly turned aside, by pointing out that it merely represents the person's opinion and not scientific 'facts'.

Other techniques that Ellis spoke of included rational-emotive imagery, written homework assignments, bibliotherapy, and behavioural homework, especially the 'shame-attacking' exercises he seemed to love so well. Shame-attacking exercises consist of one's acting foolishly or socially inappropriately in public, a sort of *in vivo* desensitisation. They were thought to be very important, since Ellis stated that 'all neurosis is due to shame or self-downing'. (However, at other times he claimed that all neurosis was due to dogmatic religiosity, to innate biological predispositions to think crookedly, and to whining). Above all, he said, it was the therapist's task to 'talk them out of their horseshit'.

There was even less mention of ABCs and irrational thinking during the supervision of individual cases by the co-directors of training, Bill Knaus and Ed Garcia. Though graduates of the fellowship training programme, neither made much use of the language or principal techniques of RET. Knaus was expert at what Ellis called 'empirical disputing' — as distinguished from philosophical disputing — and forcing abstract ideas into concrete reality.

Garcia was the 'warm-fuzzy' of RET, and looked and sounded like Leo Buscaglia long before the latter became famous in America. (Examples of their work at that time are available from the tape library of the Institute of Rational-Emotive Therapy.) In the second two-hour period each week, six fellows brought barely audible tapes of their individual therapy sessions and timidly played them for comments and suggestions.

During the first year of the two-year fellowship programme, I read nearly everything Ellis had written about therapy and listened to many of his tape-recorded sessions with clients. I attended frequent demonstrations and lectures on RET. Piecing it together, I had a clear idea about RET theory and techniques, and I was increasingly aware that they did not closely coincide with the practice of therapy at the RET Institute. With this background, I opened the door to my first client at the Institute and my development as a psychological therapist.

DESCRIPTION OF KEY CASES

The post-doctoral fellow

The man I call Ted was the first of several cases I found RET inadequate to help. Several such cases will be discussed in this section. In addition, my experiences as a trainer and supervisor of RET greatly influenced my thinking and search for better ways to get desirable therapeutic results. Several of these key incidents will be reported later.

Ted was a handsome, expensively dressed man about 29 years old. He was a commodities trader, and though he thought he was not successful enough, the amount of money he reported spending in tips each week was more than I got at that time from my fellowship stipend plus unemployment cheque. He showed no hesitation about self-disclosure. His was a sexual problem, he said. Specifically, he was impotent with his wife, whom he did not find arousing. He knew that Albert Ellis was a famous sex therapist, but decided against seeing him because the clinic rates were so much cheaper. His stated goal was to have sex with his wife.

For the next several sessions we discussed every aspect of his situation I could think of and that was recommended to me in supervision. I tried very hard to catch him at 'awfulising', or 'musturbating' (Ellis's term for speaking and presumably believing must-statements), or psychically scratching his 'I-can't-stand-it-itis'. I was able to spot some verbal irrationalities and rephrase them in ABC terms. But, he thought the ABCs were kid's stuff, and when I challenged him to cite evidence in support of his beliefs, he denied that they were beliefs — 'Of course, I don't think I *must* have sex with my wife' — or he counterattacked by saying that 'awful' did *not* mean 'more than 100 percent bad', as I parroted Ellis's definition. Persist I did, but I could not 'talk him out of his horseshit'.

Despite his lack of progress, we developed a good relationship. He liked the fact that I was male and older than him, and I liked the fact that he was like the type of businessman I had become accustomed to working with while I was a college administrator. So, we plodded on. I hypothesised performance anxiety, and speculated that he said to himself, 'I must have an erection; it's awful if I don't', when his wife wanted sex. 'No', he replied, 'I'm usually asleep and she can't wake me up'. The self-downing hypothesis was also rejected — 'What do you mean, "I think I'm a shit because I don't get an erection with my wife"!'

Slowly, as I listened to him, a picture of the problem began to emerge. His wife, whom he described as a 'cute little thing', had begun to press him to start a family. He, on the other hand, was terrified of the responsibility and of the financial strain he anticipated. He was angry with her for wanting children and for stirring his doubts about his ability to preserve prosperity. His anger came out as indifference, which he acknowledged, but I could not get him to accept the irrational beliefs that RET theory said created anger. He denied mentally damning her for raising the issue. Nor did I succeed in getting him to anti-awfulise about responsibility and threats to family finances. Either he was a DC (difficult customer in Ellis jargon) or I was a poor RET therapist. Since I knew that I was doing what I was taught and had my RET interventions accepted in supervision, I decided he was a DC. Somewhat guiltily, I decided to try another way to help him that seemed within the broad scope of 'comprehensive' RET.

My decision was aided by the client's decision to send his wife to see me because she had questions to ask about him. I agreed to see her, and told her that I did not think we were making much progress, and that her husband seemed very determined not to have children. She thanked me for confirming her judgement and left to file for divorce. Ted was very relieved. He thanked me for speaking with his wife.

Ted soon moved from the marital apartment in the suburbs to a bachelor pad in the city and a new set of problems. He was now ready to become a swinging single. He had the money, good looks, wardrobe and time, but lacked the confidence for his new role. Fresh from hearing about the merits of behaviour therapy from a guest speaker during one of Ellis's rare absences from supervision, I devised a step-by-step plan for Ted to conquer an East-side singles' bar. Into the front door and out again with an attractive woman on his arm was the behavioural goal he sought and found. He felt successful and grateful; I felt successful and guilty: he had achieved success without once discriminating or disputing an irrational belief. Sexual performance proved not to be a problem for him as he had partner after partner in those days before the reaffirmation of traditional sexual mores.

I continued to do non-RET therapy with him for several months. From time to time, I tried authentic RET with the same result: Ted began yawning. Satisfied, he asked to terminate therapy in the spring. Concerned that I had left some stone unturned, I asked that he see Ellis for at least one session. He did. Ellis declared him to be a DC borderline with whom one must do exceptionally vigorous disputing. I saw Ted a few times the next year when he had formed a relationship that was serious enough for him to contemplate marriage. Ellis had advised him to marry; I advised against it because of doubts Ted expressed. Ted liked my advice better than Ellis's and took it.

I could dismiss Ted's case as beginner's bad luck except that I remember the next client who did not respond as the books and demonstrations of RET said he would. He was a homosexual man whose lover had recently broken off the relationship. He had the normal sad reactions that follow the unwanted end to a close relationship. Today, I would tell him so; eventually, I did that, but first I tried to do RET. I used the standard 'anti-awfulising' interventions and spoke passionately of 'no shoulds exist in the universe': 'Why must you have a close relationship'? I hypothesised (i.e. made up in the absence of facts) that he believed that he could not stand it to be without a relationship. I pointed out that he was putting himself down for losing his relationship, and saying that he would never get another.

He became angry with my interpretations, and so I tried to help him with his anger problem: 'Why must you be understood by your therapist?' Though a rather passive person, he replied that he was paying for my helpful services, and despite being a low-fee clinic client, he expected more than he was getting. I decided to work on his admitted feelings of failure at losing the relationship, to avoid fine distinctions between (neurotically) needing a relationship and (rationally) wanting one, and to help him seek another lover.

I did not abandon an RET approach altogether, and resolved to employ Rational-Emotive Imagery or REI. REI begins by asking the client to picture the scene (A) and to feel the emotion (C) he or she wishes to diminish. Then, the client is supposed to report his or her thoughts, which should be irrational beliefs (iBs), according to RET theory. Next, the client is asked to change the emotion to a more 'appropriate' version of it, and to report the accompanying thoughts (rBs).

My client was very good at imagery in general, but could not do REI. He said that he knew what emotion he was supposed to feel, but could not actually experience it when directed to. That evening, I used REI with three other clients, none of whom could experience what they were supposed to. I tried REI again from time to time, but with no better results. Later, I tried Maxie Maultsby's (1977) version of REI, which is a sort of positive mental rehearsal of actions. I also used Arnold Lazarus's (1981) time projection imagery in which the client pictures him/herself weeks, months, years after a dreaded event, and explores his coping strategies. I incorporated image-provoking language into my sessions and used imagery in the form of metaphors. All of these worked well at times, but I could never use Ellis's REI to achieve the results claimed for it.

The third memorable case during training was that of Charles, a young philosophy student with a self-diagnosed 'identity crisis'. Charles seemed ideal for the philosophical disputing Ellis advocated, and soon was as effective at disputing as I was; the trouble was, he disputed my disputing. As with Ted, the relationship seemed strong and congenial, and I looked forward to his weekly visits even though I expected to finish second in the debate. When I would ask a highly recommended RET disputation, 'Charles, where is it written that you *should* . . . ?', he had several citations. What actually helped Charles was practical problem solving, for as intellectually well-equipped as he was, he had not learned to cope with everyday life; he was not 'street smart'. I did not feel guilty about giving such practical advice inasmuch as I heard Ellis doing the same in his therapy group each week, but still I knew that practical solutions were not 'elegant' philosophic solutions, and were therefore inferior to authentic RET.

By the end of the two-year fellowship programme, I was asked to join the Institute as a supervisor. Having served as Editor of *Rational Living* (now called the *Journal of Rational-Emotive Therapy*) since early 1974, I became well-acquainted with the RET literature and learned to discriminate authentic RET from an incorrect version. I had developed a model course in RET for undergraduates and understood the basics of RET as well as anyone.

I had become chair of the Department of Psychology at Pace University the year before and was now a permanent if reluctant resident of the New York area, and so I accepted the invitation. I began to teach others to do RET.

The RET supervisor

As a new supervisor, I wanted to teach authentic RET, for I subscribed to its theoretical statements and believed that postdoctoral fellows came to the Institute for the real thing. Further, I believed that we should teach RET, not general psychotherapy or clinical psychology. A pure version of RET should be taught and studied, especially if one were to conduct psychotherapy research. Of course, my own practice of RET was not in the classic mould, nor were the cases presented for supervision more suitable for the classic ABCD approach than mine were. Most of the questions raised in supervision were about clinical assessment and the management of cases and of sessions, not about what the irrational beliefs were or how to dispute them.

My own work with clients continued to develop and diverge from classic RET. I could do RET expertly and my work seemed to help clients. However, I used my RET expertise in training situations and infrequently in actual sessions with clients. I explained this discrepancy to RET-sophisticated clients as a simple matter of not sounding like Albert Ellis — a difference in style.

I worked for many months with a woman I call Bonnie, who had read *A new guide to rational living* (Ellis and Harper, 1975) and sought an RET therapist because the book appealed to her. Her problems centred on feelings of inadequacy and clearly fitted RET assumptions about disturbance. However, the intellectual disputing of her irrational beliefs seemed to get nowhere, except that she criticised herself even more for not improving. Her social anxiety and depression remained unaffected for very long by conventional RET interventions. Although she functioned well at her job, she reported having trouble in her marriage and in relating to friends. Risk-taking and time-projection imagery helped with her shyness, and she maintained gains in this area.

After a time, she began to reveal serious dissatisfactions with her marriage. Her husband was a few years younger than Bonnie, had not yet settled into a career, and at the age of 27 thought it too soon to father children. Bonnie was successful but faced the choice of pursuing her career or starting a family. Past 30, she believed that time was running out for her to have children, and criticised herself for marrying a younger man. In subsequent sessions she recognised that she chose him because he showed interest in her, and, more importantly, because she felt that she could not attract and marry a more suitable husband.

Bonnie's self-image can be summarised as 'I am so unattractive and unappealing to men that I should settle for whatever I can get'. This thought was associated with depressive affect, social anxiety resulting in withdrawal from situations wherein she might be unfavourably compared with other women, and fear that her husband would lose interest in her. At the same time, she criticised him for marrying her, thinking that he must not be much good because he settled for her.

The recognition of her implicit self-image was made more difficult by her knowledge of RET. Attempts at self-examination to discover cognitions and irrational beliefs were made more difficult by what she knew she should find. Such phrases as 'I know I think I'm a shit' and 'I must be putting myself down', were easy textbook substitutes for her own thoughts. She was self-critical and self-blaming without knowing what she was criticising and blaming herself for.

Conventional RET would focus on Bonnie's irrational beliefs or 'musturbation'. It would assume that she thought that she must be attractive to men, that she must marry well, and must be happy and have children. Typical interventions might be to ask rhetorically, 'Why *must* you be attractive to men?' 'Why *must* you marry well?' 'Why *must* you have children?' These questions invite clients to examine their beliefs by citing evidence to support them. It is not possible to cite such evidence, because it is assumed in RET that no evidence can be assembled to support absolutistic statements of what must be.

No evidence can be cited, but not due to the absolutistic nature of the statements. Rather, these are statements of personal and social values and of moral principles, and therefore fall outside the realm of scientific justification. There cannot be scientific evidence to support or refute statements of moral principles and social values. Further, principles and values are not acquired by sifting through scientific evidence. They are acquired through direct experience, modelling, absorbing explicit and implicit teachings of parents and other agents that socialise the individual in order to make him or her an acceptable member of the community.

RET technique is based on the assumption that people will surrender their irrational beliefs when they come to believe and accept the evidence. And, at times, they do. However, since their beliefs are not usually rooted in logic or in scientifically acceptable evidence, there is no reason to expect people to change their minds when they cannot find such evidence. They are more likely simply to become confused.

So it was with Bonnie. She knew that her irrational must-statements were not supported by objective evidence and that she therefore should not criticise and blame herself. None the less, she continued to do so and began to criticise and blame herself for not stopping, 'I must not be trying hard enough.' I agreed, because I followed at that time another RET principle: that people are babies who abhor the discomfort and inconvenience of the effort required for change. So I urged her to try harder. Increased effort only resulted in her feeling more guilty and ashamed of a lack of progress.

Because Bonnie had sought a rational-emotive therapist, I felt obliged to fulfil her expectations. At the same time, I tried to work on her self-image and implement my growing conviction that actions, not words, were needed to effect change. I took a broader cognitive-behavioural approach, emphasising the correcting of misconceptions and the assigning of behavioural homework, which seemed to work very well. I justified my strategy with Ellis's claim that comprehensive RET was synonymous with cognitive-behaviour therapy, a claim I would repeat with increasing frequency in RET training sessions for professionals.

The director of training

I began to do a great deal of training after the Institute's co-directors of training resigned and I assumed their responsibilities. The five-day primary-level intensive training programme had been created to introduce mental health professionals to RET by giving them supervised practice using its concepts and techniques on each other. The format of the programme challenged the training faculty to present something about RET that Albert Ellis had not already covered during the first day. I felt further challenged to teach the principles of RET as clearly as I could, for as a supervisor during these practicum programmes, I realised that most errors were made because participants did not understand how to identify an irrational belief nor what role it had in the theoretical account of disturbance.

I also realised how easy it is to teach RET concepts and techniques: the theory is simple and sessions can be structured by following the ABCD model. Anyone with basic interviewing skills can quickly learn to ask for activating experiences, emotional and behavioural consequences, and what one is telling oneself. The first stated or implied must-statement can be labelled an irrational belief, and the unanswerable 'where's the evidence?' questions posed. Since RET is purported to be educational and didactic, lessons about 'B, not A, causes C' can be readily given.

Unfortunately, this approach requires little actual experience in counselling or psychotherapy, no knowledge of psychopathology, no diagnostic acumen, and no familiarity with medication or with the literature of biological psychiatry. Perhaps this is why Ellis stated that he did not use it very much. This classic RET approach undoubtedly works with a few people, but there is nothing in RET theory that helps one identify who these people are. On the contrary, the claim is made that when classic RET does not work, what Ellis called inelegant or comprehensive RET will. But, RET is very easy to teach, so easy that, as mentioned above, the challenge is what to teach after the basic model has been presented.

My answer to this challenge was to take seriously the proposal that comprehensive RET was synonymous with cognitive-behaviour therapy. Since I was never a dedicated behaviourist or behaviour therapist, I turned to Beck's (1976) *Cognitive therapy and the emotional disorders* and Raimy's (1975) *Misunderstandings of the self*, both then newly published. I drew heavily on these thoughtful accounts for the content of my presentations, and showed that they were useful for 'inelegant' therapeutic solutions to clients' problems, as distinct from the 'elegant' solutions of real RET. 'Inelegant' solutions are accompanied by improving one's cognitive representations of reality, such as are found in Maultsby's Rational Behaviour Training (RBT). 'You can't be a "phoney" because the only phoney people that exist are department store mannequins'. 'Elegant' solutions involve philosophic changes, and are therefore changes in appraisal or evaluation: 'It would be better if I were not a "phoney" but there is no evidence that I *must* not be a "phoney"!'

Participants in RET professional training workshops had difficulty grasping the distinction between elegant and inelegant solutions, and therefore I made it a special feature of my presentations to clarify this point. Using a personal example, I showed that inelegant solutions concern one's belief that an event has happened or will happen — a truth about reality — and elegant solutions concern the appraisal of the event regardless of its actual occurrence. However, unless one believes a truth about reality, it is unlikely that one would bother to make the appraisal. In my example, I recalled flying in a jumbo jet when an announcement was made that the plane was disabled and would return whence it came to make an emergency landing. The sharp physical sensations of anxiety that followed were due to my accepting that (1) it was true that the situation was life-threatening, and (2) it was 'awful' to be in a life-threatening situation. I accepted the causal connection between appraisal and emotion that was proposed in the work of Magda Arnold (1960), R.S. Lazarus (Lazarus and Folkman, 1984), Robert Plutchik (1980), and others.

I worked out what I later called 'mini-models' of anger, anxiety and depression. These included both the empirical proposition and the appraisal in the process of creating an emotional response. For example, anger involves both the cognition that someone has trespassed against one's rules (an idea borrowed from Beck) and the appraisal that the offender is very bad (damnable) for trespassing (the RET version of anger). This implies that one can overcome anger by (1) changing one's rules, (2) getting additional information to make certain that a trespass has occurred, or (3) forgiving the trespasser.

In another part of the lesson, I taught Ellis's account of how irrational appraisals derive from irrational (by definition) must-statements. For example, the premiss that 'I must not have my rules violated' would lead, according to RET theory, to the illogical conclusions that (1) 'It is "awful" that my rule was violated', (2) 'You are to blame and be damned for violating my rule', and (3) 'I can't stand it that my rule was violated!' This bit of psycho-logic nicely fitted my professorial notions of common sense, and I spoke of it with conviction and enthusiasm.

I hypothesised that the degree of anger correlated with the extent of damnation or lack of forgiveness. This hypothesis departs from Ellis's RET in that he did not account for degree of emotion. Instead, he proposed that rational beliefs lead to 'appropriate' emotional consequences, whereas irrational beliefs lead to 'inappropriate' emotions. His terms are hard to define, especially since both rational and appropriate are defined as adaptive, self-promoting, and goal-promoting. Thus, a rational belief might lead to 'appropriate' annoyance or irritation, and an irrational belief would lead to 'inappropriate' anger and rage. By ridding oneself of the irrational belief, one is left with the rational belief and with mere annoyance or irritation; these feelings are seen as adaptive because they might in turn motivate one to take some corrective actions. The fact that my therapeutic experience did not exactly coincide with what I taught I rationalised by saying to myself that I was doing 'comprehensive' RET.

The Dutch psychologist

My thinking was greatly influenced by an association with René Diekstra of Rijksuniversiteit te Leiden and founder of the Instituut voor Rationale Therapie in The Netherlands. Our contacts resulted first in my attempting to expand RET theory and practice, and later, due to a clearer understanding of RET, to abandon its central assumptions and seek a more integrated cognitive-behaviour therapy.

Diekstra proposed, as part of an international training scheme, that an official manual of RET be created, with chapters to be written by specialists in their fields, and the whole volume revised frequently to reflect recent advances. This proposal never became reality, but I was nominated as the American editor of the manual due to my involvement in training and my editorship of *Rational Living*, the Institute's journal. Somehow the proposal resulted in my becoming third author of an RET training manual already begun by Susan Walen and Ray DiGiuseppe (Walen, DiGiuseppe and Wessler, 1980). At that time there were a few other books on how to do RET written for professionals, and my addition to the writing team was supposed to confer a stamp of authenticity on the effort. I tried to get Walen and DiGiuseppe to adopt some of my ideas about an expanded RET, but they preferred to stay with the orthodox version rather than break new ground. My chapter on group therapy which contained some of my newer thoughts was dropped from the final manuscript, and only a few paragraphs I wrote about the philosophy of RET remained in the first chapter. Otherwise, my contributions to the book were that of editor and conferer of authenticity.

I had already expanded the basics of RET by showing that there were cognitive aspects of the 'A' of the ABC model. The actual activating event was not so influential in producing emotional and behavioural consequences as one's attending to and believing that the event had occurred or would occur in a particular way. There were, I contended, cognitive aspects of 'A', and 'B' should represent rational and irrational beliefs. 'B' should represent must-statements and their derivatives of self- and other evaluations. In this expansion of the ABC model, 'A' was similar to the knowledge or cognitive component of an attitude, 'B' was the affective or evaluative component, and 'C' (the behavioural consequences) was the action component. The revised ABCs nicely fit into attitude theory, and were not simply a case of cognition squeezed into a behavioural S-R model.

Diekstra, like Maultsby, had a different version of ABC. All cognitive material was represented by 'B' and could be discovered by asking 'What are you telling yourself?' questions. Ellis had, in 1977, confronted Maultsby about his failure to go beyond 'empirical' solutions and to offer clients 'elegant' solutions that involved philosophic change rather than a different symbolic mental representation of the environment. A result of the confrontation was that Maultsby no longer claimed that his Rational Behaviour Training was synonymous with RET. In the summer of 1979, I found myself in Switzerland with Diekstra, who was teaching a very different version of RET than I taught in my training programmes. I did not disagree with the other version, but I knew that participants found it confusing that 'B' stood for all cognitions when Diekstra spoke, and for evaluative cognitions only when I spoke. I suddenly got the thought that the solution was to eliminate the ABCs.

It was only a short step from my Beck-Ellis hybrid version of ABC to dropping the alphabetic designations altogether. The model I devised incorporated another acquisition from the didactic presentations of Diekstra: the structural differential of General Semantics. I had had a causal understanding of General Semantics from my college days and got reintroduced to it by Renato Tagiuri during my short stint at the Harvard Business School. I did not take it very seriously until Albert Ellis began advocating it as therapeutic. In the mid-1970s, he wrote several books without using any form of the verb 'to be', which is forbidden in General Semantics because it symbolises essence rather than process. Ellis clearly opposed the 'is of identity' but did not mention much else about General Semantics.

The structural differential, simply stated, is a hierarchy consisting of (1) reality in process, (2) perception of reality, (3) symbolic descriptions of perceptions, (4) inferences about one's descriptions, (5) evaluations of one's inferences. Difficulties arise when one level of the hierarchy is confused with another, for example, when one's inferences are mistaken for reality. Diekstra's and Maultsby's therapeutic strategies were to reduce inferences and evaluations to more accurate descriptions of reality, descriptions that could be checked by answering the question, 'Where is the evidence that what I am telling myself is true?'

I used their hierarchy to formulate an expanded version of RET that did not mention ABC. In the original version presented in Switzerland and a week later in England, there were six steps: stimulus, description, inference, evaluation, emotional response, and behavioural response. Descriptions and inferences could be subjected to the test of accuracy, and evaluations to the test of utility. Although I thought I was expanding basic RET concepts and integrating two versions of rational psychotherapy, I realised that the six-step model did not require the use of such terms as 'rational' and 'irrational', and that these could be dispensed with. Indeed, they were confusing, because Ellis said they meant something different than did Maultsby, Diekstra and Tosi (1974), and Grieger and Boyd (1980).

In place of rational and irrational beliefs, I began to develop the notion of Personal Rules of Living, and first used the phrase in a paper read at the 1979 American Psychological Association meeting. I do not recall when I first used the phrase with clients, but I do recall the context. I was impressed that some people have a list of requirements to live up to in order to regard themselves well. Carl Rogers had years earlier spoken of 'conditions of worth', and I sought an RET way of saying something similar. I pointed out to certain clients that their lists contained numerous rules, but that the last rule at the bottom of the list was 'I must live up to all of the above rules, and I am not much of a person if I do not.' If they would change the last rule and its self-denigrating conclusion, they could keep all the others; in fact, they could retain the rule if they would separate it from negative conclusions about themselves. Rules should be guides for living, and not conditions for self-acceptance. I found that clients liked the Personal Rules of Living notion better than the rational-irrational belief dichotomy, understood it and could identify their rules more readily than their beliefs. Further, clients said they felt put down when their thoughts were labelled irrational, and frequently put themselves down for thinking irrational thoughts or not surrendering them when urged to do so. I later expanded the notion of Personal Rules of Living in ways described below, and they continue to be an integral part of Cognitive Appraisal Therapy.

These ideas eventually appeared in *The principles and practice of rational-emotive therapy* (Wessler and Wessler, 1980), a how-to-do RET book project that was proposed by Ruth Wessler. Though we had divorced in 1976, Ruth and I had remained friends, and I eagerly agreed to co-author a book with her. In it, we would propose our own version of RET which would not be radically different from orthodox RET, but would include some of the concepts we had added from our knowledge of academic psychology. In particular we agreed on the exclusion of lists of irrational beliefs (something I could not keep out of the Walen-DiGiuseppe book) and the inclusion of the expansion of the ABCs.

Ruth had been thinking of her own version of an expanded model, and our thinking corresponded closely. We adopted the term 'emotional episode' as a title for the model, and included attention to stimulus as part of the process and the feedback of reinforcing consequences to suggest a continuous process rather than a strictly linear model. There were now eight steps arranged in a more-or-less sequential fashion: stimulus, awareness, description, inference, evaluation, emotional response, behavioural response, and reinforcement. This model provided a framework for the integration of the main cognitive-behavioural approaches to psychotherapy as well as a conceptual bridge between cognition, emotion and behaviour. For example, anxiety might be treated by changing the situation (stimulus), distraction (awareness), greater symbolic accuracy in thinking about the situation (description), revising one's forecasts about what might happen (inference), 'de-awfulising' about the situation (evaluation), tension reduction by medication or relaxation (emotional response), counterphobic action (behavioural response), or altering environmental contingencies (reinforcement).

It can be seen that within the diversity of cognitive-behavioural therapy, certain approaches emphasise certain steps of the eight-step model of the emotional episode. Ellis's RET, in its most distinctive form, emphasises the evaluation step. Beck's cognitive therapy does also but, like Maultsby's RBT, focuses on inferences as well. A problem-solving or skills-oriented approach mainly works at the behavioural response step, as does a self-instructional approach like that of Meichenbaum. The eight-step model shows that there are many places for therapeutic intervention, and suggests that multiple interventions might be better than singling out one step on which to concentrate. By the end of 1980, Ruth and I had completed the manuscript for our book.

I had received an invitation from René Diekstra to spend my sabbatical leave at the Rijksuniversiteit te Leiden as guest professor. In 1981, I participated in the making of what was intended as the definitive RET film that would counteract the effects of the notorious and widely seen (by everyone but me, it seemed) 'Gloria' film. I packed off in August for a year in Europe. Except physically, I never returned.

The turning point of no return occurred in Leiden while lecturing graduate students in clinical psychology. I gave a series of lectures on the cognitive-behavioural approaches to therapy. In order to tie them together, I decided to explain their theoretical accounts of anxiety and show how the therapeutic interventions aimed at theoretically defined targets. I took my lectures very seriously, much more than the students did, for they were more concerned with political causes than with techniques of therapy, more interested in theory than in practice.

I had scheduled the two lectures on RET for the end of the series, for I was after all an authority on the subject and I wanted to save the best for last. I was well into the familiar account of anxiety, speaking slowly so as to be clearly understood. Dutch students speak excellent English, and understand it even better, but none the less seemed to appreciate my slow and careful rendering of ideas. The relatively slow pace of my sentences gave me time to listen to myself talking and to think about what I was saying.

As I spoke the words, anxiety comes from 'musts', I suddenly had a thought I had never before been aware of, despite having made the same basic presentation on numerous other occasions. I thought to myself, this makes no sense! How can 'musts' invariably lead to anxiety? Are there not other causes, maybe even more significant ones? I strongly hoped that no one would ask me to defend the position I had just stated, for I simply did not understand how I could. Worse, I hoped that no one would ask me for evidence to support the claim, for I knew that no study had ever showed what RET hypothesised to be the relationship between cognitive content and emotional response. Fortunately for my pride, no one asked anything. I bicycled home to my seventeenth-century canal house next to the Pieterskirk, where the Pilgrims worshipped before sailing the ship *Mayflower* to the New World; I felt emotionally shaken by the experience and preoccupied by the doubts it raised.

EMERGENT NEW DEVELOPMENTS

I continued to conduct training workshops in Europe, but I felt increasingly uneasy about the role of must-statements in emotional disturbance. My intent was to ease my discomfort by expanding RET, and to do so I had to find a new understanding of must-statements. This task was made all the more difficult by my not using them in my own work. I found myself using Personal Rules of Living to the exclusion of irrational beliefs, and thus did not have to deal with the thorny issue of the supremacy of the musts. At the

University of Münster, near the town great-grandfather Wessler left over a hundred years ago to come to America, I managed to confuse Professor Lily Kemmler, who had invited me, and everybody else by not mentioning irrational beliefs and speaking only of Personal Rules of Living, but calling what I did RET.

Decisions

By then I had also expanded the emotional episode to include another type of cognition that earlier accounts, and certainly the basic ABCs, did not and could not include (Wessler, 1982). What Ruth and I had left out of the eight-step model was human decisions. In so doing, we had perpetuated a fundamentally mechanistic model of human functioning that, ironically, left no provision for change, therapeutic or otherwise. If human emoting and acting were simply a matter of putting together certain cognitive ingredients, then humans indeed were mere cognitive-behavioural robots rather than thinking, decision-making human beings. My inspiration for this modification was the foremost American expert in the psychology of decision-making, Irving Janis.

Janis was also on sabbatical leave during the 1981–1982 academic year, at The Netherlands Institute for Advanced Study. We met twice and discussed counselling at length. His research showed the importance of the therapeutic relationship, and he expressed doubts that the RET idea of neutral self-regard could be attained or even approximated by real human beings. Persons fabricated in the minds of therapists might be so self-accepting as to think of themselves as neither positive nor negative. He agreed that non-rational factors play an important part in many decisions, and that people in counselling can come to trust their counsellors to the point of accepting what they say without consideration for their logic or evidence.

Alternative conceptions

In the spring of 1982, I moved to England. I presented programmes on RET at several universities and received favourable reactions except for the portion I devoted to classical RET. My own views were better accepted than those of Albert Ellis. I saw the RET film that had been made the previous summer, and heard myself give a version of RET that I no longer fully endorsed. Then I saw the infamous 'Gloria' film for the first time and was astounded. It was so at variance with what I knew and taught about RET that I resolved to publish a version of RET in which I could clarify my differences with Ellis's theory, philosophy, and methods of treatment.

I began work on a paper for the European Behaviour Therapy Congress in September. Originally, René Diekstra and I were to present a jointly written paper. However, we could not agree on its content, except that Goldfried's (1980) seeking of commonalities among the various therapies was a significant move in the right direction. In the end, Diekstra did not attend the conference, and I presented a paper that made it impossible to return to the fold of orthodox RET.

The paper was titled 'Alternative conceptions of RET: toward a philosophically neutral psychotherapy' (Wessler, 1984a). With a growing conviction that Ellis's thinking had been inspired less by the scientific method he espoused and more by his anti-religious views, I raised the question of the supremacy of the musts. Do musts always lead to disturbance? Does the belief that there are no musts in the universe dispel neurosis? And finally, could RET be expanded to the point that one need not think like Albert Ellis? The paper offered an alternative view of RET, one that differed from Ellis's philosophical and theoretical assumptions, and from his techniques of therapy. In the conclusion of the paper, I stated that I was prepared to accept the judgement that I no longer did RET. The audience in Rome did not react, but thousands of miles away in New York, Albert Ellis did.

His reaction had been prompted by a visit from our mutual friend and colleague, Windy Dryden, with whom I sought refuge after my stay in Leiden. Could a person with these views function as director of training? Of course, the answer was no, but the discussion should have taken place between Ellis and me, for even then my aim was to expand RET, not to do away with it. I sought an integration of the cognitive-behavioural approaches to psychotherapy, not to start yet another form of it.

Upon my return from sabbatical leave, Ellis and I discussed our differences, and only we truly understood them. We knew we could not work together again, that our views had diverged beyond the point of reconciliation. Though others in RET said it was just a misunderstanding and could easily be rectified, Ellis and I knew differently. He told me then that no one, except he himself, knew more about RET than I. He said that what I was doing was cognitive-behavioural therapy but not RET. I knew this was true, and I knew it was the reason I had to move on. He said in parting that if anyone would ever revise RET theory it would be he himself.

Cognitive appraisal therapy

My psychological departure from RET was easier than my reputational departure. Having co-authored two well selling books and written several journal articles and chapters on RET for edited books, some of which had yet to be published, I was still closely identified with RET. I fulfilled commitments for training programmes, but was careful to point out differences between Ellis's RET and other parts of my presentation. It proved especially confusing for groups I had previously worked with under the RET banner. I knew that I advocated cognitive therapy, and continue to think that my work comes under that generic label. However, the term 'cognitive therapy' is closely identified with A.T. Beck, whose work I very much respect and admire, and I did not want to misrepresent myself as Beckian. Lazarus's Multimodal Therapy has the spirit of psychotherapy integration I endorse, and I have lectured and conducted workshops on the Multimodal approach to assessment and treatment planning.

I searched for a new phrase to identify my approach to cognitive-behaviour therapy, and finally settled on Cognitive Appraisal Therapy (CAT). I have admired the work of Richard Lazarus and wanted to use his key term, cognitive appraisal. He declared it to be in the public domain, and I have since used it to identify my work and set it apart from RET. I did not then and do not now think that CAT is a new form of therapy; integration and not fragmentation of treatment approaches should be sought.

A simple explanation for my shift from RET to CAT is that I stopped doing as many demonstrations of therapeutic technique and started to do more actual therapy. I found it very easy to interview a volunteer from an audience, especially an audience of mental-health professionals, to discuss a specific issue and to uncover the relevant cognitions. However, the week-after-week business of therapy was another matter. Despite good therapeutic alliances and plentiful insights into cognitions, many clients did not put insights into action and were slow to make gains in therapy. I suppose that every modification of an existing form of treatment can be traced to dissatisfaction with the results obtained by the older method. Though

I had become a skilled practitioner of RET, I found that it did not obtain the results in ongoing therapy that I had claimed for it when, as a good RET supervisor, I taught others. By working with clients who did not change much or as quickly as I thought they should, I came to revise my approach in working with them and in thinking about their problems. CAT is the outcome.

As a result of working with a wider variety of clients, CAT has become less cognitive. My initial attraction to RET was academic — I thought that RET theory closely corresponded to principles of attitude change I had known from social psychology. Later, refinements in my thinking had come from training experiences — teaching other professionals to understand and how to do RET. After theory and training had provided the majority of my understanding of people, I entered a new phase, that of extensive clinical practice, with a new partner, Sheenah Hankin. As CAT has developed, it has been a joint effort of two people who see some fifty clients each week, and who spend endless hours in discussions of cases (Wessler and Hankin-Wessler, 1986). Where the word 'we' appears below, it represents our mutual thinking.

We emphasise careful diagnosis, assessment and the selecting of treatment plans that fit individual clients. An approach to treatment that heavily depends on theory, whether it is psychoanalysis or RET, is necessarily limited in its treatment of cases. Just as it is bad medicine for a physician to administer the same drug to every patient regardless of diagnosis, it is bad psychotherapy to administer the same treatment to every client regardless of diagnosis.

CAT is the principal approach we take with neurotic depression, social anxiety, marital conflict, and problems of anger and hostility. CAT contains a great deal of Beck's cognitive therapy, but is more flexible on the theoretical point of cognitive factors in anxiety and depression. In the developments discussed below, it can be seen that we accept the possibility of non-cognitive factors in some emotional processes. Of course, we fully accept the role of biochemical disturbance in some forms of psychopathology, and work closely on some cases with a psychopharmacologist.

Cognitive modality

Personal Rules of Living (PRLs) continue to be a key concept in CAT. The notion of a rule is easily understood by most people we have worked with, and their importance in one's life is readily acknowledged. PRLs guide our actions, our decisions, and even our opinions of self and others. They may be divided into two types: rules about the way things are, and rules about the way things ought to be. The former express something akin to natural law in that they are statements about regularities, e.g. 'People who work hard will get ahead'. Although they may have empirical support, most likely they were learned, usually at an early age, from some source deemed credible at the time. Ironically, in later life the source may not continue to be regarded as credible, but the message has long since become indelible. Rules about the way things ought to be are statements of personal values; they may be based on moral principles and social values, or may have been learned piecemeal and patched together in a more-or-less harmonious whole. These rules cannot be supported empirically because they do not come from the domain of fact; they come from the domain of ethics and morality. Thus, to say, 'People who work hard *should* get ahead', is a far different proposition than to say that they will succeed.

PRLs are not the same as rational or irrational beliefs. The should in a prescriptive PRL may refer to a hope, a suggestion, a recommendation, a norm, a command, a demand, or an imperative. CAT assumes that without rules human affairs would be chaotic. Fortunately, adopting rules to live by is a universal and natural tendency in the human species. There is no assumption in CAT that PRLs invariably lead to dysfunctional emotional or behavioural consequences, whereas Ellis has distinguished between conditional shoulds (rational) that lead to good emotional and behavioural consequences, and imperative shoulds (irrational) that lead to bad results. However, there is no evidence that this dichotomy in fact produces the results Ellis predicts, and the relationship between (ir)rational and results are circular by definition: rational and irrational are defined in terms of the results they bring.

PRLs are cognitive structures, but they are not necessarily conscious. The rules people are not aware of, and are therefore nonconscious, may be more important in some instances than the ones people phenomenologically know. Non-conscious rules are followed mindlessly.

We assume that rigidly held PRLs frequently lead to unhappiness and self-defeating actions; they lead to demands that neither oneself nor others can live up to because of their unyielding nature. Since PRLs are propositions about one's conceptions and prescriptions about reality, the failure of reality to meet one's expectations can be very disturbing.

We hypothesise that the most important rules are those that result in self-appraisal. Like the following of rules itself, self-appraisal seems to be an unavoidable part of life. People seem unable to suspend self-judgement for very long; in this way CAT differs from RET, which holds that it is both possible and desirable for people to have neutral self-appraisals (also known as unconditional self-acceptance).

PRLs may conflict with one another, and the clash of rules is often the focus in CAT. It is impossible to follow two or more conflicting rules at the same time. The solution in CAT is to set priorities among one's rules or to modify them. A husband is torn between furthering his career and spending time with his spouse because he has PRLs that prescribe both, and has a PRL that states that a spouse will be unhappy and leave if he does not have both a successful career and spend ample time with her. In marriage, the conflict of PRLs held by each spouse results in disappointment, hostility and breakdown of the relationship.

Phenomenological Developmental History (PDH) is another key concept in CAT. PRLs are learned; how and when they were acquired is important to the understanding of a person's PRLs and why the person might not readily modify them. We doubt that there can be an objective history of one's past, and so we work with people's past experiences as they recall them. Since humans seem to be innate storytellers with a need to understand themselves, the personal narrative gets constructed along cause-and-effect lines. I had mentioned the possibility of exploring the past in order to work on presently held cognitions in an RET book I co-authored (Wessler and Wessler, 1980). Additional experience further convinced me not only of the desirability of so doing, but its near necessity.

In practice this means that we spend time examining the past influences of parents, siblings, peers, and teachers, to help the client construct a narrative of how he or she came to view the world, oneself, and other people in the present way. Many clients at first think this practice means that we are conducting psychoanalysis, but of course this is not so; there is none of the jargon or assumptions of traditional psychodynamic theories. However, if significant figures from one's past explicitly taught or implicitly modelled the correctness of a rule, the individual will find it more difficult to reassess and re-evaluate the current, internalised version of the PRL. PRLs learned through modelling are more likely to be mindlessly followed; in other words, they are more likely to be unconscious, and the therapist's task is to help the client become aware of or gain insight into them.

A client, Mac, was able to identify his PRLs with guidance, and began to understand their role in his anxiety and apprehension about his future. His problem concerned money, and although he was not poor he felt uneasy when spending money or when thinking of his retirement ten years hence. He recalled his father's worries about money, and his resolution that he must never be poor. He further recalled his father's statements about him to the effect that Mac would never amount to anything, and his father's words took on the quality of a natural law personalised as, 'I must succeed financially, but I am unable to do so because of my inadequacies'. His insight into the sources of this PRL opened the way for his proposing a more accurate and adaptive rule for himself, and with practice he eliminated all but a residual of his old rules. His anxieties gradually diminished as he acted on his newly adopted rules, and to his pleasure he found that he was spending his money more wisely than before.

We seek to understand the client by discovering his or her PRLs and their development. We are not simply trying to identify specific cognitions activated by specific situations. We try to get the client to construct a mosaic of self-portraiture so that he or she can anticipate responses to new situations and plan to modify well-entrenched responses. Insight into the past aids in anticipation of the future. Insight into one's development and the acquisition of cognitions have received little emphasis in the cognitive-behavioural approaches to psychotherapy; the work of Guidano and Liotti (1983) is a noteworthy exception.

Affective modality

Learned Affective States (LAS) are an additional aspect of PDH, and are an example of how CAT has become increasingly less cognitive in emphasis. CAT assumes that affect (emotional feelings) as well as cognitions can be learned. Further, in each person's socialisation family, certain emotions were expressed more frequently than others, especially in stressful circumstances, and were thus more frequently available for learning. Even in households where overt emotional expression was rare, such as sulking as a way to imply anger, there were models to learn from. Affect becomes part of the self-image, and the learned affective state comes to be regarded as the best way to be.

For example, Mac covered over much of his anxiety about money and poverty by becoming angry when his wife pressed him to buy something or even to invest his money. When he did make a purchase, it was preceded and followed by bitter arguments and endless complaints about his wife as he freely blamed her for his difficulties. His anger seemed quite natural to him, and as a result he saw no need to change it despite the obvious marital disruption it caused. An investigation into his PDH revealed memories of his father's anger and of his mother's getting easily intimidated by those angry expressions. Mac himself recalled feeling terrified when his father expressed his wrath. Upon the father's death during Mac's adolescence, Mac began to become angry with his mother and younger siblings, and, expectedly, mother and siblings capitulated to Mac's demands and decisions. Mac's wife, who had been very dependent prior to assertiveness training, was similarly easily intimidated until she learned to deal more effectively with Mac's bullying. This, of course, made Mac all the more angry and he stepped up his efforts using the same tactics that had served him so well all his life. By showing him that his anger was a Learned Affective State that seemed natural because it had been so well learned, I was able to help him curb his angry tendencies and to convert his feelings into more constructive action. At that point, it became possible to focus on the underlying anxiety that prompted Mac's anger.

What we suggest here is a view that departs from RET as practised, although not necessarily from Ellis's (1962) earliest discussions of his then newly formed approach. We suggest that affect and action may result from either (1) previously learned cognitive structures (PRLs), or (2) learned affect. Cognitions may have mediated some LAS but then were forgotten, just as one learns to drive a car by specific messages directed at one's feet, hands and eyes telling them what to do; later, the messages are neither needed nor recalled, but the habits persist and seem to function autonomously.

Not all affect is cognitively mediated, nor are feelings mere conclusions from cognitions. Cognitions may later be added to affective experience as a sort of non-psychoanalytic rationalisation, an explanation we use to account for clients who cannot identify any relevant cognitions associated with their emotional experiences, and for clients who seem baffled that they react to certain situations as they do. Very often, we find, they reproduce the affective states (subjective feelings) as well as the overt affective actions they learned in childhood and adolescence. The insight that 'I am acting just like my father (mother) did — I sound just like him (her)' can be as distasteful for some people as it is surprising.

To get at affective states and associated cognitions, we attempt to raise affect in client sessions. The cerebral discussions and dispassionate reports of feelings that seem so characteristic of RET and the cognitive-behavioural approaches to psychotherapy are minimised in CAT. We attempt to provoke and heighten anger and anxiety by various means. These include the use of vivid language and imagery, both humorous and sad anecdotes, anxiety-arousing negative predictions, and asking people to sound and look anxious or angry. Affect can be raised by confronting clients with the feelings they have not yet acknowledged. We frequently use self-disclosure to evoke an affective response in clients; we speak of ourselves and of our own experiences, and we find that many clients respond by disclosing feelings of their own.

I had advocated the raising of affect during my RET training workshops but I never labelled it as such. My advocacy took the form of telling a personal experience that illustrated how cognitions many times emerge only when one is emotionally aroused. My recollection dates back to my early days in the RET training programme. I attempted to write about my experiences at Parsons College and the events that led to its eventual bankruptcy. In my fury to get words on paper — I have always been impatient about writing, which is perhaps one reason I have not published more — I began to mistype words, jam the keys of the typewriter, and generally make a mess of things. In my frustration I hit the typewriter and yelled angrily at it. Of course, the machine did not reply. I realised how foolish I had acted and discovered my PRL about blaming external causes when things do not go my way. Although the insight was not totally new for me, the emotional intensity in this particular situation focused my attention as no other had, and it has had a lasting impact on me. As I calmed down, I reasoned that I could solve the problem (rather than blame the machine) by either learning to type better, not typing at all, or living with my inadequate keyboard skills. I chose the latter alternative, and now, a dozen years later, use a word processor which is both very forgiving of my errors and too expensive to abuse.

Insight about learned Affective States and about PRLs begins the change process. For some clients, insight is sufficient to initiate changes in their lives, with little or no assistance from the therapist; at times, not even support is required. However, in most instances, insight must be followed by a plan of action, and then by action itself.

Behavioural modality

The best made plans often do not get started, or, when started, do not get carried out. It is tempting here to launch into a discussion of resistance. However, the term 'resistance' properly belongs in the domain of psychodynamic therapy; patients 'resist' interpretations by disagreeing with them or failing to follow therapists' recommendations. The term 'resistance' is not appropriate for this presentation, because it is not the therapist's ideas that are resisted in CAT, but rather the client resists the plan agreed upon by both client and therapist. Why would someone not comply with a plan he or she has freely agreed to and whose merits are fully acknowledged? There are two significant answers.

First, assuming that the agreement is genuine, non-compliance with the plan may be due to anticipating or actually getting fewer benefits for compliance than noncompliance. The rewards are greater for not doing than for doing, or, more likely, the expected rewards are greater. We do what amounts to a functional analysis and attempt to discover what the real or anticipated payoffs are for non-compliance. Such payoffs might be biological (as in addictions) or interpersonal (as in a neurotically bonded marriage). Such payoffs might, and sometimes do, involve nothing more complicated than reduction of anxiety: we do what makes us feel less fearful.

Secondly, there is a special instance of anxiety reduction that deserves specific attention. It is the anxiety that arises from surrendering one or more aspects of one's self-image and then not knowing how to fill the void or what to fill it with. The plan to alter an attitude made by therapist and client whose self-image includes the PRL 'I am a nervous person' is a person who has experienced anxiety as having some positive payoffs, and has developed a longstanding pattern of avoidance. Although such a person experiences anxiety, the anxiety is both familiar and desirable in that it fulfills the person's self-image. To agree with the plan to act against the anxiety hardly makes a person confident and is likely to generate increased anxiety as the person seems forced to give up part of his or her self-image. The client is more likely to employ unconscious security manoeuvres to avoid this experience.

Security Manoeuvres (SMs) are protective mechanisms the client unconsciously implements in order to prevent the surrender of hypothetical notions that constitute the self-image (cf. Carson, 1969). We hypothesise that everyone uses security manoeuvres to maintain their self-images, and that many security manoeuvres influence other people to respond in ways that support the actor's self-image. The most obvious security manoeuvres form observable aspects of one's distinctive personality. They include psychosomatic disorders that prevent the client from taking action, excuses from the client as to why it was not possible to implement the plan, cancelling subsequent therapy sessions for invalid reasons, failure to understand the plan fully enough to be able to act, and at times anger at the therapist. Clients may claim that therapy is not working, because they are feeling more anxious, especially when their goals include overcoming anxiety.

Thus, security manoeuvres are significant barriers to therapeutic progress, and are often responsible for the inertia therapists encounter when insightful clients show little change. (Inertia is the non-psychodynamic term we prefer to resistance.) One's security manoeuvres have a long personal history of good service in the protection of the self-image and the reduction of anxiety that results when the self-image is threatened by disconfirming information or deliberate attempts to modify it. In therapy, to change behavioural patterns that are consistent with negative self-attitudes requires the adoption of new actions that clash with one's sense of self. In the words of a bumper sticker on an old American car, 'It ain't much, but it's mine'. The potential loss of identity generates anxiety; the retention of negative attitudes generates depression.

To return to the case of Mac, his blaming of his wife for their so-called financial difficulties (which existed only in Mac's mind) not only warded off his anxiety but preserved his self-image as a competent provider. Mac came to realise that he acted as though his wife were responsible for their (non-existent) money troubles, and he could avoid the prophecy his father made that 'You will not amount to anything'. Mac could feel self-pity for getting victimised by his wife, and thus escaped self-recrimination. This realisation allowed him to understand why he could not implement his rational decision to curb his wife's spending and resist her requests that he invest his money — his SMs provided some important psychological gains for Mac, and until he could gain security in less neurotic ways, he showed little therapeutic change.

Security manoeuvres must be identified, analysed as to their nature and purpose, and then eroded by persistent attention and action that work against them. We urge clients to stay alert for them, to understand procrastination and lack of follow-through on homework as due to them, and consciously to work against them, however small the steps might be. Security manoeuvres are the primary focus of therapeutic effort with clients after initial assessment, insight, and plans for change have been made.

Therapeutic relationship

The cornerstone of our therapeutic work is a close relationship with our clients. Having found that impersonally rational and logical arguments have little lasting effect, that factual evidence can be tossed aside and not assimilated into one's thinking, and that self-demonstrations though powerful are difficult to carry out, we have reaffirmed the tenet that psychotherapy is an intimate, human relationship. We are prepared to match clients' self-disclosures with those of our own, to care for clients outside the consulting room, and to become part of their lives as they become part of ours. We have found that none of the dire predictions about iatrogenic dependence and catering to neurotic needs for love and approval that we learned from RET have been fulfilled.

Our work with clients in a more holistic, in-depth fashion has led us to continue therapy with an individual client much longer than we previously thought necessary. 'Short-term' or 'brief' psychotherapy is only short by comparison to lengthy psychoanalysis. (The phrase was originated to refer to any length shorter than full psychoanalysis. Given the mystique of psychoanalysis and the length of time needed for so-called successful outcomes, it is little wonder that anything else is labelled short term, and if not psychodynamically oriented, is considered supportive therapy, when it is regarded as therapy at all.) The nine months to three years that we now think is the normal length of treatment is short (and supportive) by psychoanalytic standards, but long by other standards, e.g. those found in cognitive-behavioural therapy writings.

IMPLICATIONS FOR OTHER THERAPISTS

Think eclectically

A good scientist is supposed to have an inquiring attitude, a mind open to doubts, and to revise his or her thinking when presented with disconfirming evidence. Indeed, this ideal is presumed to apply to clients in all therapeutic approaches that conceive of 'man as scientist': we want to know and understand, and we will surrender our hypotheses when they are undermined by new data. Therapists should ask no less of themselves than of their clients. My shift from RET occurred when I put aside its assumptions about disturbance and asked myself whether there were better ways to think of people's problems.

For me, eclectic refers to more than a collection of therapeutic principles and techniques. It includes all areas of psychology, as well as ideas from other social and behavioural sciences, especially those that do not stress psychopathology and can shed light on normal human problems. Other areas of learning are likewise necessary to understand clients better. My knowledge of the Bible, acquired in childhood, has helped with many an appropriate quotation; my growing up as a Protestant in a Catholic neighbourhood and my later employment at a Jesuit university has helped me understand the significance of religious issues in people's lives, a dimension of human experience that was not covered in graduate school, nor in very many psychotherapy publications, and certainly not in RET (Wessler, 1984b).

Avoid dogmatism

It is perhaps ironic that Albert Ellis, who has spoken out against religious dogmatism, has been so dogmatic about psychotherapy. Though publicly developed by a person committed to empiricism, RET is first and foremost a matter of faith. There is no scientific evidence for (or against) the supremacy of the shoulds, which forms the basis for the RET theory of disturbance, and there is no solid evidence about the efficacy of RET treatment, despite ample opportunities to provide it during the thirty years of its existence. The consequences of dogmatism are rigidity of thinking about new problems dogma does not cover, and worse, fitting new problems into the old categories.

Dogmatic psychotherapy forces clients into pre-existing concerns and hypotheses. The obvious difficulty that results is the misunderstanding of clients and their problems. Dogma makes it impossible to learn from one's clients, for learning implies the modification of already existing ideas.

Know thyself

I do not think that everyone in the world should strive for a high degree of self-understanding, nor do I subscribe to the view that the 'proper study of mankind is Man'. I make an exception in the case of counsellors and psychotherapists; they should know themselves. I advocate self-understanding because it is an unparalleled way to learn how to understand other people, and understanding of other people is necessary if one is to help them.

In working with new therapists and counsellors, I have been impressed with how guarded many of them are. Behaviourally trained therapists seem especially prone to regard therapy as an impersonal enterprise in which the skilled application of techniques should be the main concern. But psychological therapy is more closely related to the craft of surgery than to the science of medicine, except that the patient is awake during the procedures and is therefore influenced by the professional as a person.

One must know how he or she came to understand something about oneself, and how that insight led to action, and how action led to a more satisfying life. At the same time, one must guard against the dogmatic stance that says 'What worked for me must also work for you'. However, without personal experience, one has very little to self-disclose. (The importance of self-disclosure is that it builds relationships and communicates understanding.) One cannot learn much about oneself from a book or lecture. Learning from personal experience is crucial to self-understanding. I recommend wide-ranging experiences as an ideal way to discover one's PRLs and security manoeuvres. To my mind, PRLs and security manoeuvres add up to the salient aspects of personality I want to know about.

Discover affect

I do not think that adequate therapy can occur unless one understands a client's affect and is not fearful of dealing with it. I recall a colleague who was expert at solving practical problems clients posed, but quickly changed the subject when feelings were mentioned. I have frequently encountered this attitude among behaviour therapists, but this person was trained in and advocated RET ('emotive' is our middle name).

Therapists should dramatise their points, not just present them dispassionately. Drama has impact that the mere mustering of logical argument cannot possess. The message of a play can be summarised in a sentence or two, but to have influence it must stir feelings and create lasting images. The modelling of affect within sessions promotes client displays of affect. Further, it enables the therapeutic relationship to be strengthened through therapist's self-disclosure. The disclosing of our own experiences with shame, failure, sadness and anger also teaches appropriate emoting, a capacity many of our clients have not learned.

Therapeutic change

Here is a summary of what we attempt to do in CAT and what we recommend to other therapists.

Strive to relate well to each client in a genuinely accepting manner. This means accepting your client totally, and accepting all affective communications without criticism. Clients, especially with borderline personality disorders, do not benefit from having additional shame heaped upon them. However, the therapist should not permit abuse from the client; a caring relationship can still have limits and should.

Understand how each client acquired his or her characteristic affect and cognitions. Using CAT terms, this means gaining insight about the Phenomenological Developmental History, especially Learned Affective States and Personal Rules of Living. Insight into Security Manoeuvres is essential for understanding client inertia to therapeutically generated plans.

The goal is to create a new sense for clients of who they are. This is done through information about themselves, advice on what to do, and insight into the actions of significant others in their lives. (The latter is very important, because significant others, both past and present, have enormous influence on the sense of self.) Follow insight with plans for change. Plans lead to action, and action to experiences that build worth and change affect and behavioural patterns. Small gains, bit by bit, build a new picture of oneself. The focus on small gains means no failure to demoralise or shame an already suffering client.

Understand the relationship as it develops. It often contains elements of transference, i.e. the client interacts with the therapist as though he or she were some significant other in the client's life, or as some generalised other in the client's mind (e.g. a female client may treat a male therapist as she would 'all men'). Therapists are surrogates as well as agents of change.

Listen and learn

I have supervised hundreds of therapy sessions and listened to nearly as many of my own. Teaching others is an excellent way to learn, and supervising others is an exceptional way to gain exposure to diverse problems. At one time, I supervised by audiotape the practical work of therapists from all parts of North America and the United Kingdom. One of my first attempts to expand the practice of RET occurred while finding suggestions for Windy Dryden, now of Goldsmiths' College. I realised that my saying, 'Here is an irrational belief, there is a chance to dispute', would not be very helpful for supervising 25 client sessions, especially for a person who knew RET so well from the beginning of our work together. So I called attention to the style of interaction, to the therapeutic relationship, to ideas from other therapy approaches that might articulate with RET. I learned from what I heard.

What I heard from some therapists convinced me that most people who profess to do RET in actuality do not practice nor even understand it very well. Perhaps this statement holds true for other approaches to treatment as well. Misunderstanding results in poor treatment, and in the worst instances in antitherapeutic outcomes. Some therapists modelled themselves closely after the founder of RET and others took the phrase 'emotional re-education' to mean that clients need only be lectured not listened to; in either situation, their clients seemed superfluous to the stellar performances of the nominal helpers, except to act as an appreciative audience. One long-time practitioner of RET proudly submitted a tape on which he seemed never to hear the client, and in another instance the therapist mechanically reproduced RET without once realising that his prisoner-client (in a penetentiary) was joking with him about both his problems and his enthusiasm for RET solutions. I formerly used these tapes to train other RET supervisors, and I still retain them in my private collection of what not to do. I wonder if therapists who do not or cannot listen to their clients can listen to themselves and their colleagues. If they cannot, what hope is there for improvement?

Attend to different points of view

One result of feeling obliged to say something novel if not original whenever I supervised or conducted a workshop was my staying alert for different points of view that might expand my knowledge and contribute to the work of others. Reading widely in the therapy research literature has been an important source of ideas, although I generally feel that researchers are out of touch with the concerns of practitioners. A colleague recently told me of an informal poll he conducted among psychotheapy researchers to determine how many clients they saw each week. He reported the upper limit as five, and the modal number as zero!

In the end, my willingness to consider other points of view forced me away from RET and towards the eclectic cognitive-affective amalgam I call Cognitive Appraisal Therapy. One unanticipated result of remaining open-minded is that one's ideas are usually in flux and never quite gell. Of course, this makes it very difficult to write about one's ideas, for they may be refined or extended by the time a publication appears in print. So, as I close this reminiscence I am aware that it is only a snapshot of early 1986 and I must put aside the temptation to linger over it until it is finished.

REFERENCES

Arnold, M.B. (1960). *Emotion and personality*. New York: Columbia University Press

Beck, A.T. (1976). *Cognitive therapy and the emotional disorders*. New York: International Universities Press

Becker, I.M. and Rosenfeld, J.G. (1976). Rational-emotive therapy: a study of initial therapy sessions of Albert Ellis. *Journal of Clinical Psychology, 32*, 872-6

Carson, R.C. (1969). *Interaction concepts of personality*. Chicago: Aldine

Ellis, A. (1962). *Reason and emotion in psychotherapy*. New York: Lyle Stuart

Ellis, A. (1979). On Joseph Wolpe's espousal of cognitive behavioral therapy. *American Psychologist, 34* 98-9

Ellis, A. and Harper, R.A. (1975). *A new guide to rational living*. Englewood Cliffs, NJ: Prentice-Hall

Goldfried, M.R. (1980). Towards the delineation of therapeutic change principles. *American Psychologist, 35*, 991–9

Grieger, R. and Boyd, R. (1980). *Rational-emotive therapy: a skills-based approach*. New York: Van Nostrand Reinhold

Guidano, V.F. and Liotti, G. (1983). *Cognitive processes and the emotional disorders*. New York: Guilford Press

Lazarus, A.A. (1981). *The practice of multimodal therapy*. New York: McGraw-Hill

Lazarus, R.S. and Folkman, S. (1984). *Stress, appraisal, and coping*. New York: Springer

Maultsby, M.C., Jr (1977), Rational-emotive imagery. In A. Ellis and R. Grieger (Eds), *Handbook of rational-emotive therapy*. New York: Springer

Plutchik, R. (1980). *Emotion: a psychoevolutionary synthesis*. New York: Harper & Row

Raimy, V. (1975). *Misunderstandings of the self*. San Francisco: Jossey-Bass

Tosi, D.J. (1974). *Youth: toward personal growth*. Columbus, OH: Merrill

Walen, S.R., DiGiuseppe, R. and Wessler, R.L. (1980). *A practitioner's guide to rational-emotive therapy*. New York: Oxford University Press

Wessler, R.A. and Wessler, R.L. (1980). *The principles and practice of rational-emotive therapy*. San Francisco: Jossey-Bass

Wessler, R.L. (1982), Varieties of cognitions in the cognitively-oriented therapies. *Rational Living, 17*(1), 3–10

Wessler, R.L. (1984a). Alternative conceptions of rational-emotive therapy: toward a philosophically neutral psychotherapy. In M. Reda and M.J. Mahoney (Eds), *Cognitive psychotherapies: recent developments in theory, research, and practice*. Cambridge, MA: Ballinger

Wessler, R.L. (1984b). A bridge too far: incompatibilities of rational-emotive therapy and pastoral counseling. *Personnel and Guidance Journal, 63*, 265–6

Wessler, R.L. and Hankin-Wessler, S.W.R. (1986). Cognitive appraisal therapy (CAT). In W. Dryden and W.L. Golden (Eds), *Cognitive-behavioural approaches to psychotherapy*. London: Harper & Row

10

When More is Better

Arnold A. Lazarus

PRIOR THEORY AND PRACTICE

There have been several 'key cases' that shaped my clinical orientation over the years. One such patient was not even mine. She was a woman in her early thirties whose agoraphobic difficulties had remained refractory to heroic drug treatment and psychotherapy from some of the most reputable clinicians in Johannesburg, South Africa, in the mid-1950s. I was an undergraduate at the time and learned about this long-suffering woman from my girlfriend (subsequently my wife). Joseph Wolpe was presenting informal lectures and demonstrations at the University of the Witwatersrand, and although my own orientation was distinctly non-behavioural (I had been strongly influenced by the psychodynamic, Rogerian, and antibehaviourist climate in the Psychology Department), I nevertheless felt that since the 'tried and true' approaches had failed, Wolpe's iconoclastic methods were worth a try. (There had even been serious talk of lobotomy for the client, and despite my basic scepticism of 'behaviouristic psychotherapy' I felt that it certainly could do no greater harm than psychosurgery!).

Wolpe agreed to conduct the therapy behind a one-way mirror. As I observed him performing strange and unorthodox procedures such as deep muscle relaxation, followed by systematic desensitisation both in imagination and *in vivo* (I was even allowed to accompany the client on certain driving excursions as a paraprofessional!), I still remained sceptical. Within a few months, however, there was no doubt that measurable gains had accrued. Initially the client had been virtually housebound and had refused to go anywhere unaccompanied by her husband, but after about 12 sessions of relaxation and desensitisation, she was able and willing to remain alone in several places she had formerly avoided, and she had definitely increased her range of movement. Wolpe then added assertiveness training to the treatment regimen, and I witnessed (what he termed) 'behaviouristic psychodrama' wherein role playing and role reversal featured prominently. Further gains accrued, the school year ended, and Wolpe continued the therapy at his consulting room in the city. By that time, my scepticism had waned considerably.

My enthusiasm for the active techniques that I subsequently christened 'behaviour therapy' (Lazarus, 1958) continued to grow, and I was won over to Wolpe's theoretical and practical position (Wolpe and Lazarus, 1966). Soon thereafter, as we shall discuss, some crucial findings led me to modify my outlook.

DESCRIPTION OF THE KEY CASES

Mrs D

The first key case, whom I termed 'The Charitable Lady' (Lazarus, 1971) was very similar to the aforementioned woman who had responded to Wolpe's 'behaviour therapy'. When Mrs D first consulted me in 1966, I was directing the Behavior Therapy Institute in Sausalito, California. The client, accompanied by her husband, had arrived for her initial appointment some two hours early so that she could use the time to calm herself before meeting with me. She was housebound by anxiety and could venture no further than her front porch without feeling faint, shaky, and panicky. Although she absolutely refused to leave the house without her husband, even his presence did not mitigate most of her tensions and feelings of apprehension. The onset of her condition, some six years previously, followed an incident when her husband was falsely accused of stabbing a fellow worker. At the time, both of them were employed by the same wholesale organisation where he worked as a divisional manager and she as a private secretary. When her husband was fired, she resigned. They both obtained new employment the very next day, but on her way to work Mrs D suddenly experienced anxiety that soon reached panic proportions. She returned home and thereafter found herself anxious and panicky whenever she left her house.

Two years later, only with the assistance of heavy sedation, she went out of town to attend her mother's funeral. Upon her return, her condition had deteriorated. One of her neighbours, a psychiatrist, treated her at home for approximately 18 months. He had a psychodynamic orientation, and in addition to dream interpretation he spent considerable time examining her 'dependency needs'. In keeping with Freud's (1924) paper in which the need to expose phobic individuals to their feared situations had been emphasised, he had constantly encouraged Mrs D to leave the house, and he had gently coerced her into accompanying him on longer and longer walks. This treatment seemed to have enabled her to function as she had before her mother's demise. She could venture away from home with varying degrees of discomfort, but only when accompanied by her husband. She never went out without him. I contacted the psychiatrist with the client's permission and was told that she was 'a passive-dependent personality who . . . had regressed to a pre-oedipal level of fixation'. Prognosis, he added, was poor.

Mrs D had consulted me in my heyday of behavioural zeal. After history taking and the development of rapport, the first therapeutic objective was to enable her to come for her visits accompanied by someone other than her husband. An initial hypnotic induction showed that she was 'hypnotisable' and this was factored into various coping images wherein, under hypnotic relaxation, she would picture herself coming for her sessions with a friend or acquaintance. She found an escort and succeeded in taking public transportation to and from the Institute with her trusted friend. She was seen twice weekly. Using positive hypnotic suggestions and systematic desensitisation based on relaxation, it took 16 sessions (less than 2 months) before she was able to come from her appointments alone.

Imaginal and *in vivo* desensitisation remained the treatment of choice. The aim was to extinguish her 'territorial apprehension', which extended to situations such as crowded places, restaurants, movies, shops and city-centre streets. These items were added to her anxiety hierarchies, and were systematically whittled away. Hypochondriacal fears were also dealt with by desensitisation wherein, under hypnosis, she would be deeply relaxed while picturing herself experiencing various bodily discomforts for which she was to conjure up benign explanations. Further progress followed, with minor setbacks from time to time.

It then appeared that her husband was undermining her therapy. It seemed that he had encouraged (if not somehow provoked) her dependency. He was interviewed, and, after some initial denials, stated that he felt a sense of security in knowing that his wife was always at home and was so dependent on him. He added that if she became mobile and too self-sufficient, he feared that she would leave him for another man. It then transpired that this fear was a product of his own sexual ineptitude. Conjoint sessions were arranged with the main emphasis directed at enhancing their sexual relationship, as well as examining other ways of improving their marriage in general.

Assertiveness training also featured prominently in Mrs D's therapy. A seemingly pivotal area concerned her relationship with her father. A domineering man, the very idea of standing up to him was something she could not even contemplate. Through behaviour rehearsal (Lazarus, 1966) this objective was eventually accomplished. At this juncture, Mrs D had been seen a total of 38 times over a 5- to 6-month period. She enjoyed taking long walks alone, and was able to go shopping, visiting and travelling within a 20- to 30-mile radius without undue distress. In addition to being able to venture out of her home, other changes were evident. Her marriage relationship in general and her sexual experiences in particular were more gratifying. She was far less hypochondriacal and socially submissive. In place of her previous self-preoccupation, she took pride in her home and enjoyed a wider range of social outlets. Who could dispute that some impressive improvements were evident?

The 'key' incident occurred at the point where I was ready to discharge her as 'much improved'. Although she was delighted by her new-found ability to remain relatively anxiety-free while travelling and engaging in the niceties of social interaction, she confided in me that her level of self-esteem was extremely low. She stated that therapy had enabled her to function like a relatively independent 12-year-old, but that she remained 'kind of blah!' She referred to herself as 'the height of mediocrity', and denigrated her intelligence, appearance, education, knowledge and overall value to society. Despite her impressive gains in behaviour, her greatly attenuated anxiety, and her augmented social and interpersonal skills, given her negative self-statements, what would probably occur if therapy terminated at this juncture? Most likely, her gains would have been short-lived.

Accordingly, using a form of cognitive disputation borrowed from Ellis (1962), I endeavoured to correct her self-downing and other dysfunctional beliefs. These sessions went beyond the parameters laid down by Wolpe and other 'behaviour therapists'. Whereas they accepted the need to 'correct misconceptions', my cognitive procedures transcended this specific area of discourse. A much broader philosophical realignment was attempted. Mrs D and I discussed everything from the meaning of life to the virtues of humanism. The logic of these discussions led Mrs D to conclude that 'If you want to *feel* useful, you have to *be* useful'.

Mrs D founded an organisation that distributed basic essentials, such as food and clothing, to impoverished people. She and her fellow workers began in a modest way by soliciting goods from friends and strangers. They contacted needy families and established centres in other communities. This charitable organisation, with Mrs D as the president and founder, spread to many areas of the United States, and fed and clothed thousands of needy persons. The contrast between the formerly fearful woman who would not venture beyond her front porch, now pounding on strange doors in strange neighbourhoods while pursuing her worthy cause, is quite poignant. At a one-year follow-up, she had maintained all her gains and added: 'Thanks to the fact that I exist and care, thousands of people now derive benefit.'

It was Mrs D, more than any other client, who alerted me to the realisation that behaviour therapy may not be both necessary and sufficient, and that it was sometimes (often?) important to venture beyond the boundaries of the methods outlined by Wolpe and Lazarus (1966) and by Wolpe (1969). I subsequently embarked on a series of follow-up inquiries and concluded that sustained improvements 'were often contingent upon the apparent adoption of a different outlook and philosophy of life and increased self-esteem in addition to an increased range of interpersonal and behavioral skills' (Lazarus, 1971, p. 18).

The pivotal points *vis-à-vis* the treatment of Mrs D all revolved around the fact that she was my client in 1966 when I viewed cognitive interventions as essentially secondary to the unlearning of primitive (subcortical) levels of neural organisation. 'Neurotic anxiety cannot be overcome by purely intellectual action — logical argument, rational insight — except in the special case where it stems entirely from misconceptions' (Wolpe and Lazarus, 1966, p. 12). In referring to the fact that Ellis (1962) had based an entire system of psychotherapy on the rational correction of the faulty assumptions and illogical philosophies which may underlie maladaptive behaviour, Wolpe and Lazarus (1966) stated: 'Behavior therapists, by contrast, regard rational corrections as, in most instances, merely a background to the specific reconditioning of reactions that usually belong to the autonomic nervous system'

(p. 131). Indeed, there was a pervasive terror that by exploring cognitive processes, the floodgates of 'mentalism' would be opened and we would fall right back into the quagmire of psychoanalysis. Thus, after receiving (and responding so well) to my most ardent behaviour therapy procedures, when it transpired that Mrs D remained essentially unhappy, unfulfilled, frustrated, and self-downing, it was not easy for me simply to accept that *more was needed*. It was with trepidation and considerable internal turmoil that I turned to Ellis (1962) and ventured into the areas of systematic cognitive disputation. And when entering into the domain of Mrs D's philosophical values and existential *angst*, I was happy that Wolpe could not see or hear what I was doing. My mentor would disapprove! A year or so later, when I dared to suggest that perhaps the reciprocal inhibition paradigm that Wolpe espoused was too restrictive, I was branded a heretic and summarily dismissed from the inner circle of 'behaviour therapy', from which I have been banished ever since. Indeed, my treatment of Mrs D was no minor incident in the evolution of my approach to psychotherapy.

Upon discovering that elegant treatment outcomes often require *more* than 'pure behaviour therapy', I continued to experiment with techniques drawn from a variety of sources. Here, the danger was that an unsystematic mish-mash of methods would only muddy the waters. It was clear that nothing less than a holistic approach resting on a systematic theoretical base, tied to a comprehensive yet coherent framework, would suffice. The conflict and the challenge both centred on the questions: What do we add? What do we exclude? The case of Mary Ann was the first in which the tactics that I subsequently christened 'Multimodal Therapy' were put to the test (Lazarus, 1973).

Mary Ann

Mary Ann, aged 24, was diagnosed as having chronic undifferentiated schizophrenia. She had had three admissions to psychiatric hospitals, and according to the reports her prognosis was poor. When I first saw her she was taking the following medications: Trilafon 8 mg t.i.d., Vivactil 10 mg t.i.d., Cogentin 2 mg b.d. The Multimodal Life History questionnaire revealed a background of parental guilt-induction, extreme bullying by her older sister who was five years her senior, and problems with her peers when she entered puberty, culminating in her first noticeable breakdown at

Table 10.1: Modality profile for Mary Ann

Modality	Problem	Proposed treatment
Behaviour	Inappropriate withdrawal responses	Assertiveness training
	Frequent crying	Non-reinforcement
	Unkempt appearance	Grooming instructions
	Excessive eating	Low-calorie regimen
	Negative self-statements	Positive self-talk assignments
	Poor eye contact	Rehearsal techniques
	Mumbling of words with poor voice projection	Verbal projection exercises
	Avoidance of heterosexual situations	Re-education and desensitisation
Affect	Does not express anger	Role playing
	Frequent anxiety	Relaxation training
	Suicidal feelings	Time projection, anti-depressant medication (see Drugs/Biology)
	Emptiness and aloneness	General relationship building
Sensation	Stomach spasms	Abdominal breathing and relaxing
	Out of touch with most sensual pleasures	Sensate focus method
	Tension in jaws and neck	Differential relaxation
	Frequent lower back pains	Orthopaedic exercises
Imagery	Distressing scenes of sister's funeral	Desensitisation
	Mother's angry face shouting 'You fool!'	Empty-chair technique
	Performing fellatio on God	Implosion technique
	Recurring dreams about airplane bombings	Vivid imagery invoking feelings of safety
Cognition	Irrational self-talk: 'I am evil'; 'I must suffer'; 'Sex is dirty'; 'I am inferior'	Deliberate rational disputation and corrective self-talk
	Syllogistic reasoning, over-generalisation	Parsing of irrational sentences
	Sexual misinformation	Sexual education
Interpersonal relationships	Childlike dependence	Specific self-sufficiency assignments
	Easily exploited/submissive	Assertiveness training
	Overly suspicious	Prescribed risk-taking
	Secondary gains from parental concern	Explain reinforcement principles to parents and try to enlist their cooperation
	Manipulative tendencies	Training in direct and confrontative behaviour

Table 10.1: contd.

Modality	Problem	Proposed treatment
Drugs/ Biology	Depression and auditory hallucinations (?)	Trilafon 8 mg t.i.d.; Vivactil 10 mg t.i.d.; Cogentin 2 mg b.d.

age 18, shortly after graduation from high school. 'I was on a religious kick and kept hearing voices'. Her second hospital admission followed a suicidal gesture at age 21, and her third admission was heralded by her sister's sudden demise soon after Mary Ann turned 24.

In Multimodal Therapy, the construction of a *modality profile* serves as a template or 'blueprint' that guides the course of therapy and points to the range of probable interventions. The profile shown in Table 10.1 was constructed for Mary Ann.

The treatment period covered a span of 13 months. In addition to individual treatment, Mary Ann was also in a group for 30 weeks, and was seen with her parents for eight sessions of 'family therapy'. Towards the end of therapy she became engaged and was seen with her fiancé for several premarital counselling sessions. At the end of the 13 months, her medication had been discontinued, and most of her problem areas were either substantially less troublesome or entirely absent. A follow-up one year later, and then three years after termination, revealed a stable recovery.

The treatment of Mary Ann exemplifies the multimodal tradition. In addition to familiar behaviour therapy techniques such as desensitisation, assertiveness training, role playing, and differential relaxation, several additional procedures were employed such as the empty-chair technique (Perls, 1969), time projection, and other imagery techniques that are not considered within the purview of behaviour therapy. In keeping with the doctrine of *technical eclecticism* (Lazarus, 1967, 1986), while applying methods drawn from different disciplines, the active ingredients of each technique were sought solely within the province of social learning theory. The multimodal approach is not merely holistic; it is also comprehensive and systematic.

EMERGENT NEW DEVELOPMENTS

The case of Mrs D led me to hypothesise that if long-lasting outcomes were to be achieved, specific cognitive interventions (e.g. the realignment of certain attitudes, values, opinions, beliefs and issues pertaining to self-esteem) may have to be added to action-oriented, performance-based methods — that it is not sufficient to rely solely on changes in maladaptive behaviours. Thus, my 1971 book *Behavior therapy and beyond* included a separate chapter on 'Cognitive restructuring', and argued for the synergy of cognitive-behavioural procedures. Issues such as 'dichotomous reasoning', 'overgeneralisation', and 'excessive reliance on other people's judgment' were discussed, as well as Ellis's (1962) eleven rational points of emphasis. These ideas were not well received by the mainstream behaviour therapists of the day. Nevertheless, Franks and Wilson (1976), in their opening commentaries of the *Annual review of behaviour therapy,* seemed to favour the 'cognitive theory of conditioning for humans' (p. 5), and one year later (Franks and Wilson, 1977) they explicitly discussed 'The cognitive connection', emphasising that cognitive-behaviour therapy 'is neither passing fad nor indicative of a paradigm shift, and it is to be viewed neither as an independent third force nor as a putative link between the behavioral and psychodynamic enclaves' (p. 13). Clearly, behaviour therapy had 'gone cognitive'. In terms of current theories of social learning (Bandura, 1986), cognitive factors are by no means a mere backdrop to the processes of autonomic conditioning. As Bandura (1986) stated:

> Cognitive factors partly determine which environmental events will be observed, what meaning will be conferred on them, whether they leave any lasting effects, what valence and efficacy they will have, and how the information they convey will be organized for future use (p. 454).

The first emergent theme was the 'broad-spectrum' behavioural position (Lazarus, 1971) based on the ABC paradigm (Affect, Behaviour, Cognition), which, in the light of antecedent conditions, ongoing behaviours, and maintaining consequences, would set the stage for a more thorough assessment and call for a wider range of therapeutic techniques. Although Mrs D's therapy was anything but narrow — in addition to desensitisation and assertiveness training, conjoint sessions had also been part of the treatment repertoire — the need for something extra soon became evident. Cognitive interventions were thereupon included, and enabled her to achieve a sense of well-being and personal worth in a manner that was compatible with her own particular needs. Thus, the broad-spectrum orientation was predicated on two basic objectives: (1) resolve as many problems as possible, and (2) help each client find a gratifying *modus vivendi*.

Mrs D led me to question whether I was covering all relevant bases, whether something more was needed to ensure better — more stable — outcomes. Soon, it became apparent that by specifically adding Sensory experience, Imagery and Interpersonal considerations (e.g. family systems), one would achieve a far greater degree of comprehensiveness, and the *multimodal* approach was launched (Lazarus, 1973).

A fundamental premiss was developed, viz. that clients are usually troubled by a multitude of specific problems that should be dealt with by a wide range of specific treatments. Comprehensive therapy will lead to identifiable changes in a client's behaviours, affective responses, sensory experiences, mental images, cognitive processes, and interpersonal relationships. Moreover, some clients have problems that call for biological interventions (Lazarus, 1981). This follows directly out of the main lesson learned from Mrs D and from Mary Ann, viz. that 'more is better'. Hence the following assumption: *The more coping responses a person learns in therapy, the less likely he or she is to relapse.* Thus, in addition to the correction of maladaptive and deviant behaviours, it appears to be equally important to quell unpleasant feelings, negative sensations, intrusive fantasies, dysfunctional beliefs, stressful relationships, and possible biochemical imbalances. 'To the extent that problem identification (diagnosis) systematically explores each of these modalities, whereupon therapeutic intervention remedies whatever deficits and maladaptive patterns emerge, treatment outcomes will be positive and long-lasting' (Lazarus, 1973, p. 407).

IMPLICATIONS FOR OTHER THERAPISTS

Any general rule has its exceptions. Consequently, the practising clinician must inquire under what specific circumstances less might be better than more. There may be certain problems that respond better to a highly targeted unimodal or bimodal approach. Even in the treatment of agoraphobia, after conducting a multimodal assessment, I have found it unnecessary to recommend more than *in vivo* desensitisation for some clients. According to Zitrin, Klein and Woerner (1980), approximately 29 per cent of agoraphobic individuals need no more than a couple of highly targeted treatments (e.g. imipramine and/or alprazolam, plus exposure). The other 71 per cent seem to require more interventions.

Whereas leading researchers have not acknowledged the multimodal framework, they have certainly drawn attention to the need for multidimensional treatment. Thus, Emmelkamp (1982) stressed that, in addition to *in vivo* exposure, 'other procedures such as assertion training, cognitive restructuring, marriage therapy, or treatment by drugs may be indicated for some cases' (p. 70). Goldstein (1982) referred to 'the synergistic effect of combinations of treatment modalities' (p. 212).

The case of Mary Ann underscores the need to offer a good deal more than medication and emotional support to people diagnosed as 'psychotic'. When dealing with instances of severe psychopathology, once the florid symptoms are controlled by medication, many people are amenable to interventions aimed at eliminating specific and interrelated problems in many areas of functioning. Diagnostic labels — schizophrenia, agoraphobia, anxiety disorder, etc. — are replaced by modality profiles in multimodal assessment. This provides a clear nexus between diagnosis and treatment. Consider the modality profile of a 32-year-old woman whose primary diagnosis was 'agoraphobia with panic attacks' (DSM III, 300.21):

Behaviour: Patterns of withdrawal, avoidance and procrastination. Crying spells and outbursts of temper. Goes nowhere alone

Affect: Anxiety, guilt, 'fear of fear', some degree of depression

Sensation: Frequent bouts of palpitations, dizziness, and other anxiety concomitants — faintness, abdominal discomfort, tremulousness, diaphoresis, dyspnoea. Vague, non-localised aches and pains probably due to muscular tension

Imagery: Pictures herself being hurt, not coping, losing control, being trapped, fainting, being rejected. Poor self-image

Cognition: Catastrophic cognitions (dwells on 'what if . . .'), dysfunctional beliefs (especially about perfection-

	ism), dichotomous reasoning, overgeneralisation, self-downing
Interpersonal:	Problems in marriage related to her ambivalence. Timid, inhibited, unassertive in most interpersonal contexts. Limited contact with groups of people, especially crowds
Biological:	Headaches. Obesity. Daily use of aspirin. Takes barbiturates at bedtime. Has no systematic exercise regimen and does not adhere to sound nutritional habits (indulgence in 'junk foods')

Clearly, if only one or two interventions were offered to help the client overcome her agoraphobia, so many interrelated problems would remain untouched that a salubrious outcome would be most unlikely. Had I used modality profiles in the late 1960s when treating Mrs D, her chart would have been very similar to this one. Although we managed to address each of her main problem areas, there was a certain element of trial and error, which is greatly reduced when using Modality Profiles as 'blueprints' to guide the clinician. But whatever the merits of multimodal assessment eventually turn out to be, it was Mrs D, more than any other individual, who launched me in the direction of extending, amplifying and broadening the base of behaviour therapy.

Perhaps the main drawback is that Multimodal Therapy is hard work. Often, throughout the course of multimodal assessment and therapy, there is nothing especially edifying or fascinating for therapist and client alike. Ferreting out the main problems in behaviour, affect, sensation, imagery, cognition, interpersonal relations and biological functioning is often tedious, routine, taxing, and enervating. How much simpler it is to be a Rogerian and offer nothing more than a warm and genuine relationship coupled with empathic reflections of clients' affective reactions. For those who see only families, it can be stimulating to spend one's time unravelling putative triangulations and enmeshment while bringing emotional saboteurs to justice. Following the lead of the late Milton Erickson, a new breed of psychotherapists is now proliferating. These clinicians rely heavily on anecdotes, parables and metaphors supposedly addressed to the patient's 'right brain' or 'third ear'. Certainly, it is more enjoyable for most therapists to tell fairy stories (and get paid!) than it is to decide: (1) which particular client is likely to derive benefit from Rogerian reflection (with or without additional measures); (2) when is it best to involve the entire family network; or only certain family members, or neither of the foregoing; (3) having drawn up a modality profile, where does it seem best to intervene and how should this be decided?

Indeed, it is usually easier on the therapist to be unimodal, or bimodal, or even trimodal. Working multimodally calls for a good deal of decision-making, and many questions are raised that go far beyond the issues addressed by most clinicians. Whereas a Rogerian will offer warmth and empathy to all, a Multimodal Therapist will ask: What type of relationship is this person apt to respond to? What style, form, speed and cadence should I adopt? Can I deduce what kind of treatment he or she requires? Am I well suited to this person? Do we appear likely to establish rapport? Would it be in the client's best interests to be referred elsewhere? Do I have evidence that my ministrations are likely to prove effective? These types of questions are generally not pondered by Freudians, Rogerians, Jungians, Adlerians, Sullivanians, and devotees of most other psychotherapeutic disciplines. Instead, the field is characterised by omnibus theories, overgeneralisations and fads. Those who practise psychotherapy for their own enlightenment and fascination are, unfortunately, not in the minority. Could this be why our field is still in a pre-paradigmatic stage of development?

REFERENCES

Bandura, A. (1986). *Social foundations of thought and action: a social cognitive theory.* Englewood Cliffs, NJ: Prentice-Hall

Ellis, A. (1962). *Reason and emotion in psychotherapy.* New York: Lyle Stuart

Emmelkamp, P.M.G. (1982). *In vivo* treatment of agoraphobia. In D.L. Chambless and A.J. Goldstein (Eds), *Agoraphobia: multiple perspectives on theory and treatment.* New York: Wiley

Franks, C.M. and Wilson, G.T. (Eds) (1976). *Annual review of behavior therapy.* New York: Brunner/Mazel

Franks, C.M. and Wilson, G.T. (Eds) (1977). *Annual review of behavior therapy.* New York: Brunner/Mazel

Freud, S. (1924). Turnings in the ways of psychoanalytic therapy. *Collected papers*, vol. II. London: Hogarth Press

Goldstein, A.J. (1982). Agoraphobia: treatment successes, treatment failures, and theoretical implications. In D.L. Chambless and A.J. Goldstein (Eds), *Agoraphobia: multiple perspectives on theory and treatment.* New York: Wiley

Lazarus, A.A. (1958). New methods in psychotherapy: a case study. *South*

African Medical Journal, 32, 660-4

Lazarus, A.A. (1966). Behavior rehearsal vs. non-directive therapy vs. advice in effecting behavior change. *Behaviour Research and Therapy, 4*, 209-12

Lazarus, A.A. (1967). In support of technical eclecticism. *Psychological Reports, 21*, 415-16

Lazarus, A.A. (1971). *Behavior therapy and beyond.* New York: McGraw-Hill

Lazarus, A.A. (1973). Multimodal behavior therapy: treating the BASIC ID. *Journal of Nervous and Mental Disease, 156*, 404-11

Lazarus, A.A. (1981). *The practice of multimodal therapy.* New York: McGraw-Hill

Lazarus, A.A. (1986). Multimodal therapy. In J.C. Norcross (Ed.), *Handbook of eclectic psychotherapy.* New York: Brunner/Mazel

Perls, F.S. (1969). *Gestalt therapy verbatim.* California: Real People Press

Wolpe, J. (1969). *The practice of behavior therapy.* New York: Pergamon Press

Wolpe, J. and Lazarus, A.A. (1966). *Behavior therapy techniques.* New York: Pergamon Press

Zitrin, C.M., Klein, D.F. and Woerner, M.G. (1980). Treatment of agoraphobia with group exposure *in vivo* and imipramine. *Archives of General Psychiatry, 37*, 63-72

11

From Prescription to Integration

James O. Prochaska

PRIOR THEORY AND PRACTICE

I have always been an eclectic therapist. As an intellectual relativist, it is clear that no single school of therapy has a monopoly on understanding people and their problems. Most schools of therapy do have the advantage, however, of having a more systematic and structured approach to helping people. As an eclectic, I have been struggling to develop a more systematic and integrative approach to psychotherapy.

At the time that I was working with the cases that are to be presented, I was trying to practise a type of prescriptive psychotherapy. I say trying because it is very trying to practise prescriptive psychotherapy when the research literature provides all too little leads as to the best interventions to prescribe for particular people with particular types of problems.

Ideally, prescriptive psychotherapy would provide a cookbook approach that would enable clinicians to look up a particular problem in a comprehensive cookbook and find the correct recipe for a cure. If a patient was suffering from a specific phobia, for example, a standard text might prescribe systematic desensitisation or *in vivo* desensitisation (Wolpe, 1973). For clients with specific sexual dysfunctions, a specific intervention developed in the new sex therapies would be prescribed (Masters and Johnson, 1970; Kaplan, 1974). For patients with particular patterns of depression we could prescribe a combination of cognitive therapy and chemotherapy or interpersonal therapy and chemotherapy, depending on which literature we follow.

The type of prescriptive psychotherapy that I was practising was both an empirically and experientially based eclecticism. To the extent that there was empirical evidence that a specific therapy like desensitisation was most effective with a specific problem, like a phobia, then that was the treatment I prescribed. When there was no adequate research available, such as the most effective therapy for character disorders, then I had to rely on the clinical experience of myself and others who wrote about such problems.

As an eclectic therapist, I was influenced by many major schools of therapy (Prochaska, 1984). For phobias, I relied on behaviour therapies developed by Wolpe (1973) and others. For sexual dysfunctions, I practised the new sex therapies developed by Masters and Johnson (1970) and Helen Kaplan (1974). For obsessive-compulsive disorders, I applied implosive therapy generated by Stampfl and Levis (1973).. For depression, I emphasised cognitive therapies, such as those of Beck (1976) and Ellis (1973). With marital disorders, I was most influenced by communication therapists, like Sherod Miller (Miller, Nunnally and Wackman, 1975) and transactional therapists, like Eric Berne (1964). With character disorders, I relied most heavily on Freud and other psychoanalytic therapists. As an eclectic, the therapies I prescribed ranged from remote-control aversive conditioning for self-abusive retarded individuals (Prochaska, Smith, Marzilli, Donovan and Colby, 1974) to intensive insight-oriented psychoanalytic therapy for passive-aggressive personalities.

With such a broad range of theoretical influences and therapeutic practices, it is impossible in a case or two to capture the eclectic nature of my prescriptive approach. The cases that will be presented were all clients with the same presenting complaint. Each case involved a chronic and severe form of vaginismus that made intercourse impossible. In my prior practice, this is how I would have proceeded with such cases.

First, I would obviously have to be knowledgeable about the nature of the problem. I would need to know that vaginismus is the involuntary spastic contraction of the circumvaginal muscles that close off the outer third of the vaginal barrel. When present in its most severe form, this condition makes penetration impossible. In the past, vaginismus was thought to be a rare phenomenon. It is now known that milder forms of this condition occur more frequently than many therapists or spouses realise. Often a couple experiencing difficulty with penetration mistakenly attribute the problem to inadequate lubrication. In fact, however, the difficulty can be caused by involuntary spastic contractions. In its most severe forms, vaginismus prevents any type of penetration, not only intercourse but finger penetration or the insertion of a tampon. In its severe form, vaginismus had been thought to be a chronic problem with poor prognosis for treatment.

As an eclectic, I would consider alternative formulations of the problem. In the classic psychoanalytic formulation, vaginismus was thought to be rooted in the female's hostile desire to castrate the male; the female is impelled by penis envy to capture and to hold on to the male organ (Fenichel, 1945). More recent psychoanalytic formulations view vaginismus as resulting not specifically from the female's castration wishes and penis envy, but rather from a general hostility towards the male partner.

A behaviourally oriented formulation conceptualises vaginismus as due to conditioning experiences wherein penetration becomes associated with pain or fear. A classic example of such an association of penetration with fear and pain would be the traumatic and painful experience of rape. Some women may also be taught to associate pain or fear with penetration by parents or peers who paint vivid pictures of tissue being torn and blood being shed. The anticipation of pain or even bodily damage elicits fear. The fear, if severe enough, can cause involuntary spastic muscle contractions. The contractions prevent penetration, thereby avoiding anticipated pain or damage. The avoidance of penetration reduces fear. The reduction of fear reinforces the muscle contractions. Vaginismus is maintained because it serves as an avoidance response that reduces intense fears due to anticipated pain. From this theoretical orientation the solution is not to raise consciousness of underlying conflicts but rather to reduce fear via counterconditioning procedures.

Since increasing evidence indicated that counterconditioning-type treatments were highly successful with vaginismus (Masters and Johnson, 1970; Kaplan, 1974), the prescription for the problem was straightforward. The prescription followed the relatively standard format for treating vaginismus described by Helen Kaplan (1974). The treatment includes counterconditioning procedures designed to extinguish anxiety and fear by having the person approach a feared stimulus while remaining relatively relaxed. The clients are trained in deep muscle relaxation, including voluntary relaxation of the circumvaginal muscles. The gradual approach consists of the women inserting either a dilator or a finger. In the present cases, the women used finger insertion beginning with just the first knuckle of the index finger. Then, as therapy progresses, the women gradually inserts two knuckles and her full finger. Further progress involves comparable finger insertion by her partner with the woman in control of guiding his finger. Next, control is turned over to her partner. Then, gradually, penile insertion begins with the woman in control of the progress, followed by intercourse with partners varying control of initiating penetration. Penile penetration with pleasure rather than intercourse with orgasm is generally used as the criterion for recovery from vaginismus, since lack of orgasm from intercourse may be due to factors independent of vaginismus. Hence, a woman is considered recovered from vaginismus when she can engage in intercourse with pleasure.

DESCRIPTION OF THE KEY CASES

Let us now examine what happened when standard prescriptions did not necessarily result in standard outcomes. The key cases represent the common dilemma a prescriptive approach faces — that standard prescriptions succeed smoothly sometimes, fail miserably other times, and are met with resistance and difficulties often times. The cases will be presented in a manner that encourages the reader to anticipate which of the cases was an easy success, which was a difficult success, and which was a failure.

In presenting the three cases of vaginismus, we shall highlight client characteristics that are generally considered to be predictors of outcome of psychotherapy. The information to be presented approximates the amount of information that the therapist had available at the end of the first evaluation session. Thus, the reader can begin collecting clues and formulating prognoses as to which case would be an easy success, which a difficult success and which a failure.

The first couple, Case A, were both 22 years old and married for four years. During the four-year period, they had not consummated their marriage. She was a high-school graduate and was currently employed as a sales clerk in a department store. Mrs A was average looking, had a mesomorphic or athletic body type, though she was petite, about a US size 4. She was highly anxious and entered therapy with the belief that her sexual dysfunction was just a sign of a bigger problem. She thought of herself as being neurotic. Except for not being able to have intercourse, her overall sexual adjustment was good. She enjoyed relating sexually with her husband. When they engaged in mutual caressing, both she and her husband were orgasmic. This seemed to be quite gratifying for both, though they experienced frustration at not being able to have intercourse. She had never used a tampon, had been unable to have an internal physical examination, and had never experienced finger penetration or penetration of any kind.

Her fears began in childhood when she heard acquaintances talking about experiencing painful intercourse. At the same time she also reported hearing others talking about pleasurable experiences. The overall marital relationship appeared to be good: they reported few arguments and conflicts and felt good about most of their life together. Mr A was a high-school graduate and a factory worker of working-class background. Both of them were moderately verbal, not highly talkative, yet not really difficult to engage in interaction. Mrs A described her relationships with her family and with friends as being average; she reported no notable conflicts with these persons and felt good about relating to them. Both spouses felt good about their marital relationship, reporting that they seldom, if ever, argued. After the initial session, the therapist rated Mrs A as moderately defensive and as a sensitiser rather than a repressor, a denier or rose-coloured-glasses kind of person. That is, she is the kind of person who looks for and generally finds and focuses on things related to her fears and anxieties, the kind of person who worries a good deal about her anxieties and related problems. As such, she could be rated as being moderately pathological, not in the sense of any major underlying psychotic syndrome, but rather in so far as her anxieties clearly extended beyond the specific fear of penetration. Nevertheless, she was a fairly likeable individual, one who came across as quite warm. However, she also gave the impression of wanting to be taken care of by an accepting companion who would not place strong demands on her. In regard to payment, only a minimal fee was attached to therapy.

Mrs B was an average-looking 26-year-old woman with an endomorph body type, on the heavy side but not obese. She was in her second year of graduate school and was working as a research assistant in a commercial biological laboratory. She had been married for nine months to a 36-year-old PhD research chemist who was working in a business setting. Her fears of penetration dated back to early adolescence. She, too, was not able to have any type of penetration, nor was she able to have internal physical examinations or insertions of tampons. Her conflict about intercourse, namely, wanting to have it but not being able to do so, started about a year earlier, when she became engaged.

Mr B had been married previously and had been impotent in that relationship for most of his attempts at intercourse. His impotence

Table 11.1: Client characteristics of Cases A, B and C

Client characteristics	Case A	Case B	Case C
1. Age	22	26	22
2. Appearance	Mesomorph, average looks	Endomorph, average looks	Ectomorph, average looks
3. Education	HS graduate	2 years graduate school in biology	College senior in botany
4. Occupation	Sales clerk	Research assistant in commercial laboratory	Full-time student
5. Socioeconomic class	Lower middle or working class	Upper middle	Middle middle
6. His age and occupation	22; factory worker	36; PhD research chemist in business	22; college senior social sciences
7. Religion	Both Catholic	Both Jewish	Both Catholic
8. Duration of:			
Fear	Since early teens	Since early teens	Since early teens
Avoidance	Since early teens	Since early teens	Since early teens
Conflict over intercourse	4 years	1 year	6 months
9. Relationship adjustment	Both pleased, few arguments	Very conflicted; daily arguments	Both pleased, few arguments
10. Rest of sexual adjustment	Both orgasmic with mutual caressing	Both orgasmic with caressing but frequent arguments over sex	Both orgasmic with mutual caressing
11. His sexual adjustment	Apparently OK	OK now but impotent in first marriage	Apparently OK
12. Other relationships and family	Average with friends	Average with friends; conflict with mother	Average with friends; very close to mother

13. Anxiety level	High	High	High
14. Defensiveness	Moderate, sensitiser	Moderate to high, projector	Moderate, sensitiser
15. Amount of talk	Moderate	High	Moderate
16. Pathology as seen by self	Sees self as neurotic type	Sees self with some serious problems; sees husband as neurotic	Sees self as normal with limited problems
17. Pathology as seen by therapist	Moderate	Moderate to high	Low to moderate
18. Likeability	Moderate to high	Low to moderate	Moderate
19. Attractiveness for therapy	High	Moderate to high	High
20. Fee	Low	Average private	None

was an important factor in the break-up of his first marriage. Presently he felt positive about his sexual response; he was able to get and maintain erections. But he was concerned that if his wife's condition was not cured, there might be a return of his impotence. The marital relationship of this couple was conflicted and marked not only by the specific sexual problems but by other problems as well. The spouses reported having daily arguments. In the therapy sessions they bickered and argued regularly. Their sexual relating tended to be infrequent, since sexual intimacy was one of the areas that very easily set off arguments. However, when they did engage in mutual caressing, each of them could be orgasmic. Mrs B reported having an ongoing conflict with her mother, because the latter tried to tell her how to clean her house, take care of her husband and the like. In regard to friends, her relationship with them was average.

At the beginning of therapy, Mrs B was highly anxious, not merely in regard to the specific sexual problem, but also regarding other conflicts in her life. She was highly verbal, able to talk quite readily and about many different issues. Her level of defensiveness was moderately high. One might categorise her as a projector, in so far as she tended to regard others, for example her husband and mother, rather than herself, as the source of her problems. She viewed her husband as a neurotic individual and herself as having problems, but not neurotic. In terms of overall affective tone, she came across as angry rather than warm. In regard to likeability, she was rated by the therapist as being in the low to moderate range. This couple paid an average private fee for treatment.

Ms C was a 22-year-old college senior, preparing to graduate. She was single but planned to get married in six months. Her fiancé was also a college senior. Both were honor-roll students, he in the social sciences and she in botany. Each of them felt good about their relationship and experienced sexual pleasure with each other. He saw himself as sexually well adjusted. This couple wanted and attempted to have intercourse for about six months before coming for therapy but were not able to because of the vaginismus problem.

Ms C dated her fears about penetration back to early adolescence; her avoidance of any penetration was complete and also went back to her early teens. Her relationships with friends were good. Ms C had a close relationship with her mother, who lived nearby. At the time she entered therapy her anxiety level was quite high. She could be categorised as a sensitiser, the worry-wort kind of person who looks for things to worry about and generally finds them. She viewed herself as normal with a limited, fairly isolated problem, namely, vaginismus. The therapist judged her overall problems to be of low to moderate severity. This client paid no fee for treatment.

For the sake of convenience and easy access, the characteristics of each of these clients are listed in Table 11.1.

1. Which of the cases, in your view, was the 'easy success'? Case A? Case B? Case C?

2. With which of the cases did sexual therapy 'fail'? Case A? Case B? Case C?

Having completed the above predictions the reader now has the opportunity to compare answers with those given by three groups who heard a presentation about these three cases and filled out the same questionnaire (Prochaska and Lapsanki, 1980). Group I consisted of 40 faculty and graduate students of a psychology department at a state university. The faculty members all had doctoral degrees in psychology, and the students were working towards this advanced degree. Group II consisted of 104 undergraduate volunteers in an introductory psychology course at the same university. Group III consisted of 16 professionals who were active in counselling and social work in the community. Most of these persons held master-level degrees in social work.

Most professors, professionals, graduate and undergraduate students predicted that Case C was the 'easy success'. Across all three groups 75 per cent predicted that Case C was the easy success, and 20 per cent predicted Case A. The popular choice for easy success, namely Case C, was picked by 60 per cent of Group I, 86 per cent of Group II, and 50 per cent of Group III. Contrary to these popular predictions, the actual 'easy success' was Client A. Interestingly, significantly greater percentages of Groups I and III (32.5 and 31.3 per cent, respectively), the more highly trained predictors, were correct than were the untrained freshmen (12.5 per cent). Even with a very difficult task for predicting, professional training made a difference.

Predicting the outcome of therapy is no mere academic exercise. At the outset of treatment, psychotherapists frequently make predictions concerning the process and outcome of therapy with particular clients. The predictions, often not even verbalised, may affect the way therapists and clients work in therapy, for example whether clients will be seen several times a week, once a week, or every other week.

In the case of Mr and Mrs A the therapist predicted that treatment and recovery would be relatively easy. As it happened, the couple was short on money, had only evenings available for treatment, and lived a great distance from the therapist. The therapist, on the other hand, was very short on evening hours. Treatment began in the usual way, with the couple being seen for two face-to-face sessions. Then, because the therapist predicted that they would be a relatively easy couple to work with, it was mutually decided that the couple would phone the therapist on Wednesday evenings. During these 10-minute free phone interviews, the couple reported how they were doing with their current exercises, while the therapist assessed their progress and assigned tasks for the next step of treatment. This procedure, which suited the needs of both the therapist and the couple, flowed quite naturally from the prediction that the case would be relatively easy to handle. This option would probably not have been viable if the case were predicted to be difficult.

The progress of treatment with Case A, represented in Figure 11.1, shows that 100 per cent recovery, namely intercourse with pleasure, was achieved after seven weeks in therapy. Note that at follow-up the curve goes beyond 100 per cent recovery. This is because the couple presented physical validation that the treatment was indeed effective: the woman became pregnant. Hence the bulge in Figure 11.1 can be called a 'pregnancy curve'!

Although it is not surprising that Case A recovered, it is surprising that they could recover so quickly after suffering through their problem for four years of marriage. How can we account for a troubled couple recovering after just two face-to-face interviews and five 10-minute phone calls? Later we shall examine some clinical interpretations of such rapid recovery and our current theoretical understanding which would predict a quick recovery for Case A.

Case B was probably most likely predicted by the reader to be the failure. At least the majority (over 80 per cent) of professors, professionals and students predicted that Case B was the failure. Clearly this case was the popular choice to fail in therapy. But again these predictions miss their mark, since Case B turned out to be the difficult success. Once again, however, the more highly trained predictors in Groups I and III outperformed the untrained undergraduates in Group II. Our advanced training prepares us to be either more sensitive to our clients or more cynical about researchers trying to trick us.

Figure 11.2 presents the progress curve for Case B, the couple

Figure 11.1: Progress curve for Case A

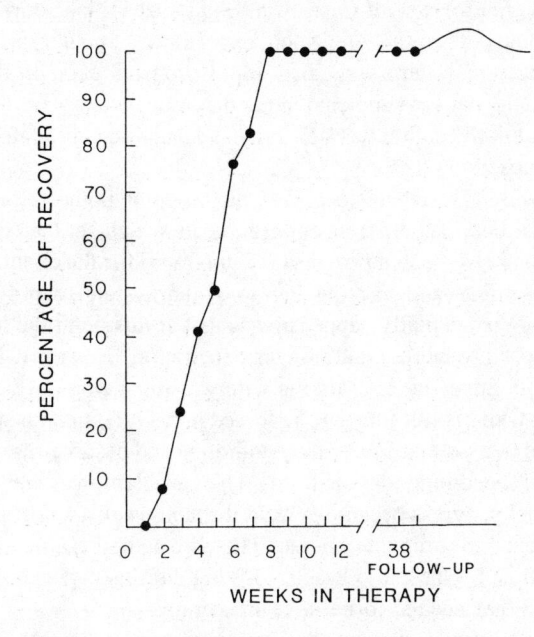

Figure 11.2: Progress curve for Case B

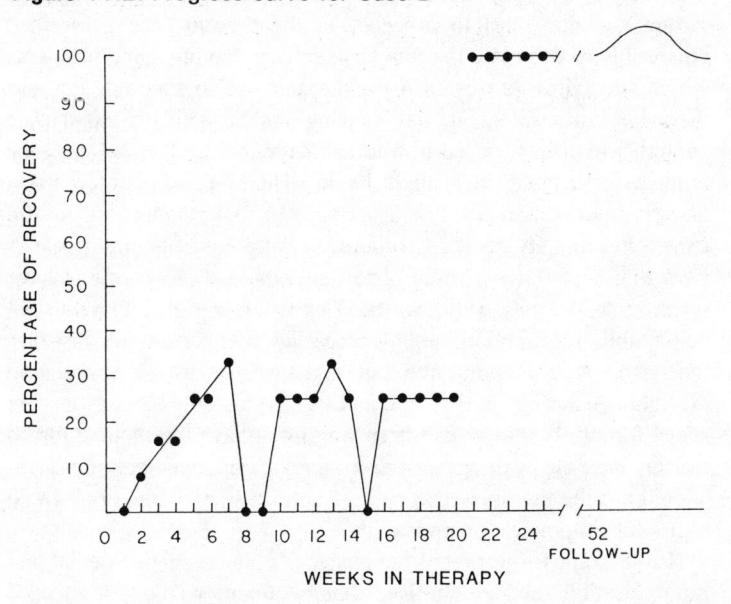

married for nine months who had a great number of arguments. The course of treatment with Case B indicates that initial improvement followed the pattern that one would expect from a counterconditioning perspective. There was fairly rapid progress early in therapy, much like the pattern predicted in the theoretical curves (see Wolpe, 1973). But at the eighth week therapy suddenly began to fail and the client relapsed.

Why did this setback occur? One might hypothesise that the couple had one of their frequent arguments which set the treatment back. It may also be that progress was too rapid for the client, arousing intense fear and causing her to withdraw and avoid further progress. What actually happened was that at this point the husband was supposed to begin gentle finger penetration. However, he tried to force his finger in. He said his wife was just being obstinate and she could take his full finger if he forced her. Of course, using force frightened her, so that she quickly withdrew and became resensitised instead of becoming desensitised. This problem was handled in therapy and progress became evident through week 14. But then her husband tried to force intercourse. The wife again became intensely frightened and relapsed to baseline. What did this pattern of results suggest? What needed to be done in therapy?

The clinician, following the scientific method, often finds it necessary to develop and test hypotheses concerning what might be wrong and how best to proceed. In the present case, it seemed reasonable to postulate that the husband was having some problems which needed to be treated if the therapy was to succeed. Perhaps the wife's improvement was causing the husband to experience anxiety which in turn led him to sabotage therapy. What evidence is there for thinking this might be so? The clue, of course, is that he was impotent in his first marriage. In that relationship he did experience anxiety about intercourse to the point of being impotent. Now that Mrs B was getting better and would soon be free to have intercourse, he may well have been experiencing anxiety about not being able to function, about repeating the pattern of his first marriage. At this point the husband rejected this interpretation outright, declaring he was fine and had no anxieties about sex. He stated forcefully that he had been waiting to have intercourse for 10 months and the waiting was making him impatient not impotent. Would not the therapist also be impatient in such a situation? I told him I felt impotent not impatient.

The therapist interpreted the husband's statements as denial and rationalisation, and emphasised that treatment would not succeed unless the husband was willing to work on his fears, since they were interfering with the couple's progress. It was suggested to the husband that he accept his wife's help in dealing with his fears, just as she was accepting his help. He agreed reluctantly and began to work on his anxieties, one of which concerned the 10-year age difference between them. He had been fantasising that if she were to become fully functional, she would be peaking sexually at a time when he would already be 'over the hill'. He would not be able to keep up with her. This would make him look bad and might lead her to seek another partner. He began to deal with his fears of failure and rejection. In the process of dealing with his fears he risked being more vulnerable with his wife present. They began to talk more openly and to argue less. Then, all of a sudden, in the twenty-first week of therapy, they announced a breakthrough. They reported going to bed and starting to practice with just her doing finger penetration with him present. He had his arms around her helping her to relax. She became very aroused and they had intercourse with pleasure.

A challenging question for Case B was what processes of change allowed them to make a surprising breakthrough after repeated relapse? What variables accounted for Case B being a difficult therapy case? What are effective procedures that a therapist can use with a difficult couple in which one spouse is apparently eager for action while the other is resistant to action? Later we shall address these questions and explore how the transtheoretical model we have developed can help a difficult couple succeed even though most observers predicted they would fail.

The couple who failed was the couple who most people predicted would be an easy success. Figure 11.3 presents the progress curve for Case C. Apparently progress was occurring initially. After the fifth week there was a setback. This relapse appeared to be precipitated by Mr C's becoming frustrated and impatient and trying to force his finger in. Mr C expressed his frustration in therapy over the fact that he believed Ms C was not really trying very hard. He said she postponed practice sessions with weak excuses and would rush through the sessions that were scheduled. The therapist tried to help Mr C deal with any anxieties he might be having about the prospect of his partner being free to have intercourse. He seemed open to considering such an interpretation but was not able to get in touch with any anxieties. Following the expression of some of his frustrations there were no further episodes in which he tried to force penetration.

What was preventing Couple C from progressing? Given that Ms

Figure 11.3: Progress curve for Case C

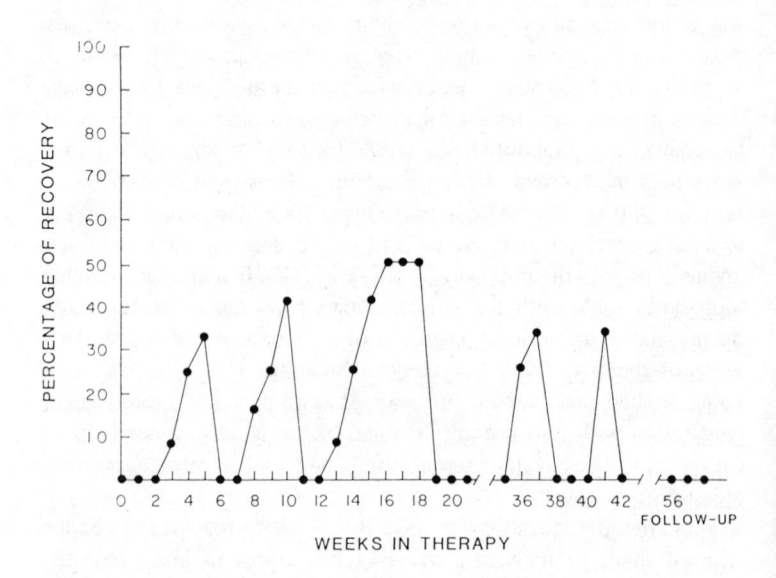

C was Roman Catholic and maintained close ties to her family it was reasonable to hypothesise that she may have been in conflict over the prospect of having sexual intercourse prior to marriage. Even though Ms C had entered therapy with the conscious goal of wanting to overcome the vaginismus before getting married, she may have been experiencing more guilt and ambivalence when the prospect of pre-marital intercourse became a reality. The therapist helped Ms C re-evaluate how she felt about remaining a virgin until marriage. Fantasy exercises were used to help Ms C imagine walking down the aisle aware that she still was a virgin on her wedding day. She felt great. When imagining walking down the aisle aware that she was a non-virgin, however, she felt anxious and guilty. She imagined that her mother would come up to her and ask her if she was still a virgin. Ms C realised that her bright blush would reveal the fact that she had violated a cardinal rule of her church.

After becoming conscious that Ms C had internalised the rule of remaining a virgin until marriage, Couple C decided to postpone further therapy until shortly after their wedding. If the hypothesis was correct that vaginismus served in fact to maintain Ms C's virginity until marriage, then the prediction followed that progress should be rather rapid once the couple was married. The relatively flat curve (which occurred just after the wedding date at the 16th week of treatment) demonstrates how quickly a good clinical hypothesis can be discredited by disappointing data.

The conflict that such cases created is how we can develop a truly prescriptive psychotherapy when people with comparable problems respond to standard treatments with unpredictable results that range from easy to difficult successes, to failures. What theoretical constructs can help us to explain how people with similar symptoms can react to similar prescriptions in such diverse ways that outcomes are strikingly different? What therapeutic approaches can guide us to more effective interventions when we are confronted with resistance to change or failure to change?

The challenge that I confronted was to develop a more comprehensive and integrative model of change that could account for how some people make successful changes relatively easy, whereas others experience great difficulty in changing and others fail to change their troubled behaviours. The key question was how do people change, whether in therapy or outside of therapy. The need was for more process research on how people change rather than outcome research that mainly addresses how much people change in therapy.

EMERGENT NEW DEVELOPMENTS

Answers to these questions did not emerge just from working with clinical cases. The first construct that helped in the understanding of such different outcomes actually emerged from research on people attempting to quit smoking on their own or with the help of therapy (DiClemente and Prochaska, 1982). This research focused on the processes of change that people use to overcome problem behaviours. What we discovered was that the processes that people use vary with the stages of change they are in (Prochaska and Di-Clemente, 1983). With a sample of 155 outpatients entering psychotherapy, we identified four stages of change: precontemplation, contemplation, action and maintenance (McConnaughy, Prochaska and Velicer, 1983). The precontemplation stage involves people who are either unaware of having a problem or are not thinking seriously about changing. They may enter therapy because of pressure from others, but they are not seriously intending to change. Contemplation is the stage in which people become aware that a personal problem exists. They are struggling to understand the problem, its causes and its cures. They are seriously thinking about changing but they have not yet made a commitment to change. Action is the stage during which people change their overt behaviours and the environmental and/or experiential conditions that affect their behaviour. Maintenance is the stage in which people work to continue the gains attained during action and to prevent a relapse to their more troubled patterns of functioning.

Which stage of change clients are in at the beginning of therapy is an important determinant of prognosis. The further along in the stages of change that clients are at the beginning of therapy, the more quickly clients can be predicted to progress. With the three cases of vaginismus, it became clear retrospectively that both Mr and Mrs A were ready for action. They put the penetration exercises into practice almost immediately without resistance. Mrs B, on the other hand, was apparently ready for action, as suggested by the readiness with which she practised the finger-insertion exercises. Mr B, however, apparently was not adequately prepared for action. He was not aware of his own performance anxieties about intercourse, in part because his wife's symptoms protected him from having to face his own sexual problems. The denial and rationalisation that Mr B used to avoid his own anxiety are defences that tend to occur much more often with clients who are in the precontemplation stage.

When therapy involves two or more clients working together, such as in marital therapy, then therapy can be expected to progress most smoothly when each of the clients is at the same stage of change. This apparently was true with Couple A. If one spouse is ready for action while the other has not contemplated what change will mean, then therapy will be difficult at best. The therapist is in the difficult position of being damned by one spouse for moving too slowly or being resisted by the other for moving too quickly. This apparently was true for Couple B, where Mr B had to sabotage the exercises in order to slow down change.

The first rule that emerged when we applied a stage model to our previous practice was that patients' responses to prescribed treatments will vary according to the stage of change that patients are in. If action prescriptions are given to patients in the precontemplation stage, they are likely to project feelings and fantasies of being coerced or pressured on to the therapist's attempts to help. Resistance will be the result. If contemplation prescriptions are given to patients ready for action, then feelings of impatience may be projected. Dropping out or acting out may be the result.

Table 11.2: The stages of change in which particular processes of change are emphasised the most and the least

Precontemplation	Contemplation	Action	Maintenance
Processes used the least	Consciousness raising		
		Self-reevaluation	
		Self-liberation	
		Helping relationship	
		Reinforcement management	
		Counterconditioning	
		Stimulus control	

A more systematic approach to eclectic therapy attempts to match the change processes prescribed by the stage of change clients are in (Prochaska and DiClemente, 1984). Table 11.2 presents the processes of change that have been found empirically to be emphasised at different stages of change (Prochaska and DiClemente, 1983). We can see from Table 11.2, for example, that counterconditioning as a change process will be emphasised by individuals during action and maintenance but not during precontemplation and contemplation. No wonder that Mr B would resist our counterconditioning prescriptions when he was not ready for action.

Table 11.2 suggests that consciousness-raising procedures will work best with clients in the contemplation stage. Self-reevaluation, which is both a cognitive and affective reappraisal of one's problem and the kind of person one is able to be given the problem, can help bridge the movement from contemplation to action. Self-liberation involves the creation of new alternatives for living and is emphasised during action. Contingency control and helping relationships are most beneficial during times of action when risks of failure are greatest and the need for reinforcement and support are heightened. Stimulus control and counterconditioning procedures can be effectively prescribed as both action and maintenance interventions.

Our emerging approach to an integrative eclecticism included the two dimensions of the processes and stages of change. The processes were originally derived from diverse schools of therapy, such as behavioural, client-centred, cognitive, existential and psychoanalytic (Prochaska, 1984). These processes were refined empirically through a series of studies on clients, therapists and self-changers (Prochaska and DiClemente, 1983, 1985; Prochaska and Norcross, 1983). These processes have not been found to be empirically or theoretically incompatible. They can be integrated within the dimensions of the stages of change. The integration of the stages and processes of change can provide a more systematic guide for prescribing particular interventions and exercises.

A third dimension is needed before we can understand the successes and failures we had with our clinical cases. This dimension involves the levels of change. Stages indicate *when* particular types of changes can be made. Processes describe *how* particular changes can be made. Levels focus on *what* needs to be changed. The levels of change are the dimension that provides structure for the content of therapy.

The levels of change represent a hierarchical organisation of five distinct but interrelated levels of psychological problems which are addressed in psychotherapy. These levels are:

(1) Symptom/situational
(2) Maladaptive cognitions
(3) Interpersonal conflicts
(4) Family/systems conflicts
(5) Intrapersonal conflicts

Historically, systems of psychotherapy have attributed psychological problems primarily to one or two levels and intervened at these levels. Behaviourists focused on the target symptoms and situational determinants; cognitive therapists on maladaptive cognitions; family therapists on the family/systems level; and psychoanalytic therapists on intrapersonal conflicts. We assume that therapy will be facilitated if therapists and clients agree as to the level to which they attribute the problem and the level or levels at which they are willing to work to change the problem behaviours. It is important that therapists engage clients at appropriate and at least implicitly agreed-upon levels for the work of therapy to progress smoothly.

Given five different levels of change, how can therapists proceed systematically across the different levels? In our transtheoretical approach we prefer to intervene initially at the symptom/situational level because change tends to occur more quickly at this more conscious and contemporary level of problems. The further down the hierarchy we focus, the further removed from awareness are the determinants of the problem likely to be. Also, as we progress down the levels, the further back in history are the determinants of the problem and the more connected the problem is with the sense of self. Thus we predict from the transtheoretical model that the more complex the level that needs to be changed, the longer and more complex therapy is likely to be. Furthermore, the further removed in history are the determinants of the problem, the greater resistance there will be to trying to change those determinants. One of the reasons for greater resistance is that deeper attributions tend to be more threatening to self-esteem than are more surface attributions. It is more threatening, for example, to believe that vaginismus is due to hostility towards men and a desire to emasculate men than to believe that the anticipation of painful intercourse elicits fear and involuntary circumvaginal muscle contractions. One of the rules of transtheoretical therapy is to use the least threatening attributions that can be justified, since our clinical formulations have the potential for producing damage in their own right.

With Case A, for example, the therapist could have attributed the vaginismus to neurotic conflicts within Mrs A, since she was already set to perceive herself as neurotic because she could not consummate her marriage. The professional's attributions would have carried considerable weight with the young woman and could have done damage to her self-concept and self-esteem. Effective and efficient change was able to be facilitated by focusing on the symptoms and situational level without causing Mrs A to perceive herself as a neurotic individual in need of long-term intensive therapy.

Unfortunately, all too frequently it is the case that problems are not resolved just by focusing on symptom and situational variables. Case A tends to be the exception rather than the rule in clinical practice. At the same time, however, we frequently cannot predict beforehand that therapy cannot be an easy success. Thus, when in doubt, as with Case A, we recommend starting at the symptom and situational level of problems.

There are cases, however, where the initial interview and assessment make it clear that much more is involved than just situational variables. With Case B, for example, it was clear from the initial interview that there were interpersonal conflicts contributing to the couple's sexual dysfunction. Sometimes, as in this case, the therapist cannot intervene at a more complex level until it is also clear to the clients that therapy will not work just by treating the symptom and the situational variables. Case B began at the first level of change with the expectation of having to go to other levels. Hopefully, the therapist remained open to the possibility that his attributions were in error, and the couple may have recovered from symptom and situational treatment without having to confront more complex interpersonal conflicts.

At other times, both the clients and the therapists agree in their attributions that presenting complaints are due to or involve more than the immediate situational variables. If they agree on the level that needs to be changed, then therapy can begin at that level with minimal resistance. Case B, for example, might have presented for therapy with a shared attribution that the vaginismus problem was being maintained by struggles for control and unresolved resentments in their current interpersonal life. Resolution of these problems may have resulted in resolution of the vaginismus problem. Prochaska and Marzilli (1973) reported that in approximately half of their cases first treated for interpersonal conflicts, the sexual dysfunctions improved along with the relationship improving. On the other hand, improvement of interpersonal conflicts could free the couple to cooperate more effectively to produce rapid change at the symptom and situational level. The transtheoretical therapist is prepared, then, to intervene at any of the five levels of change, though the preference is to begin at the highest level that clinical assessment and clinical judgement can justify.

Current interpersonal conflicts may interfere with progress at either the cognitive or situational levels. Couple B was a case where the interpersonal dynamics disrupted progress at the symptom and situational level. Shifting to the interpersonal level can be more complicated, especially if it requires two people having to cooperate in conjoint therapy. One common complication is that one spouse, such as Mrs B, may be ready for action, while the other spouse, like Mr B, may be in the precontemplation stage and may be denying any need to make personal changes.

The most common content issues at the interpersonal level are communication and control. Partners in the precontemplation stage defend against their own needs to change by blaming their spouse for any difficulties the couple is having. Mr B, for example, was blaming all of their interpersonal conflicts on his wife's vaginismus and thereby defending against his own insecurities and anxieties, including the fact that he, too, was petrified of penetration. Cross-blaming is one of the most common communication patterns of conflicted interpersonal relationships. Blaming one's partner for problems not only serves as a defence but it also is a means of trying to control the relationship. If the partner is to blame for problems, then the partner is one who has to change and accommodate, and the person who wins the cross-blaming contest is in control. No wonder cross-blaming can be so intense and that spouses can be very resistant to becoming aware of their own contributions to interpersonal conflicts.

Transactional analysis has described common forms that blaming can take, including the games of 'Now I've got you, you son-of-a-bitch', 'If it weren't for you', and 'Look what you made me do' (Berne, 1964). Couples caught in cross-blaming communicate as if they are in a court-room with the therapist serving as judge and jury. Each communicates their most convincing case for why their partner should be found guilty and be coerced into changing. Each partner is trying to convince the therapist that 'I'm OK and my partner is not OK and that is why I should be in control and my partner should change.' With Mr B we used fairly strong confrontation of his denial and projection by pointing to his repeated pattern of sabotaging progress in therapy by trying to force penetration.

As individuals begin to become aware of their contributions to interpersonal conflicts, they are obviously more open to re-evaluating themselves. If they become aware, for example, that they are frequently communicating like a parent who is trying to blame and control a problem child, they begin to question how they feel and think about relating like a parent. Their defensive tendency will be to say, 'If my partner didn't behave like a child, then I wouldn't have to act like a parent.' By becoming more conscious of the concept of circular causality, they can reverse this proposition and say 'If I didn't respond like a parent, maybe my partner wouldn't continue to act like a child.'

How to liberate oneself from interpersonal levels of problems without changing the other person is the paradox facing many patients. Rather than seeking self-help, many people would rather have help with changing other people. They tend to believe that 'If I could just get my partner, or my parent or my employer to change, then I would be free of problems.' One of the liberating teachings that can be derived from a circular causality concept of relationships is that 'If I don't like what I am getting from my relationship, then I should change my behaviour.' Rather than continue to rely on trying to change significant others through coercive strategies like the blame game, clients can begin to rely on intentional change by committing themselves to acting differently in their relationships.

When Mr B was able to break out of his angry parent ego state in which he yelled at his recalcitrant child-wife for not trying hard enough, and he was able to take more adult responsibility for part of their problems, the couple was able to make remarkably rapid progress. Effective action is more likely to be maintained if both people in a relationship have progressed through the contemplation stage and are ready to risk relating in novel ways. Once Mr B had progressed from precontemplation to contemplation and was ready for action, the couple was able to make rapid progress in overcoming their sexual dysfunctions. Their progress at the interpersonal level also included liberating themselves from an exclusive reliance on defensive and destructive blame games.

An inability to progress at the current interpersonal level is usually interpreted as due to unresolved historical conflicts. First we shift to a family systems level to determine if progress can be made by helping the patients break out of patterns passed on from one generation to the next. Individuals can be unable to make intentional changes because they have yet to become individuated and independent enough from their families of origin. Ms C, for example, appeared to be overly attached to her mother. Because she had not differentiated herself enough from her mother, she could only experience her body as still under the control of her mother's rules. Furthermore, if her mother was having trouble letting go of her emotionally, Ms C could continue to have considerable difficulty in consummating her marriage. She would not be free to follow through on the penetration exercises until she owned her body and her self as separate and independent of her family's control. Since Couple C dropped out of therapy before we could address these issues fully, we are left with clinical interpretations rather than case illustrations for the effectiveness of working at the family systems level.

IMPLICATIONS FOR OTHER THERAPISTS

Key cases and crucial data have led to a transtheoretical approach to psychotherapy. This approach views comprehensive treatment as the differential application of the processes of change at the four stages of change according to the problem level being addressed. Integrating the levels with the stages and processes of change provides a model for intervening hierarchically and systematically across a broad range of therapeutic content. Table 11.3 presents an overview of the integration of levels, stages, and processes of change.

This integrative model of change has a number of important implications for therapists. The first is that action-oriented prescriptions will be met with resistance by clients who are in the contemplation or precontemplation stage of change. Similarly, contemplation-

Table 11.3: Levels × stages × processes of change

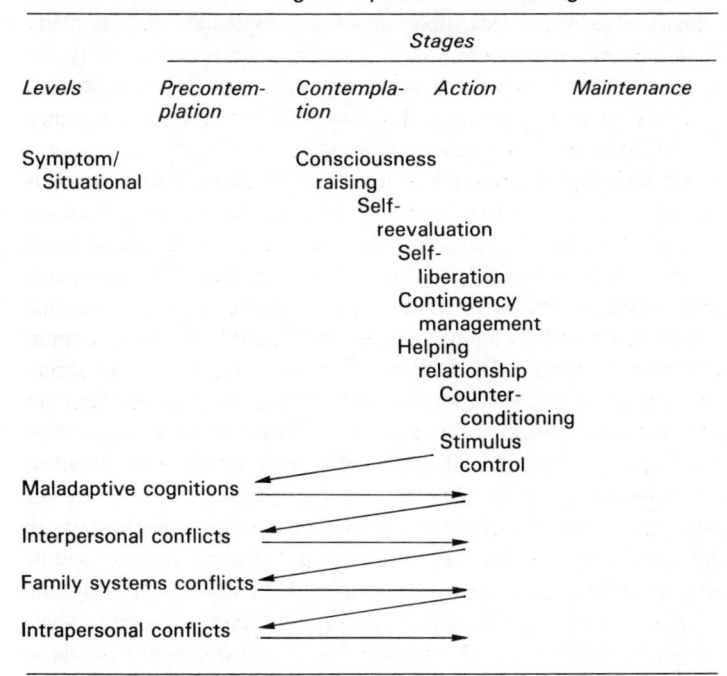

	Stages			
Levels	Precontemplation	Contemplation	Action	Maintenance

Symptom/Situational		Consciousness raising
		  Self-reevaluation
		    Self-liberation
		    Contingency management
		    Helping relationship
		    Counter-conditioning
		    Stimulus control		

Maladaptive cognitions	← →			
Interpersonal conflicts	← →			
Family systems conflicts	← →			
Intrapersonal conflicts	← →			

oriented treatments will be met with resistance by clients ready for action. Therapy will be most effective when the processes of therapy match the stage that clients are in.

A second implication is that therapists will need to change therapeutic processes as clients move across the stages if we are to help facilitate progress. Our research on self-changers and our experience with clients indicate that people can get stuck for years in a stage like contemplation as they repeatedly rely on consciousness-raising and self-reevaluation procedures rather than moving to more action-oriented procedures.

Another implication is that, to be most effective, therapists need to be at least as sophisticated about change as are clients. Most self-changers apply eight to ten processes over the course of their recovery. Most traditional therapies rely on two or three processes of change (Prochaska, 1984). If the therapist is limited to two or three processes, then the client will have to bear more of the responsibility for changing.

A fourth implication is that by working systematically, across the stages of change, we can integrate processes of change that traditionally were viewed as theoretically incompatible. Processes like consciousness raising that were originally derived from psychoanalytic theory can be integrated with behavioural processes like counterconditioning and stimulus control. Change is not just a function of increased consciousness or modified contingencies or a helping relationship. Successful change is a function of a diverse set of change processes that are systematically applied across a series of stages of change.

The transtheoretical approach also has major implications for intervening at very different levels of change. Three basic strategies can be employed for intervening across multiple levels of change. The first is a *shifting levels* strategy. Therapy would typically focus first on the client's symptoms and the situations supporting the symptoms. If the processes could be applied effectively at the first level and the client could progress through each stage of change as was true with Couple A, therapy could be completed without shifting to a more complex level of analysis. These types of cases will be our easiest successes. If this approach was not effective, therapy would shift to other levels in sequence in order to achieve the desired change. The strategy of shifting from a higher to a deeper level is illustrated in Table 11.3 by the arrows moving first across one level and then down to the next level. This is the strategy we would now recommend for Case C, with emphasis finally being placed on resolving family of origin conflicts.

The second is the *key level* strategy. If the available evidence points to one key level of causality of a problem and the client can be effectively engaged at that level, the therapist would work almost exclusively at this key level. This strategy seems similar to the prescriptive approach that I previously emphasised. Thus, if the evidence points to phobias being best treated at the situational level, then our prescription would seem to be straightforward. The key level strategy recognises, however, that the same syndrome can be caused by conditions or conflicts at very different levels of change. The previous prescriptive approach would recommend treating all cases of vaginismus, for example, at the symptom and situational level. But, as our key cases indicate, the same type of vaginismus problem can be controlled by variables at very different levels of change. The implication is that the key to one client's problem will not necessarily be the same for other clients with similar symptoms.

The third alternative is the *maximum impact* strategy. With many complex clinical cases, it is evident that multiple levels are involved as a cause, an effect or a maintainer of the clients' problems. In these cases, interventions can be created which attempt to affect clients at multiple levels of change in order to establish a maximum impact for change in a synergistic rather than a sequential manner.

Applying the transtheoretical model, therapists can develop a more comprehensive and integrative approach that ranges from prescriptions to projections. For some clients, like Case A, our original prescriptive approach will be highly successful. Clients ready for action at the symptom and situational level can cooperate without projecting any excess baggage on to our prescriptions.

Other clients, like Mr B, can project feelings of coercion and control on to the same types of prescription. The resistance that results from Mr B's projections can be taken as evidence that the therapist is intervening at an inappropriate stage or an inappropriate level. Therapeutic prescriptions can be given as projective devices that clients will restructure in accordance with the stage and level they are at.

If therapists are effective in applying the key level strategy, they are not likely to prescribe interventions that will be resisted by clients. When therapists misapply the key level strategy, they may need to analyse their attributions as projections based on countertransference reactions or theoretical predilections. Therapists who attribute every clinical problem to unresolved oedipal conflicts, or unresolved control conflicts or unresolved family conflicts may be substituting personal or theoretical projections for more accurate clinical attributions.

REFERENCES

Beck, A. (1976). *Cognitive therapy and the emotional disorders*. New York: International Universities Press

Berne, E. (1964). *Games people play*. New York: Grove Press

DiClemente, C. and Prochaska, J. (1982). Self-change and therapy change of smoking behavior: a comparison of processes of change in cessation and maintenance. *Addictive Behavior, 7*, 133–42

Ellis, A. (1973). *Humanistic psychotherapy: the rational-emotive approach*. New York: McGraw-Hill

Fenichel, O. (1945). *The psychoanalytic theory of neurosis*. New York: W.W. Norton

Kaplan, H.S. (1974). *The new sex therapy*. London: Ballière Tindall

Masters, W. and Johnson, V. (1970). *Human sexual inadequacy*. Boston: Little, Brown

McConnaughy, E., Prochaska, J. and Velicer, W. (1983). Stages of change in psychotherapy: measurement and sample profiles. *Psychotherapy: Theory, Research and Practice, 20*, 368-75

Miller, S., Nunnally, E. and Wackman, B. (1975). *Alive and aware: how to improve your relationships through better communication*. Minneapolis, Minnesota: Interpersonal Communication Programs

Prochaska, J. (1984). *Systems of psychotherapy: a transtheoretical analysis*. Homewood, IL: Dorsey Press

Prochaska, J. and DiClemente, C. (1983). Stages and processes of self-change of smoking: toward an integrative model of change. *Journal of Consulting and Clinical Psychology, 51*, 390-5

Prochaska, J. and DiClemente, C. (1984). *The transtheoretical approach: crossing traditional boundaries of therapy*. Homewood, IL: Dow Jones-Irwin

Prochaska, J. and DiClemente, C. (1985). Common processes of change with smoking, obesity, and psychic distress. In S. Shiffman and T. Willis (Eds), *Coping and substance abuse*. New York: Academic Press

Prochaska, J. and Lapsanski, D. (1980). Predicting outcome in three cases of vaginismus. Unpublished manuscript, University of Rhode Island

Prochaska, J. and Marzilli, R. (1973). Adaptation of Masters and Johnson's therapy for sexual problems to an outpatient clinic. *Psychotherapy: Theory, Research and Practice, 10*, 301-6

Prochaska, J. and Norcross, J. (1983). Psychotherapists' perspectives on treating themselves and their clients for psychic distress. *Professional Psychology: Research and Practice, 14*, 642-55

Prochaska, J., Smith, N., Marzilli, R., Donovan, W. and Colby, J. (1974). Demonstration of the advantages of remote-control aversive stimulation in the control of headbanging in a retarded child. *Journal of Behavior Therapy and Experimental Psychiatry, 5*, 285-9

Stampfl, T. and Levis, D. (1973). *Implosive therapy: theory and technique*. Morristown, NJ: General Learning Press

Wolpe, J. (1973). *The practice of behavior therapy*. Elmsford, NY: Pergamon Press

12

Key Cases in Psychotherapy: Concluding Issues

Windy Dryden

In this final chapter, it is not my intention to provide a comprehensive presentation of all the salient issues that are discussed (or are implicit) in the contributors' chapters, since I do not wish to curb the reader's independent thinking. Rather, I will discuss some of the issues that are personally relevant to my own work as a theoretician and practitioner of psychotherapy.

MORRISON

Morrison's chapter (Chapter 2) is interesting in that he resolved a conflict between his personality and the behaviourally inspired psychotherapy he practised *before* taking on the case that he describes. The case provided him with an opportunity to test out important insights which he derived from the dream that he vividly describes. His contribution clearly shows one practitioner's dissatisfaction with the approach in which he was originally trained. The sources of this dissatisfaction seemed to be (a) the lack of resonance between the approach and Morrison's personality; (b) the failure of the approach in helping Morrison to go deeply into his clients' 'psyche'; (c) the failure of the approach to help Morrison to explain the cognitive aspects of his own personal conflict; and (d) his own impatience with his progress as a therapist using a behavioural approach. This has important implications for those involved in training therapists. Morrison advances the view that training should ideally allow therapists to weigh different approaches and try different techniques until they find the most comfortable and effective approach for themselves. The issue of personal comfort with one's own therapeutic approach stands out for me as a central theme in Morrison's chapter. His hypothesis that this factor serves as a protection against therapist burnout particularly warrants investigation. Also Morrison's personal-comfort thesis would suggest that even if a given therapeutic approach was shown to be more effective than all others, not all therapists would then practise this approach. Morrison is rightly concerned with *both* the personal comfort of therapists *and* the issue of effectiveness. It is only where these conflict that important dilemmas are posed for practitioners.

A second theme that stands out for me in Morrison's chapter concerns the close parallel that appears to exist between the process of change in emotive-reconstructive therapy (ERT) and the therapeutic processes present in Morrison's dream. In both, an image provokes the expression of strong repressed feelings which lead to powerful insights, which in turn stimulate personality changes. This raises two interesting questions: (a) to what extent do therapists practise a type of therapy that is based on their own experiences of personal change?, and (b) to what extent will their clients benefit from similar mechanisms of learning? Clients differ in the ways in which they learn and thus not all will benefit from the change process implicit in ERT. This raises other questions: to what extent do therapists expect clients to accommodate to their therapeutic approach and to what extent do they actually accommodate to their clients' unique styles of learning? At present we know very little about accommodation processes in psychotherapy.

After Morrison found that his newly derived techniques were effective, he embarked on two major activities. First, realising that he was without a theory to explain why his techniques worked, he undertook a search to find such a theory and eventually settled on Kelly's construct theory as an explanatory framework. His search illustrates how important theory tends to be to psychotherapists, as has been observed by Cornsweet (1983). Secondly, Morrison carried out a series of research studies to demonstrate the effectiveness of his new approach. There exists an inherent problem whenever the person who invented a therapeutic approach carries out research on it. In this case to what extent did Morrison's personal investment in his approach affect his findings? One must query whether his results can be explained by his faith in his own approach rather than by the methods themselves. However, he is to be congratulated for attempting to investigate empirically his own approach to therapy, a venture which was also taken by Prochaska.

AVELINE

Aveline (Chapter 3) shows graphically the personal conflict that he experienced during his described case. His chapter demonstrates how a therapist's temperament can influence his or her interventions with a client. Here Aveline's strong reparative element in his personality, where he easily feels responsible and guilty, and his acute awareness of anger directed towards himself prevented him from sharing some of his feelings until later in the therapeutic process. However, his tenaciousness encouraged him to persist and to go against his reparative temperament and tendency to avoid conflict. In doing so Aveline learned that, in some therapy cases, client change inside the therapy room can have a greater impact on the client's development than change outside therapy. This realisation led to a revision of one of his previous 'practice points'.

It is a myth that therapists can be helpful to all their patients, and limiting factors such as personal temperament need to be acknowledged and whenever possible transcended. As Aveline notes, it was only when he stopped pretending that he was at one with his client that he could deal with the breakdown in their relationship. However, although Aveline was able, in this case, to transcend some of his temperamental qualities, it is a mistake to believe that therapists can transcend all their limiting factors, and a certain humility is a desirable quality to have as a therapist. Knowing oneself and one's limitations and having the ability to overcome these as far as one can are important qualities of effective therapists, as is knowing when not to persist with given clients whose therapy is not going well. None of the contributors deals with this latter issue, but it is discussed by Wachtel and myself elsewhere (cf. Dryden, 1985).

Finally, Aveline makes an important point concerning the concept of transference. He notes that exploring the transferential elements of the client-therapist can serve to create distance between the two participants, and such a strategy may not be helpful for clients like Aveline's who seem to benefit more from working with a therapist who is self-revealing. This raises the following question: to what extent can therapists relinquish ways of working that are central to *their* concept of what constitutes effective therapy when these ways are not helpful with given clients?

THORNE

Thorne's chapter (Chapter 4) is a fascinating account of a therapist being challenged to extend the concept 'core therapeutic conditions' which are so central to the practice of person-centred therapy. Thorne's faith in the wisdom of the organism, in God, and in the correctness of his own motivation encouraged him to offer a kind of therapeutic relationship which seemed to be so important in the case described, but which may be viewed as unethical by some. It is important to note that the development of such a relationship was only possible given (a) the fact that the client's husband placed a lot of trust in Thorne as a therapist; (b) the freedom from institutional constraints that in Thorne's view can inhibit his spontaneity as a counsellor; and (c) the congruence between the client's and therapist's religious values. This case illustrates Thorne's discovery of the physical (bodily) dimensions of empathy, his questioning of the limits of psychotherapy as traditionally practised, and his own enormous commitment to the development of his client.

Thorne is sure that his client would have been poorly served by his prior mode of therapy (i.e. that characterised by weekly meetings lasting 50 minutes, based on verbal exchange and focused on the present, and where discussion of religious issues is scrupulously avoided), and it is apparent that no other case described in this book challenged so many of the therapist's prior therapeutic practices as did Thorne's. His work as described here is an obvious challenge to those therapists who work within rigorous time, place and behavioural boundaries. How easy, in comparison, it is to practise therapy within rigorous guidelines, particularly given the risks inherent in extending boundaries. It should also be remembered that Thorne's work as described here is based on his belief in himself as an experienced therapist and on the absence of self-deception. His work also places a lot of emphasis on the client having great faith in the therapist's intentions. Other clients may have misconstrued Thorne's 'bodily' interventions and matters may have easily got 'out of hand'. Self-deceiving therapists are particularly vulnerable in this regard. Perhaps more than anything, Thorne's case serves as a reminder of the important role that supervision plays in the practice of psychotherapy, and particularly so when therapists are considering extending traditional therapeutic boundaries.

WILE

Wile's contribution (Chapter 5) is interesting in that his realisation concerning how difficult it is to apply aspects of his theory actually strengthens his belief in the theory itself. Wile's thesis is that squelching of ordinary feelings produces symptoms of psychological disturbance (Freud's Theory 1). He notes that while giving credence to Freud's first theory he found himself, in his described case, caught between this and Freud's second theory (namely that people's original wishes are fundamental infantile and primitive). According to Wile, Freud's second theory encourages accusatory thinking, a tendency exacerbated by everyday momentary overload. Thus, in his case, while believing in Theory 1, Wile reverts to Theory 2 (and begins to accuse his client couple) when faced with the pressure of everyday therapeutic overload. Such pressure, Wile notes, can stem from such self-imposed therapist demands as: 'I'm supposed to be the therapist around here and to know what I'm doing, but I haven't the vaguest idea what's going on.' It is the therapist's rejection of his or her own helplessness or impotence that is the problem here. The 'solution' is, as Wile recognises, very difficult. It is for therapists to encourage themselves to accept all their feelings and reactions as 'acceptable'. Interestingly, Thorne makes a similar point when discussing the sexual feelings he experienced in working with his client. Wile's 'solution' for therapists also forms the basis of his therapeutic strategy with clients who are to be urged to accept all their feelings as ordinary and 'acceptable'.

Wile goes further in his chapter and suggests that many therapeutic concepts in current usage are disguised accusations which presumably serve to impede client progress. Although he does not say so, it seems that Wile would be critical of the increasing use that psychotherapists seem to be making of psychiatric diagnostic terminology (cf. DSM-III), such as the term currently in vogue: 'borderline personality disorder'. In this respect Wile's position directly opposes the medical model of psychotherapy.

ROWAN

Rowan's chapter (Chapter 6) shows how one therapist responded to a situation where a potentially productive intervention (i.e. siding with the client) conflicted with a centrally held principle of therapy (i.e. it is the client who does therapy, not the therapist). His solution is an interesting one. It is to distinguish between doing therapy and carrying out therapeutic activities. Thus 'siding with the client' is now seen by Rowan as 'therapeutic' in the sense of preparing the way for therapy to occur rather than as part of 'therapy' itself. He notes that this distinction leads to the challenging observation that much of what is done in a therapy session is not therapy! Though some may say that Rowan's distinction is a smart way of avoiding cognitive dissonance, it does seem to lead to a clear demarcation of responsibility between client and therapist. However, his distinction may add to the problems of psychotherapy researchers, since how is one to know whether 'therapy' is taking place or not?

In his thoughtful section on implications for other therapists, Rowan emphasises flexibility as a desirable therapist quality which particularly fosters therapeutic developments. This includes being open to the ideas of others and the ability to integrate these into one's theory of therapy. However, he also recognises that serendipity is important, e.g. having the good fortune of being in the right place at the right time. But, as Rowan stresses, a therapist may have luck on his or her side but may not have the flexibility to utilise constructively such serendipitous opportunities.

BUTT AND BANNISTER

Butt and Bannister's contribution (Chapter 7) traces the gradual shift that Butt made from being a behaviour therapist to becoming a personal construct therapist (with the help of Bannister). Initially, Butt's response to impasses in behaviourally oriented social skills training was to provide 'more of the same', until he realised that he had been helping clients to find silly answers to silly questions. This situation arose because he accepted uncritically clients' initial complaints and assumed that they wanted unreservedly what they said they wanted from therapy. It was when Butt began to realise that 'people cannot don an ill-fitting role, however much they might appear to want it' that he began to see the value of helping clients to find better questions rather than better answers to unhelpful questions. And yet to ignore completely clients' stated goals is to court therapeutic failure. Butt and Bannister rightly distinguish between accepting uncritically clients' initial goals and taking them seriously but not at face value. What clients say they want may not coincide with what they are prepared to accept, but they may be most prepared to revise what they want when they see that they are not prepared to accept its implications.

Butt's theoretical change paralleled the personal change achieved by clients in the sense of being gradual rather than sudden. In both areas of change, 'new propositions are tried on for size gradually, and for a time exist side by side with old'. Clients and therapists are similar, say Butt and Bannister, in that both cannot be left without a theory and that for both a new role has to connect with the old.

Butt and Bannister note the different responses that therapists can make when facts do not fit theory: find a new theory, adopt an eclectic stance or keep the old theory and distort the facts. Note that both the chapter by Butt and Bannister and that by Rowan give eclecticism a 'bad press', whereas 'technical eclecticism' is advocated by Lazarus. As I have discussed elsewhere (Dryden, 1984), there are different types of eclecticism and the term appears to be employed in different ways by different authors in this book. However, note once again the important role that theory plays in Butt and Bannister's presentation as it does elsewhere in the book (cf. chapters by Ellis, Morrison, Rowan, Wessler and Wile). At a time when therapists appear preoccupied with technical developments, at least half of the book's contributors are preoccupied with what seem to be predominantly conceptual concerns.

ELLIS

In Chapter 8, Ellis discusses changes in his theorising about disturbance. His first key case helped him to consolidate his thinking about the biological basis of human irrationality and played an important part in the origin of rational-emotive therapy. Note how, in this case, Ellis uses his client's questions to stimulate himself to do some rapid 'on the spot' thinking. These questions seem to bring to the surface knowledge of which Ellis was previously only dimly aware. He literally gets the answer to some of his own questions about disturbance through open 'arguing' interchange with his client. This is particularly interesting in light of the many criticisms rational-emotive therapists receive concerning their 'arguing' style of therapeutic interaction. 'Arguing' in RET really means 'debating', and should not be confused with being argumentative. At the end of his first key case, Ellis advocates that therapists can learn from clients particularly if they are prepared to treat every session as an experiment and are prepared to listen carefully to the doubts that their clients have about their 'arguments'. Note also that Ellis experienced little conflict in this first case since prior conceptual change had already been initiated. It was as if Ellis' client helped him to consolidate his ideas. This process of consolidation is also described in Wile's chapter.

In Ellis' second key case, he begins to see more clearly the role that discomfort disturbance plays in psychological problems. Prior to this case he had thought that ego disturbance was more pervasive than he now considers it to be. According to Ellis discomfort anxiety (DA) is less dramatic than ego anxiety (EA) and it is only when his second client reports still feeling 'anxious' after making great strides in overcoming his feelings of shame (EA) that Ellis sees with greater clarity the distinction between EA and DA.

WESSLER

In the following chapter, Wessler, formerly Director of Training at the Institute for Rational-Emotive Therapy in New York, traces the development of his increasing disenchantment with RET. Indeed, it is interesting to note that his dissatisfaction with the traditional version of RET was present at the outset of his own training as a rational-emotive therapist. Wessler rose quite quickly through the ranks at the Institute for RET and very soon became Director of Training. Although he does not explicitly say so, it seems to me that Wessler squelched his dissatisfaction with RET (see Wile's chapter) throughout his period of office as training director. It is difficult to teach any system of therapy as well as being primarily responsible for organising training programmes while being explicitly aware of one's major dissatisfactions with that system. It is also difficult to acknowledge openly such dissatisfactions when one belongs to a professional community based on that system. Thus it is possible to argue that it was difficult for Wessler to 'listen to himself' with any clarity until he took sabbatical leave from his office at the Institute.

Wessler's chapter raises important issues concerning the role of professional communities in the life of psychotherapists. Such communities offer practitioners a forum for an exchange of ideas and, perhaps more importantly, a sense of belonging. However, they may not be very helpful in encouraging open critical debate when the object of that debate is the therapy system that provides the *raison d'être* for the community itself. Also, given Wessler's experience and my own hypothesis concerning the constraining impact that his professional community had on the development of his thought, perhaps all psychotherapists should take sabbatical leave from such communities in order to discover what they really think about therapy!

LAZARUS

In Chapter 10, Lazarus traces the development of his therapeutic approach from unimodal (behaviour) therapy to bimodal (cognitive-behaviour) therapy to multimodal therapy. During this journey he learned that: 'the more coping responses a person learns in therapy, the less likely he or she is to relapse' and that 'clients are usually troubled by a multitude of specific problems that should be dealt with by a wide range of specific treatments'. Initially Lazarus experienced conflict about alienating his mentor, Joseph Wolpe, but he decided to take a risk, 'came out of the closet' and renounced the unimodal aspects of behaviour therapy. He was indeed banished by Wolpe, and 20 years later the aftermath of the Wolpe-Lazarus split can still be seen in periodic exchanges of letters in professional journals. This underscores the fact that dissociating oneself publicly from a previously held position may have negative consequences for the therapist concerned, as Wessler also discovered.

Lazarus' chapter challenges the position of therapists who rely upon a restricted number of therapeutic procedures in their practice of psychotherapy. He suggests that such therapists are attracted to unimodal and bimodal therapies partly because these do not require as much hard work as does multimodal therapy, and partly because such therapies are intrinsically enjoyable to practise. These factors seem to be negative elements of the personal-comfort thesis advanced by Morrison in Chapter 2.

PROCHASKA

Prochaska's chapter (Chapter 11) shows how his developing ideas on transtheoretical therapy were firmly rooted in his ongoing research on levels, processes and stages of change. Prochaska is the only contributor in the book whose therapeutic developments stemmed *from his own ongoing research*. Morrison's research on emotive-reconstructive therapy was initiated after he developed this therapeutic approach, and Lazarus, who argues that therapeutic procedures need to be empirically based, essentially relies upon the research findings of others. It seems as if Prochaska learned more from his research than he did from his clients. In this sense he is in the minority, both in this book and among American psychotherapists (see Morrow-Bradley and Elliott's (1986) research discussed in Chapter 1).

SOME FINAL REFLECTIONS

Editing this book has been a gamble, since I did not have a clear idea, at the outset, what the finished product would look like. I am generally pleased with the diversity of views expressed in the book, which seems to parallel the diversity of opinions existing in the field of psychotherapy today. My biggest regret is that most contributors failed to make clear (even after editorial promptings) what conflicts they experienced during the conduct of their key cases. It is interesting to me that the contributors who succeeded in clearly articulating their conflicts were those who wrote about personal conflicts (Thorne, Aveline and, to some extent, Morrison). Perhaps it is more difficult to articulate one's experience concerning conceptually based conflicts.

Nevertheless, I consider the book to be a worthwhile addition to the literature on psychotherapy and I particularly hope that it will provide some guidance and comfort for novice and experienced therapists as they encounter their own key cases.

REFERENCES

Cornsweet, C. (1983). Nonspecific factors and theoretical choice. *Psychotherapy: Theory, Research and Practice, 20*(3), 307–13

Dryden, W. (1984). Issues in the eclectic practice of individual therapy. In W. Dryden (Ed.), *Individual Therapy in Britain*. London: Harper & Row

Dryden, W. (1985). *Therapists' dilemmas*. London: Harper & Row

Morrow-Bradley, C. and Elliott, R. (1986). Utilization of psychotherapy research by practising psychotherapists. *American Psychologist, 41*(2), 188–97

Index

ABC theory 178, 179, 180, 190–1
academic environment 50–3
acceptance, unconditional 50–2, 209
accusatory statements 85–8, 89–91, 94, 257
　reasons for 92–4, 95–6
　see also cross-blaming
accusatory thinking in psychiatry 96–100, 257
affect see emotions; feelings
agoraphobia 213–18, 222–4
'allies' in therapy 117
alternatives, limited view of 141–2, 143
American Psychological Association 162, 192
anger
　and depression 99
　and personal rules 189, 203
　as a tactic 202
　at past events 7–8
　over others' behaviour 165, 166
　pleasurable components of 168–9, 171
　transferred 99–100
anticipation 143–4
anxiety 231, 234–5
　about inadequacy 83–4
　financial 201, 202, 205–6
　from changing self-image 136–8, 204–5
　from disowned potentials 105–6
　general 164
　sexual 238–9, 240–1; see also repression, sexual
　social 130–2
Apfelbaum, B. 80
approval/disapproval 155–6
assertions, accusations as 91, 95

assertiveness 135, 136, 137–9, 170
　training 216
assessment interview 27
assumptions, questioning 119–21
assumptive world 25
audiotapes 210–11
avoidance 229, 231
　of real issues in therapy 121

Bandura, A. 128–9, 221
'basic drives' 99
Beck, A.T. 197, 228
behaviour therapy 6–7, 127–9, 130–3, 144, 213–14, 215–16, 217–18, 228
　tediousness of 6
Behaviour Therapy Institute 214
behavioural factors 204–6
behaviourism 41, 143, 229
　cognitive factors in 6
'being and becoming' 23–4
'being in the world' 24
'being known' 25–6, 34–5, 44
beliefs
　groundless 151–2
　'rational'/'irrational' 162–3, 178, 189; see also musturbatory beliefs
　unconscious 172
Bergantino, L. 124
Berne, Eric 228
Binder, J.L. 45
birth, understanding of 72
body, befriending of 55–6, 57–8, 61, 73–4
body work 58, 59–62, 64, 66, 68–9, 73–4
boundaries in therapy 53, 69–70, 117, 256
Buscaglia, Leo 180

cathartic breakthrough 106

change
  dilemmas in 135–9, 143, 204–5
  experimenting with 139–40
  goals of 135–7
  in construct systems 13, 14–15
  in relationship between client and therapist 35
  levels of 244–8, 250
  stages of 241–3, 248–50
charities, involvement with 217
child abuse 10
childhood experiences 7–9, 10–11, 12–13, 30, 31, 108–11, 218
children 29–30
Christians/Christianity 50, 53–4, 59, 60, 69, 240
cognitive appraisal therapy (CAT) 192, 197–211
cognitive approach 12, 128–9, 216–18, 221–2, 228
cognitive factors 6, 199–201; see also beliefs; self-statements
cognitive structures 199
'cognitive therapy' 197
cognitive-learning theory 5–6
collaborative process, therapy as 161
communication in therapy 49, 62–3, 64
communication therapy 228
complaints, taking at face value 134, 146, 258
conditioning 229
consciousness-raising procedures 243, 250
construct systems
  change in 13, 14–15
  simplistic 12–13
constructive alternativism 138–9, 144–5
consumer-oriented approach 14–15, 17
control, struggles for 246–7
'core conditions' 48, 75, 256
core-role constructs 136–8
corrective emotional experiences 24
Corsini, Raymond 160
counterconditioning treatments 229
counter-transference 44
cross-blaming 246–7
'culturally sanctioned accusations' 94, 96–7, 101

decision-making 195
defences/defensiveness 85, 105
definitional concepts 152–5
demoralisation 22–3
dependency 28, 29, 31, 215
depression 6, 27
  and anger 99
  as a result of traumatic experiences 107–12
  positive components of 168–9
desensitisation 215
diagnostic procedures 16
dialogues with clients 49, 81–2, 83, 85–8, 151–7, 165–7
Diekstra, René 190, 193, 196
'difficult customers' (DCs) 171, 182
DiGiuseppe, Ray 190
discomfort anxiety/disturbance see low frustration tolerance (LFT)
disputing irrational beliefs 161–2, 179–80, 184, 186, 259
disturbances, origins of 153–6, 157, 158–9
dogmatism in therapy 160, 207–8; see also theories, psychological, as obstacles
dominance v. submission 131
Dostoevsky, Feodor 16
drama in therapy 209
drawing/painting in therapy 114, 115, 123–4
dreams 112–13, 114, 123
Dryden, Windy 196, 210

eclecticism 141, 207–11, 227, 243, 259
  dangers of 122–3
  technical 220

'ego analysis' 80, 90, 101
'elegant' v. 'inelegant' therapy 188–9
Ellis, Albert 127, 177–80, 181, 183, 184, 185, 195–7, 199, 202, 207, 217, 228
Emmelkamp, P.M.G. 223
'emotional episode' 193
emotions
   'appropriate' v. 'inappropriate' 189
   realm of 201–4, 208–9
   see also feelings
emotive-reconstruction therapy (ERT) 11–15, 254
   techniques of 13–15
   theoretical basis of 11–13
empathy 49, 50, 57, 62–3, 64, 65–6, 68, 72
Erickson, Milton 224
'everyday momentary overload' 81, 93, 95, 257
experimentation in therapy 160–1
experimenter expectancy effect 177

Facilitator Development Institute 56
family systems 248
fear 54–5, 61
   of intimacy 86–7
   of sexual penetration 229, 231, 234
   of violence 135–40
feelings
   discovery of 91–3
   exploration of 111–12
   expression/non-expression of 91–2
   heightening of in therapy 203
   justification/condemnation of 78–9, 81, 94–5, 100–1, 257
   see also emotions
Fenichel, O. 80
Ferrucci, P. 123–4
'fixed role enactment' 139–40
flexibility in therapy 13, 198, 258
Frank, J.D. 25
Franks, C.M. 221
Freud, Sigmund 42, 44, 78–81, 215
   neuroticism of 79–80
Freudians 149, 160, 172; see also psychoanalysis
friendship in therapy 43
frigidity 53–65
futility, sense of 27

Garcia, Ed 180
genuineness 65, 71
Gestalt theory 12
'Gloria' film 195–6
goals 135–7
Goldstein, A.J. 223
'good wife' role 133
grief 183
group work 104, 129, 131
guilt 57
   destructive 59, 60–1, 63, 64, 78–9
Guntrip, H. 42

Hankin, Sheenah 198
'hatred of men' 86, 229
Heidegger, A. 24
helplessness, feelings of 93
Hobson, R.F. 42
homework 60–1, 69, 150
homosexuality 183
hostility 135, 136, 137–8, 140, 150, 229
humanist existentialism 43
humanistic approach 105
hypnotic trance, spontaneous 9–10
hypnotism 215

'identity crisis' 184
ideology 120
imagery 7–8
   work with 9–10, 11, 13–14, 110–11, 113–17, 123
images of therapy 41–2
imaginative approach to therapy 170, 123–4

implications for other therapists 15–17, 40–5, 71–6, 96–101, 122–5, 145–6, 159–62, 172–3, 222–5, 248–51
implosive therapy 228
impotence 83–4, 181–3, 231, 234, 238–9
indoctrination, early 149–50, 199, 200–1
inquisitiveness 139–40
Institute for Rational-Emotive Therapy 162, 176, 180, 184, 187
intensity, emotional, in therapy 49
intent v. effect 97, 99, 142–3
interpersonal conflicts 246–8
interpersonal focus 23, 41
interpretations, therapist's, client's rejection of 98–9
intimacy, fear of 86–7
intimate relationships *see* relationships, marital; relationships, sexual
'intraceptive capacities' 9
intuition 68–70

James, W. 43
Janis, Irving 195
Janov, Arthur 7
Johnson, V. 228
Jones, Gwynne 128
Julian of Norwich 60–1
Jung, Karl Gustav 43, 104
justification/condemnation 78–9, 81, 94–5, 100–1, 257

Kant, Immanuel 159
Kaplan, Helen 228, 229
Kelly, George 12, 140, 141–5, 146, 254
Kemmler, Lily 194–5
key level strategy 250, 251
Knaus, Bill 180
Kohut, H. 110

Lake, Frank 103
Lane, Frank 70
Langs, R. 42, 97

Lazarus, Arnold 183–4
Lazarus, Richard 197
laziness 70
learned affective states (LAS) 201–2
learning by therapist 210–11
Levin, D.M. 119
Levinson, E.A. 43–4
Levis, D. 228
Lewin, K. 178
Lomas, P. 43
loneliness 27, 28
love, concept of 60, 74–6
low frustration tolerance (LFT) 164, 166–9, 171–2, 173, 260

Mahrer, Alvin 105, 111
Mair, M. 42
male violence 10–11, 238
marital relationships/problems *see* relationships, marital
Masters, W. 228
Maultsby, Maxie 183, 188, 191
maximum impact strategy 250–1
memories 10, 13, 23, 33, 58–9, 63
Miller, Sherod 228
misunderstandings 83–4, 88
modality profile 219–20, 223–4
modelling 119, 201
mortality, acceptance of 72
multimodal therapy 218–20, 222–5, 261
musturbatory beliefs 163, 165–7, 172–3
mutuality in therapy 52, 57, 69

nakedness 61, 62, 64, 68, 73–4
'neurosis' 245
'neurotic paradox' 132–3, 134–5, 145
nonconformity 28
non-verbal communication *see* physical responses to client

oedipal conflict 98
oppression, by family 109–10
outcome and process research 16–17, 254, 261–2

'paranoia' 149–50
parents 10–11, 27, 28, 30, 32, 85–6, 108–11, 118, 153–7, 248
'passive aggression' 100
payoffs from behaviours 204–5
'peak experience' 7–9
Peck, Scott 70, 75
Pelagius 76
person-centred approach 48–9, 56, 65–73, 256
personal construct theory 12, 135–40, 141–5, 254
personal rules of living (PRLs) 192, 199–201
Peterfreund, E. 98
phenomenological developmental history (PDH) 200–1
philosophy 159–60
phobias 128–9
physical responses to client 55–6, 57–8, 61, 62, 64, 68–9, 73–4
potentials, disowned 105–6
power
　in therapy 39, 89
　struggles for 87, 246–7
predicting outcome of therapy 235–6
prenatal experiences 63, 70–1, 108
prescriptive therapy 227–8
present, emphasis on 23
primal integration 163–5
'primitive' impulses 80, 81
process of therapy sessions 38
professional communities 260–1
progress curves 237, 240
projection 234
psychiatric diagnostic terminology, as disguised accusations 257
psychoanalysis 6, 24, 41, 43, 44, 128, 148–9, 206, 228
　and sexual difficulties 229
　stock formulations of 98–100
'psychological burnout' 16
'psychosis' 223
psychosomatic symptoms 78

purism, dangers of 122

Radley, A.R. 135–6
rational behaviour training (RBT) 188, 191
rational-emotive imagery (REI) 180, 183–4
rational-emotive therapy (RET) 148–73, 176, 178–80, 181–94, 198, 202, 203, 207–8, 210, 259–60
regression 62–3, 66, 70, 104
regression-integration therapy *see* primal integration
relationships
　between client and therapist 22, 27–40, 43–5, 55–6, 57–8, 60–7, 74–6, 131; *see also* therapeutic relationship
　marital 81–5, 132, 133, 134, 150, 182, 185–6, 215, 230–1, 234, 238–9
　sexual 28, 29, 30, 31–2, 33–4, 58–9, 132–3, 234
　with children 29–30
　with parents 10–11, 27, 28, 30, 32, 85–6, 108–11, 118, 153–7, 248
repression
　emotional 79–80
　sexual 53–65, 73, 240–1
'rescue fantasies' 8, 9, 85, 91
research *see* outcome and process research
resistance 89–90, 204, 245
responsibility
　client's 113, 116, 145–6
　therapist's 51–3, 67
rights, client's 14–15, 17
risk-taking in therapy 57–8, 61–2, 64, 68, 74, 106, 256
Rogerians 224, 225
Rogers, Carl 48, 192
role-playing 14
roles
　and 'fixed role enactment' 139–40
　unsuited to individual 135,

137–8, 143
Rosen, John 113, 123
sabotage
 of own happiness 132–5
 of therapy by spouse 215–16, 238–9
schizophrenia 39–40, 218–20
Schopenhauer, Arthur 159–60
Schutz, Will 116
security manoeuvres (SMs) 205–6
self, 'true' 120–1
self-appraisal 200
self-constructs 12
self-disclosure by therapist 203, 208
self-downing 164, 171–2, 173, 180, 216–217; *see also* worthlessness, feelings of
self-esteem 156–7
 low *see* worthlessness, feelings of
self-image 135–9, 204–5
self-sacrifice 154–7
self-statements 153–5, 156–7, 158, 159; *see also* musturbatory beliefs
self-understanding by therapist 208
'sensitiser' type 231, 234
sensuality 74
serendipity 123
sex therapy 229–30, 238–41, 242, 245, 247–8
sexual difficulties
 frigidity 53–65
 impotence 83–4, 181–3, 231, 234, 238–9
 vaginismus 228–41, 242, 245–8
sexuality
 acceptance of 73–4
 repression of 53–65, 73, 240–1
 therapist's 56, 57–8, 61, 64
Shafer, R. 41–2
shame-attacking exercises 164, 180
Sharaf, M.R. 9

'shift change' 141
short-term therapy 15, 206
'siding with the client' 103–25, 258
'significant acts' 24–5, 33–4
Simon, B. 97
situational variables 245–6
skills approach 143
social skills training 129, 130–2, 137–40, 258
spiritual realm 50, 60, 64, 65–6, 69, 72–3, 74–6, 104, 207
'squiggle technique' 124
Stampfl, T. 228
statements
 powerful 93–4
 see also accusatory statements; self-statements; 'you statements'
Stattman, Jay 116
stock formulations 98–100
Storr, A. 42
structural differential 191
struture of therapy sessions 53, 69–70
Strupp, H.H. 45
stuckness in therapy 54, 55, 67
subpersonalities 112–13, 124
suicide, therapist's anxiety about 52–3, 112
Sullivan, H.S. 43, 74–5
superego 113, 124
Suzuki, R. 120
Swartley, Bill 103
synthesis in therapy 41

Tagiuri, Renato 191
Tarot cards 124
tenderness in therapy 69, 72, 73
termination of therapy 99
theories, psychological
 as obstacles 84–100
 used as weapons 85–8, 89–90, 245, 257
theory v. facts 140–1
therapeutic aids 117–18
therapeutic relationship 22, 25–6, 39, 41–5, 52, 65–7, 161, 206

therapist
    client's view of 28, 29, 30-1, 32, 34-6
    conflicts within 262; *see also* risk-taking in therapy
    finding personally appropriate therapeutic orientation 15-16
    personal history of 26
    sexuality of 56, 57-8, 61, 64
    temperament of as factor in therapy 255
    see also under individual headings, e.g. learning by therapist; self-disclosure by therapist
transactional analysis 247
transactional therapy 228
transference 41, 44, 210
transtheoretical approach 248-51, 261
Trower, P. 145
trust 54, 55, 61, 64, 72-3

unconscious beliefs 172
'unconscious' wishes 87-8
unhappiness, general 132

vaginismus 228-41, 242, 245-8
values 57, 59, 60, 61-2, 64-5, 71-6, 186
verbal emphasis in therapy 49-50, 55
vulnerability 28, 33-4, 40, 67

Walen, Susan 190
Walsby, Harold 120
Wessler, Ruth 192-3
wholeness, personal 56, 60, 65-6, 71-4, 75-6, 103-5
Wilber, Ken 121
Wilson, G.T. 221
Winnicott, D.W. 124
Wolpe, Joseph 213-14, 218, 228, 261
Woodworth, R.S. 178
workshops 56-7, 67
worthlessness, feelings of 61, 70-1, 150, 151-7, 185-6, 216-7

Yates, A.J. 160
'you statements' 87-8, 89
young people 50-3

Index compiled by Peva Keane